Drawn to Television

Drawn to Television

Prime-Time Animation
from *The Flintstones* to *Family Guy*

M. Keith Booker

The Praeger Television Collection
David Bianculli, Series Editor

Westport, Connecticut
London

Library of Congress Cataloging-in-Publication Data

Booker, M. Keith.
Drawn to television: prime-time animation from
  The Flintstones to Family guy / M. Keith Booker.

     p. cm. — (The Praeger television collection, ISSN 1549-2257)
Includes index.
ISBN 0-275-99019-2
1. Animated television programs—United States.   I. Title.
PN1992.8.A59B66   2006
791.45'3—dc22   2006018109

British Library Cataloguing in Publication Data is available.

Library of Congress Catalog Card Number: 2006018109
ISBN: 0-275-99019-2
ISSN: 1549-2257

First published in 2006

Praeger Publishers, 88 Post Road West, Westport, CT 06881
An imprint of Greenwood Publishing Group, Inc.
www.praeger.com

Printed in the United States of America

The paper used in this book complies with the
Permanent Paper Standard issued by the National
Information Standards Organization (Z39.48-1984).

10 9 8 7 6 5 4 3 2 1

For Skylor Booker
Who taught me to appreciate cartoons.

Contents

Introduction:
A Very Brief History of
Prime-Time Animation

Animated programming has been a prominent part of American popular culture since at least the 1930s, when the first feature-length films from the Walt Disney Studios began to appear along with the first animated shorts from Warner Brothers (in the "Looney Tunes" and "Merrie Melodies" series). It was thus only natural, as the new medium gained popularity in the 1950s, that animated programming would come to television. Animated programming has been an important element of American television ever since, no doubt in large part because animated programs, mostly aimed at children, have been a crucial part of the experience of American childhood. The most successful of these programs have had staying power far beyond the norm for television, maintaining a strong nostalgia value even as the children who watched them grew into adulthood. Such children's programs have typically aired on Saturday mornings or weekday afternoons—at times when children would be expected to constitute a larger-than-usual percentage of the viewing audience. A number of programs, however, have been aimed at adults from the start (or at least at a mixed audience of children and adults), and these programs have often aired in prime time. The following volume traces the development of this phenomenon through a discussion of the most important prime-time animated programs in American television history.

The history of prime-time animation begins with the airing of *The Flintstones* in the fall of 1960. This series would go on to provide some of the most familiar images of American popular culture in the remainder of the twentieth century, and it remains well known to both children and adults well into the twenty-first century. Its immediate success triggered a brief explosion in prime-time animated programming in the early 1960s, with Hanna-Barbera Productions, makers of *The Flintstones,* leading the way. In the next few years, programs such as *Matty's Funday Funnies, Bugs Bunny, Calvin and the Colonel, Top Cat, The Alvin Show, The Bullwinkle Show* (aka *Rocky and Bullwinkle*), *The Jetsons,* and *Jonny Quest* could all be seen in prime time. None of these programs was particularly successful, however, and all soon disappeared from the prime-time lineup, though several had second lives as Saturday-morning programs and many are still well known today, more than 40 years after their demise in prime time.

The failure of these programs to draw large audiences in prime time, accompanied by a decline in the popularity of *The Flintstones* itself, led to a widespread perception in the television industry that animated programs could succeed *only* as children's fare on Saturday mornings. As a result, with the removal of *The Flintstones* from prime time in 1966, animated programming disappeared from prime time and remained in a state of exile from the evening schedule for more than 20 years. (It is worth noting that the animated shorts that had been shown in theaters prior to feature films since the 1930s also disappeared during roughly this same time period.) All of this began to change at the end of the 1980s. For one thing, *The Simpsons,* which would ultimately go on to become the most successful animated program in American television history, premiered on the fledgling Fox network in 1989. For another, the rapid proliferation of cable systems for the home delivery of television programming was by this time beginning to provide important new venues on which much of the subsequent prime-time and adult-oriented animated programming of the coming years would appear.

Like *The Flintstones, The Simpsons* is essentially an animated version of the family sitcom, a staple of American television from the very beginning. Not surprisingly, then, many of the programs that followed in the wake of the success of *The Simpsons* adhered to this same format. However, perhaps remembering the failures of the 1960s, network executives were hardly anxious to jump on the animation bandwagon, and it was not until 1997, with the premiere of *King of the Hill,* also on Fox, that *The Simpsons* had its first major successor in this format. The subsequent success of this series (still on the air as of this writing in early 2006) demonstrated that *The Simpsons* was not a one-of-a-kind phenomenon. On the other hand, most of the animated family sitcoms that appeared in the next few years were, like the flurry of animated programs in the early 1960s, short-lived. Programs such as *The Oblongs* and *God, the Devil, and Bob* were quickly canceled, though Fox's *Family Guy* lasted somewhat longer, despite veering into highly controversial territory. Still, *Family Guy* was canceled in 2002, after the end of its third season on Fox. However, the subsequent popularity of that program in syndication on the late-night "Adult Swim" block of the cable Cartoon Network, accompanied by hefty sales of DVD releases of the program, led Fox to bring *Family Guy* back onto prime time in the spring of 2005, accompanied by *American Dad*, an even edgier program, if only because the subject matter was more political, from *Family Guy* creator Seth McFarlane.

In the meantime, the landscape of prime-time animated programming had been radically changed by the appearance of a number of series that did not adhere to the family sitcom format. This phenomenon was particularly aided by the proliferation of cable networks, though the first major non–family sitcom animated program to appear in prime time was *The Critic*, which aired for one season on ABC and one on Fox in the period from 1994 to 1995. Cable then made its first major original contribution to prime-time animation with the appearance of *Dr. Katz: Professional Therapist*, which ran on the Comedy Central network from May 1995 to December 1999, for a total of 78 episodes. New broadcast networks such as UPN and the WB also joined the fray by the end of the 1990s, airing (briefly) such programs as *Dilbert*, *Home Movies*, and *Mission Hill*. *Clerks*, based on the Kevin Smith cult film of the same title, ran even more briefly on ABC in the spring of 2000.

The rapid failure of this succession of programs, reminiscent of the quick demise of most of the prime-time animated programs of the 1960s, might have suggested to network executives that the non–family sitcom animated program was not really a prime-time winner. It should be mentioned, however, that the animated science fiction spoof *Futurama* (from the creators of *The Simpsons*) was moderately successful on Fox from 1999 to 2002. In addition, the most important animated program to come on the air in the late 1990s, Comedy Central's *South Park*, also departed from the family sitcom format. By far the most successful animated program ever to air on cable, *South Park* established once and for all the importance of cable as a home for animated programming. For one thing, the program managed to draw a substantial audience as well as significant and serious critical attention, despite running on a relatively obscure cable network, which *South Park* itself ultimately made much less obscure. For another, the brash, intentionally outrageous style and subject matter of *South Park*, which would almost certainly not have been allowed on network television in 1997 when the series premiered, established cable as an important site for groundbreaking animated programming.

The success of *South Park* has changed a number of fundamental audience expectations concerning animated programming, opening the way for network programs such as *Family Guy* and *American Dad*. It has also paved the way for a new generation of daring, often risqué animated programming on a variety of cable networks in the early years of the twenty-first century. Many of these programs seem almost specifically designed to try to outdo *South Park*. Comedy Central's *Drawn Together*, Sci Fi's *Tripping the Rift*, and Spike-TV's *Stripperella* all fit in this category. *Hopeless Pictures*, a thoughtful animated entry from the Independent Film Channel (IFC), also breaks new ground, though it differs significantly in tone from the other series, which often seem to present outrageous material just for the sake of being outrageous.

Finally, no survey of adult-oriented animated programming would be complete without a nod to the Adult Swim block, which, while not appearing in prime time, has provided a second home for a number of programs that originally aired during prime time. Adult Swim also produces a significant amount of its own original programming, serving as a sort of laboratory for experimentation with new forms of animated television that could probably never make it directly onto a network in prime time. As of this writing, the Fox network continues to air *The Simpsons, King of the Hill, Family Guy,* and *American Dad,* making it the only outlet for prime-time animated programming among the major broadcast networks. However, the innovative programs on Adult Swim have joined with the various programs airing on other cable networks to make the early years of the twenty-first century the richest time yet for adult-oriented animated programming. As cable and satellite television continue to expand, and as continuing improvements in computer animation make it cheaper and faster to produce high-quality animation, indications are that the future will be even brighter.

CHAPTER 1

Animation Comes to Prime Time: The Case of *The Flintstones*

William Hanna and Joseph Barbera were first paired together as a team in 1939, when the two were assigned to produce animated shorts for Metro-Goldwyn-Mayer (MGM). They worked successfully in that capacity (most particularly in the *Tom and Jerry* series of shorts) until MGM shut down their animation studio in 1957. The pair then went into business for themselves, founding Hanna-Barbera Productions to make cartoons both for use as theatrical shorts and for afternoon television, beginning with the *Ruff & Reddy* series in December 1957. With the broadcast of the first episode of *The Flintstones* on Friday, September 30, 1960, on ABC television, Hanna and Barbera became the producers of what is widely regarded as the first animation program on prime-time series television. Actually, though, it was the second. *The Flintstones* premiered at 8:30 P.M. eastern time, right after *Harrigan and Son*. But the latter was preceded, at 7:30, by *Matty's Funday Funnies*, an animated series that had run on Sunday afternoons the year before and that thus, strictly speaking, became the first animated series in prime time. However, *Matty's Funday Funnies* (which ultimately evolved into *Beany and Cecil*) was initially an anthology series that featured a number of different cartoon characters, including Casper the Friendly Ghost, Herman the Mouse, Tommy the Tortoise, and Little Audrey. *The Flintstones* was thus the first animated prime-time series that focused on a single scenario and set of characters that were originally created for prime time.

In any case, ABC's turn to prime-time animated programming in the fall of 1960 was a bold and unprecedented programming experiment, though it probably came about as much from desperation as inspiration. ABC at that time was having a very difficult time competing with its older and more established rivals, CBS and NBC. On the other hand, *The Flintstones*, which turned out to be one of ABC's most successful programs, might not have been as boldly experimental as it seemed. In fact, the formula of *The Flintstones* was in many ways tried and true. Animated or not, *The Flintstones* was essentially a family sitcom, a form that had produced some of the biggest hits of the 1950s. *The Flintstones* drew in particularly direct and obvious ways on *The Honeymooners*, a now legendary sitcom—though one that, oddly enough, had not been a huge hit in its own right and had appeared mostly as segments within other programs rather than as an independent series. Ultimately, of course, *The Flintstones* would make an even more important contribution to American popular culture than had *The Honeymooners*, while principals Fred Flintstone (voiced by Alan Reed), his wife Wilma (Jean Vanderpyl), and neighbors Barney (Mel Blanc) and Betty Rubble (Bea Benaderet, replaced by Gerry Johnson in the fifth and sixth seasons) would become among the best known and loved characters in television history.

What was special about *The Honeymooners*—other than the sterling per-formances by Jackie Gleason and Art Carney as bus driver Ralph Kramden and sewer worker Ed Norton, the predecessors of Fred and Barney—was the extent to which it captured the travails of ordinary working-class Americans in their attempt to come to grips with the radical changes that were trans-forming American society in the 1950s. The series was especially aware, for example, of the growth of technologies such as television itself and of the concomitant increase in American affluence that made a variety of modern labor-saving appliances not only available but affordable. The Kramdens and Nortons were not so affluent and couldn't quite afford all the best that modern consumer capitalism could offer, but they were well aware of developments in the society around them and felt considerable pressure to try to keep up.

The Flintstones, though set in mock prehistoric times, was broadcast slightly later, at a time when many of the new conveniences (especially television) that Ralph Kramden often resisted had become an integral part of the fabric of American life. Unlike the Kramdens, the Flintstones have all the latest household appliances, such as vacuum cleaners and garbage disposals, even if they can't always afford the fanciest brands or the latest models. Indeed, a key source of humor in *The Flintstones* involves the comic reproduction of the entire range of modern technological wonders via the materials of the Stone Age, usually constructed from rock or through the use of small animals to supply the necessary power, or even the entire appliance. Thus, Wilma's vacuum cleaner is simply a small elephant-like creature that sucks dirt and dust up into its trunk (sometimes causing it to sneeze a cloud of dust back out into the room), while her garbage disposal is a small pig-like creature that sits underneath the sink and devours whatever comes through the drain. The Flintstones' famous cars, among the show's best-known images, though several different cars appear in the series, are generally constructed of logs, with stone wheels and tops made of animal skin; they seem to be powered entirely by the driver and passengers, who sit in their seats and propel the vehicles by running along the ground with their bare feet—though the cars do seem capable of coasting for fairly long distances.

The Stone Age technology of *The Flintstones* extended even into space-flight, a key interest of American audiences in the early 1960s. In one first-season episode, "The Astr'Nuts" (March 3, 1961),[1] Fred and Barney, having accidentally joined the army, end up enlisting as astronauts in order to avoid normal army duties. The episode was very timely. On April 12, 1961, only one month after the broadcast of the episode, Soviet cosmonaut Yuri Gagarin became the first human to be launched into space. Alan Shepard became the first American astronaut in space less than a month after that, on May 5, 1961. In keeping with the typical technology of *The Flintstones*, the rocket Fred and Barney hope to ride into space is merely a hollow log launched via a giant slingshot. This rocket was developed by a German scientist (Dr. Pebbleschmidt), just as the U.S. space program was directed by former German scientist Werner von Braun. As it turns out, however, the Stone Age rocket doesn't quite make it to outer space: it lands on an artillery range, whose craters make Fred and Barney mistake it for the moon.

The show's incongruous mixture of prehistoric elements with modern technology—the Flintstones have never heard of shoes, but have a television, a telephone, and a car—can be quite amusing, but it also serves a serious function. By transplanting what is essentially a 1960s American lifestyle into the Stone Age, where its various elements seem humorously out of place, *The Flintstones* creates a continuous sense of estrangement that allows the show's viewers to see their own society, which they might otherwise simply take for granted as the natural way for a society to be, in new ways, reminding them of how unusual and relatively new their affluent, high-tech way of life really is.

This estrangement goes well beyond technology to include culture in its broadest sense, which is perhaps the biggest difference between *The Honeymooners*, which shows contemporary American life in an ordinary realistic setting, and *The Flintstones*, which provides an oblique look at contemporary America. Both series, however, tracked developments in the society around them. Thus, while Ralph Kramden resists the incursion of television into his daily life (though he finds the medium irresistibly entrancing once he does acquire a set), television for his successor Fred Flintstone is not a novelty or a convenience, but a necessity. It is, however, an expensive one, and a running motif in the show is Fred's ongoing difficulty in paying for the television set he so loves. The Kramdens and Nortons also differed from the Flintstones and Rubbles in that the former lived in urban New York, while the latter lived in suburban Bedrock, indicating the movement of the perceived center of gravity of American society from the cities to the suburbs in the late 1950s and early 1960s. Finally, the Flintstones and the Rubbles were slightly more affluent than their *Honeymooner* predecessors and had more hope of upward mobility. Thus, while Fred and Ralph are both avid bowlers, Fred also plays golf in several episodes, sometimes in the company of wealthy golfing partners, while Ralph, hoping in vain to impress his boss and get a big promotion, only pretends to be a golfer.

Otherwise, the characters and the relationships between them—which were the central foci of both *The Honeymooners* and *The Flintstones*—were quite similar in the two series. The friendships between the lead male characters of the two series were particularly crucial to their success. Both Ralph and Fred are loud, overweight, domineering figures, though (perhaps with an eye toward a larger audience of children) Fred was less extreme in these respects than was Ralph. He never, for example, offers to send Wilma "to the moon" with a blow of his mighty fist. Similarly, both Norton and Barney are patient, loyal, and somewhat subservient, though willing occasionally to poke fun at their blustering friends. Indeed, Ralph and Fred do not dominate Norton and Barney nearly to extent that they themselves seem to think. In addition, while both Norton and Barney can seem a bit slow-witted at times, they are typically more sensible and less impetuous than their larger friends, often providing hints that they may be a bit more intelligent than they appear—and often helping to curb the sometimes extreme actions of their more emotional counterparts.

Marital relations were also important in both *The Honeymooners* and *The Flintstones*. Wilma and Betty are stay-at-home housewives, as were Alice Kramden and Trixie Norton, though, oddly enough, Wilma and Betty are probably more conventionally devoted to husband and home than were their predecessors. Indeed, partly because of their more affluent suburban lifestyles, Wilma and Betty fit much more into the mold of the idealized housewives promoted by such 1950s sitcoms as *Leave It to Beaver* and *The Donna Reed Show* than did Alice and Trixie. Still, both *The Honeymooners* and *The Flintstones* differed from the classic 1950s family sitcom in that they depicted gender roles as potentially unstable and open to revision.

The masculinity of Ralph Kramden was particularly embattled, because, of the four husbands in the two shows, he seemed to have the hardest time supporting his family and remained in the most precarious financial position. Both *The Honeymooners* and *The Flintstones* were early enough that the husbands were still expected to be the breadwinners while the wives were expected to stay at home, preparing that bread and having it on the dinner table ready to be consumed when the husbands arrived from work. Meanwhile, the wives were still labeled as "girls," while the husbands continually referred to them via a variety of condescending diminutives, as in Fred's tendency, when talking with Barney, to express their mutual affection for Wilma and Betty in terms such as "bless their little hearts."

In seasons three and four, respectively, Wilma and Betty cemented their roles as model housewives by becoming mothers, thus adding another dimension to the relationships in the series and making the Flintstones and Rubbles even more typical reflections of American suburban family life. Indeed, much of season three was devoted to a roughly continuous arc of episodes building toward the eventual birth of Fred and Wilma's daughter, Pebbles, beginning with "The Little Stranger" (November 2, 1962), in which Fred (long opposed to parenthood) mistakenly concludes that Wilma is pregnant and surprisingly finds that he is thrilled by the idea. The very next week, in "Baby Barney" (November 9, 1962), the baby motif is combined with Fred's incessant efforts to get rich. Here, hoping to curry favor and thus win an eventual inheritance, Fred has told his rich uncle, the Texas oil millionaire Tex Flintstone, that he and Wilma have a baby boy named "Little Tex." Then, when Uncle Tex decides to pay a visit, Fred gets Barney to pose as the baby—with near-disastrous results.

In "The Surprise" (January 25, 1963), Wilma announces that she is, in fact, pregnant, triggering a sequence of episodes leading up to "The Blessed Event" (aka "Dress Rehearsal," February 22, 1963), in which Pebbles (also voiced by Vanderpyl) is finally born. This episode not only added a new dimension to the family dynamic of the series, but it momentarily restored the series' fading popularity. It was, in fact, the single highest rated episode in the entire run of *The Flintstones*, echoing the phenomenal success of the

"Lucy Goes to the Hospital" (January 19, 1953) episode of *I Love Lucy*, in which Lucy's son Little Ricky is born.

In the fourth season, *The Flintstones* dealt with unusually mature material for the television of the day, as the Rubbles struggled to come to grips with their inability to bear a child of their own. In "Little Bamm-Bamm" (October 3, 1963), their dream of having a baby seems literally to have come true when they discover a baby boy abandoned on their doorstep. They take the boy, who turns out to have superhuman strength, in as their own, but find themselves embroiled in a custody battle against the wealthy Pronto Burger, who also wants to adopt the boy. Given Burger's superior resources, which include the ability to hire ace attorney Perry Masonry, it doesn't look good for the Rubbles—until Burger's wife becomes pregnant and he decides to drop the attempt to adopt the club-swinging little Bamm-Bamm (Don Messick). Bamm-Bamm and Pebbles then become fast friends, of course, and the show's family units are complete at last.

If parenthood made the Flintstones and Rubbles all the more conventional as examples of the American nuclear family, there is still a strong sense in the series, as there had been in *The Honeymooners*, that conventional gender roles were becoming increasingly inadequate and needed revision in the light of the changes being undergone by American society at the time. The wives were often depicted as more practical and intelligent than the husbands, while the breadwinner-husbands often found bread extremely difficult to win. Even the seemingly more affluent Fred and Barney are continually beset by money difficulties and seem aware (as are Ralph and Norton) that the society around them offers opportunities for wealth that have somehow eluded them.

Still, both Ralph and Fred dream of cashing in on these opportunities through a variety of get-rich-quick schemes, though Ralph's dreams are typically a bit more mundane, largely involving the hope of raises or promotions at the bus company. However, in the early episode "Songwriters" (December 11, 1954), Ralph conceives a plan to strike it rich by writing hit songs and actually even gets one song recorded, thanks to Norton's help. In "The Hit Songwriter" (September 15, 1961), Fred and Barney retrace virtually the same territory, though they have to overcome a scam on the part of a con artist and then enlist the help of ace songwriter Hoagy Carmichael, voiced by the real-world Carmichael himself, in order to get their first song published.

In general, the upward-mobility dreams of the Flintstones, and to an extent, the Rubbles, were typically much more concerned with making it big in show business than those of their predecessors in *The Honeymooners* had been. This change, like most of the differences between the two series, reflected real changes in American society, in this case the increasing penetration of everyday life by various forms of popular culture, a movement fueled most importantly by the explosive growth of television, but also by phenomena such as the rise of rock music. Many episodes of *The Flintstones*, in fact, were simply about popular culture itself and did not involve the efforts of the characters to break into show business.

These "pop culture" episodes were often quite clever and highly amusing. "Alvin Brickrock Presents" (October 6, 1961), for example, is an extended take-off on Alfred Hitchcock's classic film *Rear Window* (1954), filtered through Hitchcock's anthology series *Alfred Hitchcock Presents*, which ran on American television in various incarnations from 1955 to 1966. In this episode, Fred and Barney make a pastime of eavesdropping on the incessant fighting of new neighbors Alvin and Agatha Brickrock. Then, when Agatha suddenly comes up missing, Fred, inspired by his reading of detective comics such as *Weird Detective*, concludes that she has probably been murdered, just as Hitchcock's L. B. Jefferies concludes that his neighbor Lars Thorwald is a murderer. In this case, however, a variety of comic misadventures lead to the conclusion that Brickrock (whose appearance and voice are modeled not on Jefferies, but on Hitchcock himself) is innocent and that Agatha has merely gone off to New Rock City. However, the show ends with an ironic twist when Brickrock appears for a final farewell—just as Hitchcock did with his television program. Here, Brickrock suggests, but does not state outright, that he may have disposed of his wife's body by feeding it to his rare pet piranhakeet, a man-eating bird long thought extinct that he had discovered in the course of his work as an archaeologist.

In other episodes, the Flintstones and Rubbles encounter various show-business personalities as just plain folks in the course of their day-today activities. In "Rock Quarry Story" (October 20, 1961), Wilma's favorite movie star, Rock Quarry, decides that he wants to escape from the bright lights of show business in order to lead a simpler and more authentic life among the common people. So he bolts from a publicity tour and heads for Bedrock, where he is involved in an auto accident when Fred runs a stop sign and crashes into him. Fred brings the man home for dinner to try to make amends. Wilma, the put-upon housewife, is furious—until she realizes the identity of her guest.

In several episodes, Fred himself seems on the verge of movie stardom—always with unfortunate results. Typical of these episodes is "Fred Meets Hercurock" (March 5, 1965), in which Fred is discovered by a producer of low-budget films who immediately signs him up to star in his next film, giving him the name "Rock Quarry," apparently forgetting that the name had already been used in the first season of the show. Fred then undergoes an extensive training regime to get himself in shape to play the lead role in the coming production of the film *Hercurock and the Maidens.* But this exhausting and demanding training turns out to be nothing compared to his performance in the film, which consists primarily of stunt scenes in which he undergoes a variety of violent and painful ordeals. Disgusted, Fred quits—but Barney steps in to finish the film, including a big scene in which he is surrounded by amorous slave girls. Fred returns to his original job as a crane operator (the crane is a dinosaur, of course) in a quarry, though his boss Mr. Slate attempts to capitalize on the whole experience by charging admission to the public in exchange for a chance to see an ex-movie star at work.

One key sign of the early-1960s times of *The Flintstones* was the prominence given rock music in the show. Then again, *The Flintstones* began in the pre-Beatles days of 1960, and their version of "rock" music in the early seasons is a more a kind of Beatnik jazz than what would ultimately be thought of as rock 'n' roll. The second episode ever telecast, "Hot Lips Hannigan" (October 7, 1960) introduces this motif early on. Here, Fred and Barney go out to a club where the hipster trumpet player of the episode title is performing with his band. As it turns out, Fred and Hannigan are old pals, Fred having played in Hannigan's first band back when he was in high school before giving up his aspirations to a career in music in order to settle down and marry Wilma. Hannigan, it turns out, is just a regular guy, his beatnik persona having been invented to attract young audiences. The episode thus introduces a running theme of the treatment of popular culture that runs throughout the series: The producers of this culture, financially driven by the need to attract fickle teenage audiences, are constantly struggling to find the next big thing, which creates a great deal of innovation but also a great deal of superficiality and inauthenticity. In an insight about the direction of American popular culture that would prove prescient, the show depicted this culture as one of spectacle in which surface appearance is all.

Hannigan himself bemoans the decline in musical quality of his new songs for the teenage crowd. In response, Fred decides to perform one of their "old" songs with the band—which turns out to be the gospel-inflected jazz classic "When the Saints Come Marching In." This oldie-but-goodie is a hit with the teenage crowd (which includes Wilma and Betty in disguise, unbeknownst to Fred and Barney), suggesting both that Fred might have some talent as a singer and that teenage audiences might actually be able to appreciate some of the older classics if given a chance.

By the time of the later first-season episode "The Girls' Night Out" (January 6, 1961), this latter suggestion would fall by the wayside. Here, Fred and Barney finally take their wives out for an evening of fun. Unfortunately, they take them to an amusement park that the women don't find very amusing. Fred, perhaps still dreaming of his early days as a singer, records a song ("Listen to the Rockin' Bird") in a "Make a Record of Your Own Voice" booth, but Wilma isn't impressed and they end up leaving the record behind. Some teenagers find and play the record and love it, declaring that the anonymous singer has now replaced Hot Lips Hannigan as their musical idol. Eventually, the record falls into the hands of the Keen-Teen Record Company. The company adds a musical background track and releases the record, which quickly becomes a hit. Ultimately, they are able to identify Fred as the singer, assigning a mustachioed Southern colonel—based apparently on Elvis Presley's manager Colonel Tom Parker—to make Fred over into a presentable teen sensation. The colonel (a version of a recurring character who appeared in different auspices in numerous episodes of the series) gives Fred new glasses, clothes, and hair—and even a new name, Hi-Fye. They go on the road and are a smash hit with teenage audiences. Wilma, however, soon tires of life on the road, and in any case feels that Fred is making a fool of himself. Of course, she might also simply be jealous, and this episode potentially places her in an unusually negative light. She then torpedoes Fred's promising career by starting a rumor that Hi-Fye is secretly a square. The rumor spreads like wildfire among Hi-Fye's teenage fans, bringing his popularity to an instant halt. Fred comes back to earth and returns to his old life.

The fickleness of teenage audiences is thus verified, as is their importance as consumers of popular culture, while the culture they consume is once again depicted as lacking substance. On the other hand, the episode also hints that the Colonel (who had, in an apparent—if inaccurate— reference to Elvis, earlier engineered the rise of "that boy from Georgia" with "long sideburns") may be a master manipulator of images who is driving the tastes of the teenage audience, rather than being driven by them. In fact, *The Flintstones* consistently depicts show business as a factory of false images, while those in show business are typically depicted as self-serving hypocrites. On the other hand, this critique of American popular culture is conducted with a light touch and with considerable humor that makes the suggested failings of the culture industry seem rather harmless.

Elvis is again an important focus of the engagement of *The Flintstones* with rock music in "The Twitch" (October 12, 1962). Here, Wilma has had no luck landing a big act for her Ladies' Auxiliary charity benefit (especially as she can pay only $35), but Fred assures her he can use his friendship with Sam Stone, show business superagent, to get a big star for the show. Stone, however, is a typical back-biting show-business type who provides no real help. Still, the proud Fred refuses to admit to Wilma that he has failed. Then, when he sees pop-music sensation Rock Roll singing his hit song "The Twitch" on a television program modeled on *The Ed Sullivan Show*, he declares to a delighted Wilma that the Elvis-like Rock Roll will be performing in her show, even though he has no idea how to land the big star.

When Fred and Barney tearfully beg, the personable down-home Rock Roll surprisingly agrees to do the show gratis, just to help them out—and to give him a chance to try out his hit song in front of a live audience. He also confesses that he invented the popular "twitch" dance as a result of his involuntary writhing due to his allergy to pickled dodo eggs. Unfortunately, that same allergy later renders him unable to perform in Wilma's show, so Fred himself is forced to don Rock's costume, as well as his wig and fake sideburns, and then lip sync Rock's song. The performance goes well, and the show is saved. Impressed with his success, Fred quits his job at the quarry and decides to go into show business, despite the fact that his Rock Roll–inspired singing drives Betty and Wilma to don earmuffs to shut out the noise.

Fred seems to have some talent in "The Girls' Night Out" and none in "The Twitch," but then *The Flintstones* was never all that concerned with consistency or accuracy. Indeed, these two companion, but contrasting, episodes potentially make an important point about the popular music business: Success depends not on whether or not one has talent, but on whether or not one is able to come up with a marketable image. Moreover, in both cases the show implies that Fred's ambition to be a rock star is misguided and that he would be better off staying at home in the more authentic surroundings of his suburban home, loving wife, and loyal friends.

By the beginning of the sixth and final season of *The Flintstones* in the fall of 1965, the Beatles had appeared on *Ed Sullivan* and the rock music revolution was well underway. In that season's opener, "No Biz Like Show Biz" (September 17, 1965), Fred and Barney find that they are unable to watch the Saturday football game on television because all of the stations have been taken over by programming devoted to rock music for teenagers. Bored and disgusted, Fred falls asleep and dreams that Pebbles and Bamm-Bamm, able to sing even before they can talk, have become the latest rock sensations. Fred, dreaming of the millions they will bring in, is at first thrilled, but is later horrified at the disruption in family life caused by the babies' soaring careers. He is thus greatly relieved to awaken and find that all has returned to normal.

Wilma seems to understand better than Fred the show's message that normal life is better than show business, though there are also several episodes of the series in which she seems on the verge of launching her own show-business career, sometimes in spite of herself. In "The Happy Household" (February 23, 1962), for example, Wilma tires of Fred's constant complaints about her spending habits and decides to seek employment to supplement the household budget. Betty joins her, and the two of them go to an employment agency, which then sends them to the studios of Bedrock Radio and Television Corporation to interview for clerical jobs. As luck would have it, however, they arrive just as the producer of the *Happy Housewife* television show has become desperate in his attempts to find a new host for the program. When he hears Wilma sing, he immediately signs her to a contract to host the next season of the show. Wilma decides to give it a shot, but Fred is furious, especially when he realizes that, instead of serving him his dinner each night in the manner to which she has become accustomed, his wife is now spending her evenings cooking on TV. "A woman's place is in the home!" he angrily declares, and then marches down to the studio. The studio and their slick lawyers are not impressed with his threats, however, and he is unable to get Wilma out of her contract, especially as her show is a big hit. Then a rival network hires Fred to host the *Neglected Husband* show, which will thoroughly discredit Wilma's on-screen image as the perfect housewife. Wilma's show is canceled and she returns home to an ecstatic and triumphant Fred. But Wilma, always a good sport, is happy as well—she never really wanted to be in show business in the first place. As the Flintstones and Rubbles gather happily together in domestic bliss, Fred addresses the women in the audience with a friendly reminder of their marital duties. "I hope all you wives out there are taking notes," he says.

The satire in this episode seems aimed not at Fred and his old-fashioned attitudes (he is a caveman, after all), but at the producers of *Happy Housewife*, who have absolutely no scruples about using the image of the perfect housewife to hawk the products of their sponsors (in this case, Rockenschpeel Fine Foods), while at the same time making it impossible for their own star to fulfill her wifely domestic duties.

Of course, one could take this episode as a warning to wives that their selfish husbands may simply regard them as domestic servants, but there is no evidence in the episode to suggest that this subversive interpretation was its intention. Instead, the show seems to deliver a thoroughly conservative endorsement of Fred's declaration that women belong at home, serving their husbands. Indeed, other episodes make similar points, as in

"The Entertainer" (January 19, 1962), in which Wilma encounters her old school chum Greta Gravel, now a successful businesswoman. However, it is Greta who envies Wilma, who has the husband and home that Greta lacks. Realizing that they should appreciate how lucky they are, Wilma and Betty both start to give especially good (nonsexual) service to their husbands after the encounter.

Actually, Wilma had already had failed opportunities to break into show business, even before "The Happy Household," which was the second episode in a matter of weeks to deal with that motif. In "A Star Is Almost Born" (January 12, 1962), Wilma is discovered by a television producer Norman Rockbind, who seems completely smitten with her when he sees her out shopping. In this case, however, Fred is completely supportive, immediately rushing Wilma into expensive acting lessons (and conning poor Barney into helping to pay for them) so that she can be better prepared for her new career. Fred, in fact, is far more excited about the possibility of Wilma becoming a star and the Flintstones becoming rich than is Wilma herself. When it turns out that Rockbind merely wants to use Wilma as a hand model in a skin lotion commercial, Fred refuses to allow her to participate—until he realizes that there can be big money in such commercial work. So he rushes back to Rockbind, only to discover that the part has already been recast—with Betty! Wilma's commercial career is over before it ever began, but Fred, meanwhile, has quit his job in order to become Wilma's manager. Luckily, Wilma once again saves the day by convincing Mr. Slate to give Fred his old job back.

In the first-season episode "Hollyrock, Here I Come" (December 2, 1960), Wilma actually lands a role in a TV sitcom entitled *The Frogmouth* after she and Betty win a trip to Hollyrock in a slogan-writing contest. (The slogan is for Mother McGuire's Meatballs, whose commercials feature dancing and singing meatballs that strangely anticipate the Meatwad character of the Adult Swim animated program *Aqua Teen Hunger Force*.) When Wilma and Betty go to tour a television studio while in Hollyrock, a producer spots Wilma and immediately casts her in a starring role as the loyal, suffering wife of the title character of his show *The Frogmouth*, an abusive, loud-mouthed bully. Finding that the bachelor life back in Bedrock is not quite as exciting as they had expected, Fred and Barney soon follow the wives out to Hollyrock, where the producer realizes that Fred would be perfect in the title role of his program and casts him as well. Pumped up with his newfound sense of self-importance, Fred soon proves to be an obnoxious prima donna—so much so that the producer is forced to torpedo his own show by intentionally giving Fred stage fright as the live broadcast of the show begins in order to rid himself of his new star. Once again, the Flintstones head back to Bedrock having narrowly escaped a brush with show business.

At the beginning of the third season, in the episode "Dino Goes Hollyrock" (September 14, 1962), even the Flintstones' pet dog, who is actually a small dinosaur, but with the personality of a dog, attempts to break into show business—encouraged by Fred, who hopes to cash in on his otherwise annoying pet's apparent talents. Dino, who is greatly infatuated with the TV star "Sassie" (transparently based on the canine star of the then-popular CBS program *Lassie*), gets a chance to audition for the *Sassie* program. Motivated by the desire to meet the object of his affections, he performs brilliantly. However, when Fred takes Dino to the television studio to shoot a screen test, Dino is a bit disappointed by the cast, who all seem to be stuck-up Hollyrock types. Dino gets the part, and Fred sadly goes home without his pet, whom he had expected to be glad to be rid of. Then, when Dino discovers that Sassie is completely unattractive without her television makeup, he gives up on show business and returns home, where Fred greets him with great enthusiasm.

The ultimate gist of the various "show business" episodes of *The Flintstones* is that the ordinary lives of humble folks like the Flintstones have rewards (like friendship and love) that make them preferable to the superficial pleasures experienced by pretentious show-business types. In this sense, these episodes are quite similar to those in which Fred poses as, is mistaken for, or switches places with someone rich and famous, ranging from "The Split Personality" (October 28, 1960)—in which one of the many blows to the head suffered by Fred in the series causes him to think he is a suave aristocrat—to "King for a Knight" (December 3, 1964)—in which Fred is enlisted to impersonate the King of Stonesylvania, who has gone AWOL on the eve of an important event that will allow his country to secure a large loan. In all of these cases, Fred eventually returns to normal and is glad to do so, suggesting that he is much better off where he is. The ultimate implication of such episodes, like that of the show-business episodes, is the quite conservative one that working-class people like the Flintstones are better off staying where they are rather than attempting to rise above their stations in life.

Fred himself never seems to learn this lesson. On the contrary, he remains devoted to the dream of upward mobility, believing that capitalism offers opportunities that will eventually make him rich. His endorsement of capitalism, even in its most ruthless forms, can be seen in the very early episode "No Help Wanted" (October 21, 1960), in which Fred accidentally causes Barney to lose his job and so helps him to find another one—as a furniture repossessor. Unfortunately, Fred is well behind on the installment payments for his television, and Barney is immediately assigned to repossess the set. Realizing that the kind-hearted Barney is having trouble coming to grips with the requirements of his new job (though not knowing that these requirements include reclaiming his own television), Fred urges Barney to pursue his job without hesitation. "In business you've got to be ruthless," says Fred, who is always willing to give expert advice even about things of which he knows little or nothing. "Your only friend is a buck and the more bucks you got, the more friends you got. . . . You do whatever your job calls for. That's your duty." Armed with this advice, Barney grudgingly takes the set, but then uses his own money to make the overdue payments and get the set back for his friend.

This episode is typical of the way in which this seemingly lighthearted series, much like *The Honeymooners* before it, often addressed the very contemporary concerns of its original audience. Though Fred's espousal of a ruthless and coldhearted business ethic is clearly not to be taken as a serious recommendation on the part of the makers of the series, his very description of business in those terms does suggest a quite serious anxiety over the ethics of a corporate capitalism that, after a decade of unprecedented growth in the 1950s, was playing a bigger and bigger role in the everyday lives of ordinary Americans. Ultimately, of course, the episode chooses Barney's genuine human feelings for Fred over the friendship with a buck advocated by Fred himself, which could be taken as an expression of a nostalgic preference for old-fashioned precapitalist values over those of modern American corporatism, though it could also be read simply as a reassurance that friendship and other such traditional forms of human relation can be preserved even amid the explosive rise of American consumer capitalism as the dominant economic force on the planet.

Meanwhile, Fred's all-out capitalist boosterism is typical of his own unquestioning acceptance of the values of an economic system whose benefits, as a working-class American, he did not necessarily share on an equal footing with higher-ups like his boss, Mr. Slate. Indeed, Fred seems to have accepted without question the American ethos of upward mobility and remains (despite one disaster after another) convinced that he will eventually rise in economic status if only he can come up with the proper scheme. Sometimes these schemes involve suddenly striking it rich; sometimes they simply involve getting a better job or starting a business. And sometimes they involve both, as in "At the Races" (November 18, 1960), in which Fred and Barney hope to make enough money betting on dinosaur races to be able to start their own business, a pool hall. Similarly, in "Cinderellastone"

(October 22, 1964), Fred's Cinderella dreams become literalized when his fairy godmother momentarily transforms him into a wealthy sophisticate—who convinces Mr. Slate to finally make Fred a foreman, giving him the increase in status and pay that he has sought for so long.

In "The Drive-In" (December 23, 1960), Fred and Barney again hope to start their own business (this time a drive-in restaurant), especially after Fred insists that owning their own business is the only way they will ever be able to be truly happy. The plan, however, leads to near disaster when Wilma grows jealous and suspicious in reaction to Fred's odd and secretive behavior. Indeed, Fred's efforts to start his own business invariably go awry, forcing him continually to return to his old job, usually after Wilma begs Mr. Slate to rehire him. But Fred never gives up, retaining his entrepreneurial spirit to the very end. In the final-season episode "Circus Business" (October 15, 1965), he even succeeds in buying his own carnival—though the acquisition of the failing business is essentially an accident. Fred ultimately manages to unload the carnival back on its original owner, but he still fails to learn his lesson. On the way home from the carnival, he nearly buys an oil well, though Wilma and the Rubbles talk him out of it. Immediately after they leave, of course, the well comes in, and oil gushes into the sky. Fred's final business venture occurs in "The Gravelberry Pie King" (November 12, 1965), when he puts Wilma's favorite pie recipe into production to supply a local chain of supermarkets. Unfortunately, Fred agrees to sell the pies at a price that is lower than the cost of production, so they lose money on each pie. Wilma again saves the day, this time by selling the recipe itself to the owner of the supermarkets, thus recouping their losses and even turning a modest profit.

In "A Haunted House Is Not a Home" (October 29, 1964), Fred again hopes to score an inheritance from a rich uncle. This time, in a plot largely borrowed from "The Missing Heir," a 1961 episode of the Hanna-Barbera series *Top Cat*, it is J. Giggles Flintstone who has apparently just died, leaving a fortune to Fred if only he can manage to survive one night in the uncle's haunted mansion. The uncle's ghoulish staff of servants, who supposedly stand to get the inheritance if Fred fails to stay the course, apparently spend the night attempting to murder him and Barney, who accompanies him. In the end, however, it all turns out to be an elaborate joke on the part of Uncle Giggles, who just wants to see if Fred has a sense of humor similar to his own. He doesn't, and the episode ends with an unamused Fred chasing his uncle with murderous intent.

At times, Fred fancies himself an inventor, hoping to come up with a marketable product that will make him rich. It never works, of course, as in "Itty Bitty Freddy" (October 1, 1964), where he comes up with a weight-reducing formula he is convinced will make him a millionaire. Unfortunately, the product works all too well: When Fred samples it, he shrinks to a tiny size—even smaller than Pebbles. The episode thus becomes a sort of parody of the 1950s science fiction classic *The Incredible Shrinking Man* (1957), which itself was a highly interesting exploration of masculine anxieties of the period. Indeed, Fred's own greatest concern about his new size is that Wilma will no longer find him adequate as a husband. In the end, in typical *Flintstones* fashion, Fred attempts to parlay his predicament into a career in show business, though the formula wears off and he returns to normal just as he seems on the verge of success via an appearance on the *Ed Sullistone Show*.

The *Flintstones* forayed into science fiction territory quite often, especially in the later seasons. This was primarily part of an effort to find ways to attract new viewers as ratings for the program began to slide. In the same way, they also attempted to tap into the success of other contemporary programs, as when "The Gruesomes" (November 22, 1964) features bizarre new neighbors reminiscent of the characters in *The Addams Family*, which had just started its run on ABC that September. Similarly, in "Samantha" (October 22, 1965), the Flintstones are visited by Samantha and Darrin Stephens from *Bewitched*, one of ABC's most successful programs at that time. But the movement into science fiction was an especially appropriate development for *The Flintstones*. After all, the series is in many ways a work of science fiction to begin with, a sort of alternate history narrative that imagines, with tongue in cheek, the impact of modern (sort of) technology on the prehistoric past. Moreover, *The Flintstones*, like science fiction, depends for its effects on placing the audience in an unfamiliar situation that provides a perspective from which they can view their own reality in new and different ways.

The episode "Time Machine" (January 15, 1965) is a typical example of *Flintstones* science fiction. Here, the Flintstones and Rubbles attend the Bedrock World's Fair, which features displays of all the latest scientific and technological marvels. This motif, clearly derived from the 1964 New York World's Fair, which was open from April until October in both 1964 and 1965, is one of many cases in which *The Flintstones* attempted to tap into the current interests of the American public. The 1964 World's Fair was a sort of showcase for the latest products of American industry, and the Bedrock fair is somewhat similar. For example, the Flintstones and Rubbles attend a display of the "latest labor-saving appliances," including an automatic dishwasher and automatic blender, both powered by monkeys, though Fred describes these items simply as "new ways to put a dent in our pocketbooks." Ultimately, the four go to the Hall of Science, where they try out an experimental time machine that sends them traveling to various points in the future, including Nero's Rome and King Arthur's England. They are also present for Benjamin Franklin's famous kite experiment and Columbus's discovery of America. Ultimately, and appropriately, they wind up at the 1964 New York World's Fair itself before finally returning home, concluding (predictably, given the stay-where-you-are emphasis of the entire series) that they prefer their own time to the futures they have visited.

Probably the best-known examples of science fiction in *The Flintstones* occur in the final season, in which Bedrock is visited by the Great Gazoo, a little green alien from another planet. In "The Great Gazoo" (October 29, 1965), Fred and Barney first encounter the alien, who declares himself their servant and takes them out to an expensive restaurant, only to disappear and leave them to pay the bill. The Great Gazoo makes periodic appearances throughout the rest of the final season of the series. In "The Stonefinger Caper" (November 19, 1965), the alien uses his magical powers to save the Flintstones from some spy-movie villains who have come to life. In "Seeing Doubles (December 17, 1965), *The Flintstones* becomes even more science fictional when Gazoo creates clones of Fred and Barney so that they can go bowling and go out to dinner with their wives at the same time. And, in "The Long, Long, Long Weekend" (January 21, 1966), Gazoo takes Fred and Barney on a time-travel trip into the twenty-first century, where Fred learns that interest on a $4 loan from Mr. Slate now amounts to $23 million. This episode thus addressed contemporary anxieties about mounting consumer debts in the *Flintstones* audience in the 1960s.

Gazoo's powers also helped Fred to fulfill, at least temporarily, his dreams of upward mobility. In "Two Men on a Dinosaur" (February 4, 1966), Gazoo's advice helps Fred and Barney win big at the races—which only serves to get them in trouble with a dangerous gangster. In "Boss for a Day" (February 25, 1966), Gazoo makes Fred the boss of Slate and Company for a day, while in "My Fair Freddy" (March 25, 1966), the alien helps transform Fred into a cultured sophisticate so that he can impress the members of a posh country club. In both cases, Fred's foray into the lives of the rich predictably turns to disaster, and he is relieved to return to his old self.

The Great Gazoo did add a new dimension to *The Flintstones*, but his appearance also signaled that the show was gradually losing its original identity. It was thus perhaps not surprising that the show ended its prime-time run on ABC after the season in which he appeared. Nevertheless, the Flintstones and Rubbles were only beginning their run as icons of American culture. In 1966, Hanna and Barbera topped off the prime-time run of *The Flintstones* with the release of a feature-length theatrical film, *The Man Called Flintstone,* a spy spoof that hooked into the popularity of such predecessors as the early James Bond films—much like its contemporary, the similarly titled *Our Man Flint* (1966). Despite this generic tie-in (and the insertion of numerous musical numbers), *The Man Called Flintstone* is essentially an extended episode of the television series, built on the mistaken-identity premise that was often central to the series itself. Here, Fred turns out to be a dead ringer for ace spy Rock Slag and so is enlisted to fill in when the latter is crippled in an attack by enemy agents just before a crucial mission to try to prevent the evil genius Green Goose from launching his deadly interrockinental missile. The assignment takes Fred first to Paris and then to Rome, and he brings Wilma, Barney, Pebbles, and Bamm-Bamm along on the pretense of a family vacation, though he is not allowed to reveal his mission to any of the others. Mass confusion—including an obligatory attack of jealousy on the part of Wilma when she discovers Fred meeting with a female agent—reigns as Fred bumbles his way through the episode, but of course Fred and Barney ultimately thwart the Green Goose, launching him and his minions into space aboard the missile. Given that this plot could have probably been encompassed by a single episode of the original series, the film is slow in places, and the musical numbers seem to have been added mostly to help extend the film to feature length. But the very similarity of the film to the series meant that fans of the series tended to find it charming.

After the cancellation of the ABC prime-time program, *The Flintstones* (with slightly varying series titles) returned to production in a series of Saturday-morning cartoons—on NBC from January 1967 until September 1970, then on CBS from September 1972 until January 1974, then back on NBC from February 1979 until September 1984. These subsequent series remained very much in the spirit of the original, though they were aimed more at children, among other things by giving an increasing role to Pebbles and Bamm-Bamm. Indeed, still another Saturday-morning series, *The Flintstone Kids,* which ran on ABC from September 1986 until September 1989, specifically featured the younger generation.

A sequence of made-for-TV movies also helped to keep the Flintstones and their fellow Bedrockians alive in the popular imagination, as did products such as the Fruity Pebbles and Cocoa Pebbles breakfast cereals and the Flintstones line of chewable children's vitamins, first introduced in 1968 and still a major seller in a variety of different formulas for the giant Bayer pharmaceutical conglomerate well into the twenty-first century. *The Flintstones* television programs have inspired a whole series of comic books, while the original *Flintstones* cartoons have continued to run in syndication since the show was first aired, with this phenomenon receiving a significant boost from the proliferation of cable channels in the 1990s. *The Flintstones* has been a particular mainstay of the Boomerang cable channel, which spun off from the Cartoon Network in 2000 and which, like its parent network and the *Flintstones* franchise itself, is owned by corporate media giant AOL Time Warner. The nostalgia-themed Boomerang network is testimony to the ongoing cultural power of animated series, driven in this case by Baby Boomers who hope to re-experience fondly remembered programs from their youth and to introduce their own children (or even grandchildren) to those programs.

The release of *The Flintstones* as a live-action theatrical film (directed by Brian Levant and featuring John Goodman as Fred) in 1994 signaled a similar form of cultural nostalgia. While replacing the animated characters and settings of this beloved series with live actors and real sets provides a certain amusing ironic jolt, the striking thing about the film is the extent to which it tries to be true to the original series on which it was based rather than simply poking fun at it, as many similar nostalgia-driven films have done, including *The Brady Bunch Movie* (1995) and cartoon-derived live-action films such as *The Adventures of Rocky and Bullwinkle* (2000) and *Josie and the Pussycats* (2001). The plot of the film involves a scheme on the part of corrupt Slate and Company executive Cliff Vandercave (Kyle MacLachlan) to dupe Fred into being the fall guy for Vandercave's scheme to embezzle funds from the company. All turns out well in the end, of course, and the film does an excellent job of bringing Bedrock and its inhabitants to life on the screen. As with the earlier *Man Called Flintstone*, however, the plot could have easily been encompassed within an episode of the original series—and would have made for a fairly weak episode at that. Levant's 2000 follow-up prequel, *The Flintstones in Viva Rock Vegas* (now with Mark Addy as a young Fred), once again showed blue-collar Fred defeating the scheme of an evil rich antagonist. However, it did cover some new ground by going back to the early days when bachelors Fred and Barney first met Wilma and Betty. Unfortunately, the film lacks energy and never really gets off the ground, partly because the ironic charge from seeing Bedrock come to life had already been used up in the first film.

The influence of *The Flintstones* on American culture also extends beyond the original prime-time run of the series in that the initial success of that series spurred a boom in prime-time animated programming. None of these subsequent series was successful in prime time, but several of them have become highly recognizable emblems of American popular culture. These series, including *The Jetsons, Top Cat,* and *Rocky and Bullwinkle,* are discussed in the next chapter.

NOTE

1. Dates given in parentheses after episode titles indicate the date of first broadcast of the episode in the United States.

CHAPTER 2

The Sixties Animation Explosion: The *Flintstones* Fallout

The well-known tendency of hit television programs to trigger imitations was already established by the early 1960s, so it was only natural that numerous other animated programs followed *The Flintstones* into prime time. Actually, in the fall of 1960, *The Flintstones* was already joined on ABC by *Matty's Funday Funnies* and *The Bugs Bunny Show* as the only animated programs on prime-time network television. Of these, *The Flintstones* was the biggest commercial success, ranking in the top 20 programs of that year in viewership, so it was not surprising that it returned to the ABC prime-time lineup for the 1961–1962 television season. It was also accompanied by a flurry of other animated programs in that season. ABC again led the way, supplementing *The Flintstones* with a second season of *Matty's Funday Funnies* and *Bugs Bunny*, while adding *Calvin and the Colonel* and *Top Cat* to its prime-time lineup. CBS joined the fray in the fall of 1961 with *The Alvin Show* (featuring Alvin and the Chipmunks), while NBC jumped onto the animated bandwagon with *The Bullwinkle Show*, a program that already had a substantial track record on afternoon television.

This explosion in prime-time animation was short-lived. By the end of the fall of 1962, all of these programs, with the exception of *The Flintstones*, had been removed from the prime-time schedule, though most of them lived on as part of the Saturday-morning children's programming schedule. ABC continued the animation experiment in the 1962–1963 season with *The Jetsons* and in the 1964–1965 season with *Jonny Quest*, but each of these programs was removed from prime time after a single season as well. The 1960s animation boom was over. *The Flintstones* lasted in prime time until 1966; after that there would not be another regularly scheduled prime-time animated program on network television until *The Simpsons* premiered in 1989.

Even though none of the animated programs that came to prime time in the wake of the success of *The Flintstones* was itself very successful in prime time, some of them became important parts of American popular culture. Several of them also built upon earlier pop cultural phenomena. *Calvin and the Colonel* was perhaps most notable for its echoes of the legendary *Amos and Andy* radio program. It was, in fact, created (and its title characters voiced) by Freeman Gosden and Charles Correll, who had been the voices of Amos and Andy on radio for years. *The Alvin Show* built upon the success of the late-1950s novelty recording group Alvin and the Chipmunks, voiced by Ross Bagdasarian (aka David Seville), who also did the voices of the chipmunks in the animated series. *Matty's Funday Funnies* was an anthology series that had run on Sunday afternoons since October 1959. However, it did not establish a distinctive identity for itself until it evolved into *Beany and Cecil* during its second season in prime time and then for several years afterward at various other times. The characters of Beany and Cecil themselves grew out of Bob Clampett's puppet show *Time for Beany*, which had run in syndication since the early 1950s.

Another show that drew upon the past was *The Bugs Bunny Show*, which featured an all-star cast of characters from the legendary Warner Brothers "Looney Tunes" cartoons. In addition to the wise-cracking, carrot-chomping title character and his ubiquitous stalker Elmer Fudd, the series featured cartoons starring Daffy Duck, Porky Pig, the Road Runner, Tweety and Sylvester, and Yosemite Sam, among others, most of whom dated back to the 1940s and all of whom were voiced by Mel Blanc. After two seasons in prime time, the series was moved to the Saturday-morning lineup, where it remained in various incarnations for the next three decades. Many of its characters also appeared in the feature film *Space Jam* (1996), in which basketball icon Michael Jordan helps them play a basketball game in which they must win their freedom from alien slavers. This film was only a moderate success, but it did lead to a sort of follow-up in 2003's *Looney Tunes: Back in Action*, which attempted to recapture the spirit of the original Looney Tunes cartoons with a mixture of the original characters and live actors. This film was a box-office bust, but its animated characters remain among the best-known characters in American popular culture. Bugs Bunny, in particular, is arguably the most important character in the history of American animation, as witnessed by the fact that he placed first in a 2002 *TV Guide* list of the 50 greatest cartoon characters, edging out Homer Simpson. It is certainly the case that the characters of *The Bugs Bunny Show*, taken as a group, are more important to the history of American animation than the collective cast of any other program that has appeared in prime time. However, Bugs Bunny and his cohorts are primarily important for their appearances in shorts made for theatrical distribution for nearly three decades prior to the prime-time program and in the Saturday-morning shows that ran for three decades afterward.

The lovable Bullwinkle the Moose (Bill Scott) and Rocky the Flying Squirrel (June Foray) of *The Bullwinkle Show* are also among the central icons of American television animation. These characters, created by Jay Ward and Bill Scott, not only headlined the show, but also established a presence beyond its bounds, especially in commercials for General Mills cereals, the program's sponsors. Their commercials for Trix, Cocoa Puffs, and Jets children's cereals are among the most memorable in American television history, though Rocky and Bullwinkle came to be associated especially closely with Cheerios, for which they appeared in numerous commercials that often seemed almost like segments from their television program.

The program itself began as *Rocky and His Friends* and ran for two years as an afternoon program on ABC before moving to prime time on NBC on Sunday evenings in the fall of 1961, changing its title to *The Bullwinkle Show*. It retained that title when it moved to Sunday afternoons and then Saturday mornings after its single year in prime time. Syndicated reruns of the program then ran on ABC from 1964 until 1973, and then again in 1981–1982. Despite the different titles and various airing times (and networks), the program remained pretty much the same throughout its run, and the collective four seasons of original programs are often together referred to as *The Rocky and Bullwinkle Show*. They are currently available on DVD under still another title, *Rocky and Bullwinkle and Friends*.

The program was marked by unusually crude and limited animation (backgrounds were especially rudimentary), but also by unusually sophisticated yet often painfully corny humor. In any case, the highly stylized animation was actually quite appropriate, enhancing the absurdist orientation of the entire program—which taps into a tradition in American comedy in which the films of the Marx brothers are probably the central examples. Each episode consisted of a series of brief animated sketches of various kinds. The show began and ended with brief (three–four minutes) cartoons featuring the adventures of Rocket J. Squirrel (aka Rocky the Flying Squirrel) and the dim-witted Bullwinkle the Moose, usually doing battle with their evil archenemies, Boris Badenov (Paul Frees) and Natasha Fatale (Foray).

These cartoons spanned a series of continuous plot arcs, with each segment ending in a cliffhanger in the mode of the old movie or radio serials. In each segment, a voiceover narrator (William Conrad) provided rousing, and sometimes sarcastic, commentary that was key to the overall effect. In between these main segments, the program proceeded through a series of other brief animated features, such as the parodic how-to feature "Mr. Know-It-All," in which Bullwinkle would amply demonstrate that he in fact knew very little. Other brief segments that appeared in various programs included "Aesop and Son," in which a cartoon version of Aesop would tell his son various instructional tales that parodied Aesop's Fables; "Adventures of Dudley Do-Right," in which the excessively dutiful Royal Canadian Mountie of the title battled the evil Snidely Whiplash, frequently saving damsel-in-distress Nell Fenwick; "Fractured Fairy Tales," in which narrator Edward Everett Horton would tell warped versions of various well-known fairy tales; and "Peabody's Improbable History," in which the brainy dog scientist Mr. Peabody and his pet boy Sherman would use their "Wayback" time machine to visit a variety of crucial historical turning points, usually finding that their intervention was required in order to make history turn out the way it was supposed to in the first place. The "Aesop," "Fairy Tale," and "Mr. Peabody" segments were distinguished by their punch-line endings, usually featuring an awful pun, often of a kind that children in the audience would be unlikely to understand. For example, when Mr. Peabody and Sherman discover an Alexander Graham Bell who clearly still has a great deal of work to do before he can invent the telephone, the dog explains that this was why Hemingway entitled his novel *For Whom the Bell Toils*.

From the very beginning, one of the most distinctive features of the *Rocky and Bullwinkle* shows was their self-consciousness and satirical engagement with popular culture, or even high culture, often in ways that were filled with fairly sophisticated humor and references that seemed to be meant more for adults than children. The last names of the villains Boris and Natasha, for example, apparently refer to the important Russian opera *Boris Godunov* and to the character of the femme fatale (especially prominent in film noir), neither of which would be likely to be recognized by children. The engagement with popular culture in the series might involve specific works or general phenomena. For example, the second season (which still aired on ABC in the afternoon) featured a sequence entitled "Metal Munching Mice," in which Boris and Natasha manage to gain control of an army of six-foot mechanical mice from the moon—a typically absurd motif—then set the mice to work devouring all of the television antennas in America. Their reasoning is simple: Americans are so addicted to television that, with their reception impeded, they will all immediately emigrate to other countries where television reception is still available. With the country deserted, Boris and Natasha will be free to take over. Rocky and Bullwinkle are ultimately able to defeat the plot, with the help of the little green moon men Gidney and Cloyd, who inadvertently supplied the mice to the villains in the first place. Ridiculous plot aside, this sequence makes some telling comments on the growing reliance of Americans on television to fill their idle hours. It also provides a reminder of what commercial television is for as it shows network moguls scrambling to come to grips with the fact that they are no longer able to deliver advertising to their audiences while the antennas are out of commission. As the network chief puts it, "We're pitching, but they're not catching."

Of course, "Metal Munching Mice" can also be taken as a gentle mockery of American Cold War paranoia, the ludicrous plot by Boris and Natasha perhaps suggesting that fears of elaborate Soviet plots against the United States were a bit silly as well. The Cold War was in fact consistently central to the satire of *Rocky and Bullwinkle*, and it is no accident that Boris and Natasha are blatantly Russian, even though they are officially identified as being from "Pottsylvania." That they are also blatantly stereotypical villains suggests an awareness of the extent to which conventional notions of the evil and savage Other, which had been a central element of the American national narrative from the very beginning, were simply carried over and applied to the Soviets in the Cold War years.

The prime-time run of *The Bullwinkle Show* began with the relatively brief sequence "The Three Moosketeers," which ran for eight segments at the beginning of the fall 1961 season. In typical punning fashion, this sequence is set in the province of Applesauce-Lorraine, which is ruled by the good king Once-a-Louse. Younger children might be unamused by these warped versions of Alsace-Lorraine and King Wenceslaus, but even more obscure (at least to children) cultural referents are there as well, as in the naming of François Villain, the principal bad guy of the sequence, after fifteenth-century French poet-thief François Villon. Villain, the half-brother of Once-a-Louse, unseats his kindly brother and then immediately begins to raise taxes, causing Athos, the last remaining musketeer, to go off in search of Porthos and Aramis, his former comrades. He finds instead Rocky and Bullwinkle, mistaking them for the two musketeers because of his bad eyesight. He brings the two back to Applesauce-Lorraine, where the three manage to restore Once-a-Louse, and low taxes, to the kingdom—even though Athos admits that he isn't a real musketeer either, else he would have been dead for hundreds of years.

In the sequence "Lazy Jay Ranch," Rocky and Bullwinkle buy a ranch in Wyoming that they see advertised in the want ads. They then leave their home in tiny Frostbite Falls, Minnesota, to travel out West to start their new life as ranchers. The ranch, which they have bought from Lazy Jay himself (the world's laziest man), turns out to be largely desolate, though it does have one thriving crop: worms of all kinds. Rocky and Bullwinkle spend much of the episode comically attempting to herd worms, with Boris and Natasha trying as usual to undermine them, especially after the two villains mistakenly conclude that there are large deposits of valuable minerals on the ranch. The ensuing plot wanders almost aimlessly from one nonsensical episode to another, but Rocky and Bullwinkle eventually return home to Frostbite Falls, none the worse for the wear, having reinvigorated the town of Squaw's Ankle, Wyoming, by supplying it with the worms, which have now been electrified by a lightning strike.

This sequence provides several excellent examples of the self-consciousness of the series; for example, it includes a number of moments in which the characters speak directly to the audience, or even to the narrator. The story begins as Bullwinkle becomes obsessed with watching westerns on television, which eventually causes him to get carried away and shoot his television set during an on-screen gun battle. With no television, Rocky and Bullwinkle then try to pass the time in various ways, at one point becoming desperate enough even to try reading. Finally, they decide to go West themselves, a move Rocky, who repeatedly worries about the show's viewership during the sequence, endorses because he figures it might be good for their ratings. At one point, Boris grabs the script for the episode they are in and destroys it, wanting to act on his own rather than in a manner dictated by the writers. He then has to piece the script back together in order to try to figure out what to do next. In the following scene, Rocky and Bullwinkle become confused and Bullwinkle speaks a line that was meant for Rocky, while Rocky speaks a line that was meant for the narrator.

The final sequence of *Bullwinkle* on prime time was "Topsy-Turvy World," which ran for 14 segments, beginning on January 7, 1962. Here, Rocky and Bullwinkle realize that the April weather in Frostbite Falls is unaccountably warm. Their investigation then reveals that the entire earth has tilted on its axis, causing strange weather events around the globe. The two heroes manage to right the planet and the weather fairly easily—via a series of events that is even sillier than usual, as when they are forced to battle a tribe of Polynesian cannibals (led, unaccountably, by Badenov) whom the shift has transferred to the North Pole. On the other hand, this sequence now appears almost prescient in retrospect, given contemporary concerns about shifts in the weather due to environmental effects.

The highlight of the single prime-time season of *The Bullwinkle Show* was probably the sequence "Missouri Mish Mash," which ran in 26 segments beginning on November 12, 1961. Here, in a nonsensical series of events that nicely illustrates the absurdist roots of the series, Rocky and Bullwinkle decide to travel to Peaceful Valley, Missouri, to attend a moose convention. Traveling on foot, because they can't afford other transportation from Minnesota to Missouri, they find themselves besieged by Boris and Natasha, even though Fearless Leader has ordered the two villains to make sure that the moose and squirrel reach Missouri safely. At one point, a blow to the head turns Boris into a do-gooder, which causes him to do everything he can to undermine the plans of the evil Fearless Leader. Boris, of course, fails in his efforts to stop the two heroes, but when Rocky and Bullwinkle finally reach Peaceful Valley they find themselves in the midst of a bitter feud between the Hatful and Floy families, which seem to include all of the inhabitants of the area. Eventually, it becomes clear why Fearless Leader wanted the two safe. He is searching for the Kirward Derby, a hat that makes its wearer the smartest man on earth—and that Fearless Leader is confident will give him the intellect to conquer the world. Unfortunately, it can only be located by a real idiot, so Fearless Leader hopes to dupe Bullwinkle into finding it for him.

Bullwinkle does, in fact, locate the magical derby. Then, after some wrangling for possession of it, Rocky and Bullwinkle decide to take the hat to Washington so that the government can avail itself of the hat's powers. Unfortunately, they still can't afford transportation, so Rocky quickly gets himself elected to Congress to represent Peaceful Valley by promising the Floys he will expel all Hatfuls from the county and promising the Hatfuls he will expel all Floys. Rocky and Bullwinkle are thus sent to Washington at public expense—with Fearless Leader and Boris and Natasha in hot pursuit. In Washington, the moose and squirrel encounter their old friends, the moon men Gidney and Cloyd, who are also seeking the derby, which turns out to have been created by a wizard on the moon in an effort to smarten up an incredibly stupid prince so that he could rule the moon more wisely. (The hat was loaned to Gidney and Cloyd to aid them in their first trip to earth, but they accidentally left it behind when they returned home.) In the end, the hat is returned to Gidney and Cloyd, who take it back to the moon, once again foiling Fearless Leader's quest for world domination.

The naming of the Kirward Derby was typical of the show's lighthearted play with American popular culture. It was obviously a warped version of the name of Durward Kirby, at the time a fairly well-known television personality (among other things, he was co-hosting the *Candid Camera* program at the time). But the name was clearly used in fun and did not seem intended as any particular commentary on Kirby, though the latter actually threatened a lawsuit over the name. The suit, however, was dropped after Jay Ward responded, "Please sue us; we love publicity." This episode and many other details regarding the background of the program are detailed in the excellent book *The Moose that Roared: The Story of Jay Ward, Bill Scott, a Flying Squirrel, and a Talking Moose* (published by St. Martin's Press in 2000) by Keith Scott, himself a talented voice artist who worked on the 2000 theatrical film based on the series.

Fearless Leader is a particularly interesting villain. Though he is the boss of the spectacularly Russian Boris and Natasha, he himself is clearly depicted as a leftover German Nazi military officer. From the point of view of the early twentieth century, this depiction reminds us of how recent World War II still was when the series was originally made. But it also serves as a central reminder of one of the major strategies of American Cold War propaganda, which consistently attempted to equate German and Soviet "totalitarianism" (with a special attempt in the early Cold War years to equate Josef Stalin with Adolf Hitler). This strategy took advantage of ongoing anti-Nazi feelings on the part of Americans who still remembered World War II and the associated shocking revelations concerning the Nazi death camps such as those at Auschwitz and Dachau. On the other hand, it made no sense and ignored the fact that the Americans and Soviets had been allies against the Germans in the recent world war—and that it was, in fact, the Soviet Red Army that was principally responsible for the German defeat.

One could, of course, read the lumping together of German Nazi military officers with stereotypical Russian spies in *Rocky and Bullwinkle* as a critique of this Cold War strategy, but there is little in the program itself to indicate that this critique was actually intended. On the other hand, the inclusion of Fearless Leader among the show's villains does contribute to the show's satirical suggestion (however mild) of the American tendency to demonize enemies and to view them in stereotypical ways, lumping them all together without regard to their actual characteristics. The treatment of Rocky's congressional campaign and his subsequent debut in Congress (where he becomes a great hit with his colleagues by accidentally beginning his maiden speech by calling for Congress to adjourn) is also mildly satirical in its treatment of the American political process, but such critiques in *Rocky and Bullwinkle* are always good humored, couched in such silliness that they are unlikely to offend or inspire anyone.

Still, the very presence of such material indicates the extent to which the show was aimed at an audience that was expected to include at least a reasonable number of adults. The same might be said for the show's consistent consciousness of its status as a fictional artifact, which anticipated the rise of postmodern "metafiction" later in the 1960s. The show's ability to appeal to viewers of a variety of ages no doubt accounts for the ongoing popularity of the series, which has remained a presence on American television in the decades since it was originally canceled in 1964. Reruns aired as part of the regular ABC Saturday-morning lineup until 1973, then in syndication. Occasional continuing appearances in television commercials helped to keep the moose and squirrel in the public consciousness as well.

Rocky and Bullwinkle inspired a series of live-action films, beginning in 1992 with the made-for-TV film *Boris and Natasha* (directed by Charles Martin Smith), in which the villains from *Rocky and Bullwinkle* got their own full-length spin-off, starring Dave Thomas and Sally Kellerman in the title roles. Here, the end of the Cold War does nothing to discourage Fearless Leader (Christopher Neame) from pursuing his nefarious quest for world domination. So he sends his best agent, the mysterious Agent X (Larry Cedar) to America to attempt to recover a new top-secret time-travel device that will give him the power to rule the world. Meanwhile, he sends along the bumbling Boris and Natasha as decoys to divert attention from his real agent. Just as it appears that Fearless Leader might succeed in his quest, all ends well for the world when Boris and Natasha use the device to return to the beginning of the film and negate everything that just happened. *Boris and Natasha* is a comedy of errors filled with sight gags and bad one-liners, though it has its entertaining moments. Surprisingly, though, Rocky and Bullwinkle do not really appear at all—though we learn near the end of the film that Boris and Natasha's (human) neighbors in the United States are actually secret agents who are the moose and squirrel in disguise—via "extensive surgery."

In 1999, Dudley-Do-Right got his own self-titled theatrical film, directed by Hugh Wilson and starring Brendan Fraser as Dudley and Sarah Jessica Parker as Nell. In 1997, Fraser had starred in *George of the Jungle,* based on a Saturday-morning carton series also created by Jay Ward, so he was a natural for the role, especially as that film had been a substantial hit, grossing more than $100 million at the box office. *Dudley Do-Right,* though, was a dud—with both critics and audiences.

By most accounts, Des McAnuff's *The Adventures of Rocky and Bullwinkle* (2000), which finally brought the moose and squirrel themselves to the big screen, completed a clean sweep of truly awful live-action theatrical films based on *Rocky and Bullwinkle*. Actually, this film, which features a computer-generated cartoon Rocky and Bullwinkle amid a cast of otherwise live actors, is probably not as bad as its reputation. It certainly has its hilarious moments, as in one scene in which Fearless Leader (played by Robert De Niro, no less) speaks with Boris and Natasha (Jason Alexander and Rene Russo) by videophone, then goes into De Niro's famous "are you looking at me" routine from the film *Taxi Driver*. In fact, this film, built around a plot in which Fearless Leader attempts to take over all of America's television channels with programming so bad that the entire population is reduced to mindless zombies, does an excellent job of capturing the spirit of the original series, including the excellent imitation of the original narrator by Keith Scott, who also does the voice of Bullwinkle in the film. That spirit is probably better suited to the original format of brief cartoon segments than to a full-length live-action film, but this film is still worth watching, at least for fans of the original series.

Despite the prominence of such characters as Bugs Bunny and Bullwinkle the Moose, the 1960s programs created especially for prime time were dominated by those produced by Hanna-Barbera, with *The Flintstones*, of course, leading the way. Indeed, both *Top Cat* and *The Jetsons* bore a clear family resemblance to *The Flintstones*, though *Jonny Quest* moved in a new direction by seeking to bring the action and adventure of classic comic books and radio serials to television animation. In fact, the show was originally conceived as a direct adaptation of the old *Jack Armstrong* radio serial, but problems with securing the rights to the serial led to the show's reconceptualization as an original drama, ultimately inspired as much by the "Terry and the Pirates" comic strip as by *Jack Armstrong*. Designed by comic book artist Doug Wildey based on the conception of the show by Hanna and Barbera, *Jonny Quest* showed a strong awareness of its historical context in the Cold War—an awareness that itself showed the influence of more contemporary Cold War works such as the early James Bond films, which had begun to appear in 1962. As such, the show often featured high levels of violence, while its plots typically involved ominous threats to the security of Western civilization—materials that were really more suitable for an adult audience. From the beginning, though, the show was designed to appeal to children through the use of the young boy Jonny Quest (voiced by Tim Matthieson, who later changed the spelling of his last name to "Matheson") as its central figure, along with his stereotypical turban-wearing Indian sidekick Hadji (Danny Bravo) and his lovable dog Bandit.

The adult protagonists of *Jonny Quest* were he-man superscientist Dr. Benton Quest (Jonny's father, voiced by John Stephenson in the prime-time season) and intelligence agent "Race" Bannon (Mike Road). Bannon is a pilot and martial arts expert who has been assigned by his employers—presumably the C.I.A.—to serve as a bodyguard and, essentially, babysitter for Jonny. They fear that the boy will be kidnapped by Quest's enemies, who have apparently already killed Jonny's mother and who might seek to trade the boy's safety for some of the extensive top-secret data to which Dr. Quest has access. Quest's scientific background helped to bring a strong science fiction element to the show, while Bannon's particular skills enhanced the action and adventure elements.

Though it was never quite specified, *Jonny Quest* seemed to be set in the near future, which allowed it to project scientific and technological advances that were not yet available when the show was produced. For example, the first episode of the show, "The Mystery of the Lizard Men" (September 18, 1964), features a mad-scientist villain who has developed a superlaser that he plans to use to shoot down the rocket that is launching the first manned mission to the moon. The action thus seems to be set several years in the future (the first actual moon mission was in August 1969), even as it draws upon contemporary interest in the space race in 1964. Meanwhile, the mad scientist is protected by a small army of the lizard men of the title, though they actually turn out to be ordinary men in lizard suits. Dr. Quest foils the villain by using a large mirror to reflect the laser beam back onto its source, destroying both the laser and the mad scientist. The moon launch is thus saved, even though there is never any explanation of why the villain had wanted to destroy it in the first place. Then again, within the Cold War logic of the show, no explanation is required. According to this logic, it is simply a given that the United States is surrounded by sinister forces bent on destruction of the American way of life and the sabotage of key American projects, such as the effort to be the first to land a man on the moon.

These sinister forces were often represented by mad-scientist villains reminiscent of those appearing in the Bond films, vaguely reflecting anxieties about what was perceived as the coldly scientific worldview of the Soviet Union, even if the villains were not typically identified specifically as Soviets. On the other hand, the sense of being threatened and besieged that informed the American mindset during the Cold War extended well beyond the Soviets. For one thing, Communist China was also perceived as a serious threat to American security, especially after the Korean War of 1950–1953 had brought American troops directly into conflict with Chinese forces. Indeed, China was perceived by many as considerably more frightening than the Soviet Union, based on the perception that the Chinese were driven by an "Oriental" mode of thought that made them illogical and unpredictable.

This particular kind of stereotypical thinking has a long and shameful history that extends back well before the Cold War. It is, in fact, central to the phenomenon of "Orientalism" that the late eminent scholar Edward Said described in his seminal book of the same title (New York: Vintage-Random House, 1979). Focusing especially on the Middle East, but with ramifications for the rest of the non-European world as well, Said demonstrates how thoroughly European descriptions of the rest of the world have, at least since the eighteenth century, been based more on stereotypes originating in Europe than on the actual characteristics of the cultures and peoples being described. Further, Said notes that this kind of stereotypical thinking has done a great deal of harm and that it has served as a particularly important ideological underpinning for such projects as European colonialism.

The new global political situation of the Cold War, in which the United States replaced Great Britain as the principal standard-bearer of Western modernity in the non-Western world, brought the United States to an unprecedented level of involvement with the kinds of peoples and cultures that had long been subject to Orientalist stereotypes in Britain and the rest of Europe. With little experience in dealing with these non-Western cultures, the Americans all too often simply accepted the stereotypes that they inherited from their British predecessors—with an extra dash of Cold War paranoia that often led Americans to think of Asians, Africans, and other non-Western peoples as dangerous, untrustworthy savages who threatened our Western way of life. Then again, such stereotypes had already been established in American culture as well, as in the depiction of virtually all black Africans as savage cannibals in the popular Tarzan novels of Edgar Rice Burroughs, which themselves had inspired numerous successful film adaptations from the 1930s onward. Meanwhile, the Soviets were often described in American Cold War propaganda using essentially the same stereotypes about savagery and unreliability, though the Soviets were also paradoxically described as excessively rational and scientific in their thinking, while typical Orientalist descriptions saw non-Western people as virtually incapable of rational thought.

Given the prevalence of Orientalist thinking in the rhetoric of the Cold War years, it should come as no surprise that a program such as *Jonny Quest*, which was so thoroughly situated within Cold War politics, would often fall prey to Orientalist stereotyping as well. Of course, the show inherited these Orientalist tendencies from such predecessors as *Jack Armstrong* and *Terry and the Pirates*, but it tended to give them a new Cold War spin. Thus, the antagonists who shoot down and attempt to steal an American missile in the second episode, "Arctic Splashdown" (September 25, 1964), seem vaguely Oriental and thus sneaky and conniving, but they are also high-tech pirates who fit more into the mold of the typical James Bond mad scientist than the typical Oriental. In any case, a high percentage of the episodes of *Jonny Quest* were set in various Third-World locales, which presumably opened up opportunities for exotic adventures.

After the first two mad-scientist episodes, the next five episodes in succession were all Orientalist episodes, followed by a switch back to the science fiction mode in episode eight, "The Robot Spy" (November 6, 1964). Of these Orientalist episodes, two are set in India, including "Calcutta Adventure" (October 30, 1964), a flashback episode that explains how Hadji became the ward of Dr. Quest. Perhaps most telling among these five episodes are the first two, "The Curse of Anubis" (October 2, 1964) and "Pursuit of the Po-Ho" (October 9, 1964). In the former, oily Arab Ahmed Kareem dreams of uniting the Arab people and building a great Arab nation. However, Arabs being what they are in the Orientalist view that pervades this episode, he concludes that he must use forces such as hatred and superstition rather than logical argument to convince his people to band together. He thus concocts a plan to lure the Quest team to Egypt ("a cruel country, at least by our standards," remarks Quest on arrival), where he has already conspired to steal a sacred statue of the god Anubis. Kareem then traps Dr. Quest and Bannon in a tomb with the stolen statue so that they can be found there with it. He reasons that the Arab people will be so outraged that one of their sacred treasures has apparently been stolen by these Americans that they will unite in their common hatred of the United States. The evil plan fails when Jonny and Hadji rescue their adult counterparts, and when a resurrected mummy visits the curse of Anubis on Abdul Kareem, but the episode does nothing to suggest that the devious Kareem is anything other than a typical Arab or that his own view of Arabs as motivated primarily by hatred and superstition is anything but accurate.

"Pursuit of the Po-Ho" switches its focus to the jungles of South America and to the Po-Ho Indians, repeatedly described in the episode as "savages" and "devils." Here, first a colleague of Dr. Quest, who is apparently in the region doing research, and then Dr. Quest himself, who comes there in an attempt to rescue his friend, are captured by the Po-Ho. The Indians seem motivated by little other than pure malice, though they also plan to sacrifice the outsiders to appease their savage gods. Luckily the Po-Ho, vicious though they may be, are also extremely dim-witted, so Bannon is able to rescue the two captives relatively easily, partly by disguising himself as one of their gods in order to take advantage of their superstitious nature.

India in *Jonny Quest* is treated as relatively modern. Thus, the two early India episodes are both mad-scientist episodes, though they still tend to depict Indians as a collection of schemers, con artists, and beggars. These episodes exemplify the mixture of science and the supernatural that were quite typical of the series, though the emphasis was clearly on the former. Indeed, as with the lizard men of this first episode, supernatural or fantastic elements were often introduced in the show, only to be revealed to have a perfectly rational basis—they were usually used by villains to frighten off curiosity seekers—in keeping with the show's fundamentally scientific worldview.

All in all, *Jonny Quest* lasted only through a single season of 26 episodes, though these episodes were rerun on Saturday mornings for years afterward. An updated version of the program was briefly produced in 1987, followed by another version, *The Real Adventures of Jonny Quest*, which ran from 1996 to 1999, primarily on the Cartoon Network. *Jonny Quest* was also the basis for the 1995 feature-length made-for-TV animated film *Jonny Quest vs. the Cyber Insects*. The program was again resurrected (after a fashion) in 2004 (after a 2003 pilot) with the appearance on the Cartoon Network's Adult Swim segment of *The Venture Brothers*, a *Jonny Quest* spoof.

If *Jonny Quest* was ostensibly the most serious of Hanna-Barbera's primetime cartoons from the 1960s, *Top Cat* was ostensibly the lightest, though its comedy could be quite sophisticated. Indeed, while it employed a cast of lovable humanized cartoon animals (a classic staple of children's cartoons), *Top Cat*, with its snappy dialogue, relatively complex plots, and relatively little reliance on slapstick or other cartoonish sight gags, was perhaps the most adult-oriented of the Hanna-Barbera series of the 1960s. Meanwhile, just as *The Flintstones* was largely inspired by *The Honeymooners*, *Top Cat* drew much of its inspiration from the classic Phil Silvers sitcom *The Phil Silvers Show*, which was subtitled *You'll Never Get Rich*, the original title of the series when it first aired in 1955.

The character of Top Cat himself (voiced by Arnold Stang), a lovable rogue who constantly schemes and cons to try to get ahead but who is a good soul deep down, clearly has much in common with Silvers's Sergeant Ernest Bilko, so much so that Stang has reportedly said that he had to struggle during the making of the series to avoid sounding too much like Silvers. On the other hand, much of the humor of the Silvers show was derived from its satirical treatment of army life—and, by extension, of bureaucracy in general. *Top Cat* dealt with much broader concerns and—like *The Flintstones*, though less obviously—could be read very much as a general commentary on the new American consumerist society that had arisen out of the transformational decade of the 1950s.

Top Cat lives in Manhattan, just off Madison Avenue in "Hoagy's Alley," an apparent reference to "Hogan's Alley," the New York dwelling place of the Yellow Kid, the central character of one of the first comic strips to appear in America. This fairly arcane reference was typical of the series, which often featured sly in-jokes and allusions recognizable only to the cartoon cognoscenti. Top Cat is poor and often doesn't know where his next meal is coming from, but he remains optimistic that he will some day strike it rich, meanwhile doing his best to live as if he already were. He may have to sleep at night in a trash can, but he has embellished the can with a television antenna and a "Do Not Disturb" sign. Further, it is placed immediately next to the police telephone box intended for the use of the local human beat cop, Officer Dibble (voiced by Allen Jenkins). Top Cat himself makes extensive use of the phone, much to Dibble's dismay. Thus, like Fred Flintstone, he has ironic access to the latest technological innovations (a stray cat would be no more likely than a cave man to have a phone and television). However, because of his poverty, Top Cat has to scheme and steal in order to have such niceties, providing a potential reminder of the fact that some Americans had more access to the contemporary economic and technological boom than did others. Meanwhile, though elements such as the alley and the trash can are vaguely derived from the real conditions under which stray cats live, the show is more about human struggles than feline ones. In fact, the struggles of Top Cat and his gang to get by from one day to the next, all the while dreaming of the one big strike that will make them rich forever, must surely have looked familiar to many of their viewers at the time. Part of the genius of the series was its ability to deal with potentially serious issues while maintaining enough ironic distance from reality to ensure that its treatment of these issues remained amusing rather than sobering.

Top Cat is very much dominated by its fast-talking title character, who differs substantially from his Hanna-Barbera counterpart Fred Flintstone. Fred can be an inconsiderate, loud-mouthed lout, but he is basically a stable, hard-working family man. Top Cat is a rakish bachelor dedicated to avoiding work, though, like Fred, he is at bottom a kind soul with a heart of gold. Moreover, Top Cat is not nearly as much of an irresponsible individualist as he might appear. He serves as a father figure for the gang of stray cats that joins him in the alley, making the gang a family of sorts. While he is clearly the boss of the gang and sometimes takes advantage of their devotion to him, he also feels responsible for their welfare and does what he can to ensure that they are provided for.

The genuine affection and mutual devotion that bind together this gang of stray cats provides the series with a sense of warmth that a program based on a group of scam artists might otherwise have lacked. Extra interest is also added by the fact that these characters are quite fully developed, each with his own distinctive look, voice, and personality. Providing another link to *You'll Never Get Rich,* Top Cat's closest lieutenant is Benny the Ball, who is voiced by Maurice Gosfield, the same actor who had played Private Doberman, the principal sidekick of Sgt. Bilko. Benny, who has much in common with both Doberman and Barney Rubble, is slow witted but good natured and sometimes insightful, given to asking sensible, if naïve, questions that help to keep Top Cat from getting completely out of control with his scheming.

Choo-Choo (Marvin Kaplan) is perhaps Top Cat's most enthusiastic follower, though his impulsive and energetic attempts to follow his leader's instructions often get him into trouble. He speaks with a thick Brooklyn accent and has a weakness for extremely glamorous lady cats, though he is painfully shy with the opposite sex and usually has little success with courtship, even with the help of Top Cat and the rest of the gang. In contrast, Fancy-Fancy (voiced by John Stephenson in imitation of Cary Grant) is a suave, debonair ladies' man who spends most of his time successfully wooing various female felines, though he is always willing to drop what he is doing and come to the aid of Top Cat and the gang whenever needed. The Brain (voiced by Leo de Lyon) is both ignorant and stupid, but follows Top Cat with a charmingly innocent loyalty, even if he often has no clear understanding of just what it is his boss is trying to achieve. Finally, Spook (also voiced by de Lyon) is the group's hipster-beatnik, a jazz-loving cool cat who has at least some pretensions to being an intellectual. He is clearly coded as white, though he is a virtual enactment of Norman Mailer's seminal 1957 essay "The White Negro," in which Mailer argued that the white beatnik culture of the late 1950s was largely inspired by African American cultural models. In this light, of course, Spook's name could have racial, or even racist overtones, though no one ever seems to have complained about them—and it is certainly the case that his portrayal in the series seems innocuous.

Authority figures such as Officer Dibble are almost invariably human (and white) in *Top Cat,* while the members of the gang are all feline, potentially adding a racial coding to the confrontation between upper-class authority and the gang's lower-class resistance. But the political edge of this series, which constantly hovers on the verge of the subversive, is always muted, so it is no surprise that the series avoids this racial coding, making the multicolored cats "white" as well. Dibble, meanwhile, is far from a simple antagonist to the cats. He is himself very much a part of the ensemble cast, and the love-hate relationship between Dibble and Top Cat is a key element of the series. Dibble is a dedicated, well-meaning, honest cop, and his relatively positive portrayal further serves to short-circuit potentially subversive readings of the series as a confrontation between oppressive authority, as represented by Dibble, and individual freedom, as represented by the cats. The cats constantly scheme against Dibble, of course, sometimes getting him into big trouble with his sergeant, but they tend to come to his aid if this trouble gets too serious, preferring to have Dibble, whom they know how to handle, as their beat cop rather than some potentially more difficult adversary.

While such elements as this relationship with the police are specific to *Top Cat*, the various adventures of Top Cat and the gang are, when examined closely, extremely similar to those encountered by the Flintstones. In several episodes, for example, they inadvertently become involved with criminal elements (generally human), though in this case these episodes serve the function of making the cats, who live on the edge of the law, more sympathetic by setting them apart from real criminals (also generally human), who venture far beyond the edge. Sometimes, in fact, these episodes set the cats in direct opposition to criminals. In "The Golden Fleecing" (February 7, 1962), Benny garners $2,000 in an insurance settlement, but then is fleeced of it in a poker game by a group of con artists, including a Marilyn Monroesque (feline) torch singer named Honeydew Melon, for whom Benny develops an infatuation. Top Cat saves the day, however. Not only does he win back the money at poker, but he even captures the gang and hands them over to Dibble. Other episodes also seem designed specifically to make the cats more sympathetic, such as "T. C. Minds the Baby" (January 17, 1962), in which the cats find a human baby, then decide to adopt and take care of him, though Officer Dibble eventually helps to restore the infant to its mother.

Some episodes of *Top Cat* feature attempts by the cats to break into show business, one of the most common *Flintstones* motifs. In "Naked Town" (November 22, 1961), for example, the cats learn that an episode of the popular television series *Naked Town* (obviously modeled after *Naked City*, which ran on ABC from 1958 to 1963 and which was, in fact, shot on location at various spots in New York City) is to be shot in Hoagy's Alley. Unfortunately, real-life criminals Knuckles and Ape also find out about the shooting, which will involve a simulated robbery of a warehouse just off the alley. Posing as the TV crew, they rob the warehouse themselves, enlisting the aid of the cats, who think they are acting in the program, to help load their truck. Dibble is suspended for allowing the robbery—he also believed they were shooting for television—while the cats are arrested as accessories to the robbery. In the end, the cats, having escaped, join with Dibble to apprehend the felons, winning Dibble a reinstatement and a month's vacation. Unfortunately, all is not well for the cats, as his replacement during that month cracks down on them in his absence and makes them clean up the alley.

The most representative episodes of *Top Cat* are those in which T. C. and the gang scheme to get rich or at least to improve their meager standard of living. These schemes were often very much a product of their time. In "Space Monkey" (February 14, 1962), for example, Top Cat reads of the luxurious lifestyle of a chimp that is training for the space program. So he maneuvers to enter the program as well, only to find that he is so successful at proving his superiority to the chimp that he is tapped for the first space-flight, narrowly escaping by switching places with the chimp. Sometimes, these episodes nod toward the new awareness of international culture that had been forced upon the American populace as a result of the emergence of the United States as a global military, political, and economic power after World War II. However, such episodes tended carefully to avoid the aspects of this awareness that might cause anxiety—in particular the growing realization of the relative poverty of most of the world relative to the increasing affluence of the United States. Thus, in episodes such as "The Maharajah of Pookajee" (October 4, 1961) and "The $1,000,000 Derby" (October 18, 1961), Top Cat poses, respectively, as a wealthy Indian maharajah and an Arab oil millionaire, in both cases hoping to score special favors from those who wish to profit from their relationship with him. Such episodes played upon Orientalist stereotypes about the vast wealth and power of Oriental potentates, while at the same time casting the American Top Cat in the sympathetic role of underdog, reversing actual international relationships.

More commonly, Top Cat's schemes involved more straightforward attempts to cash in on the possibilities for upward mobility presumably offered by American capitalism. The only thing he is not willing to do in order to make money is actual work, and the fact that his plans invariably fail sends a clear and completely conventional pro-work message to the audience. Time and again, Top Cat seems on the verge of striking it rich, only to have something go wrong at the last minute. In "The $1,000,000 Derby," for example, he bets a bundle on a big horse race, and his horse seems to be about to win in a photo finish. Unfortunately, the vain horse stops just short of the finish line to pose for the photo. In "The Tycoon" (December 27, 1961), the wealthy mogul of the title watches a television show (clearly based on *The Millionaire*, which ran on CBS from 1955 to 1960) in which a rich philanthropist distributes his wealth to the needy. The tycoon decides he would like to do the same, but is so cut off from everyday life that he doesn't know how to find any poor people. When he spots Benny selling raffle tickets (for 25¢ each) in one of Top Cat's numerous moneymaking schemes, he mistakes the gang for a needy family and gives Benny a check for $1,000,000. Benny hands the check over to Top Cat, who assumes Benny has accepted a 25¢ check for one of the raffle tickets. Exasperated, Top Cat tears up the check and throws it away.

Canceled after its first 30-episode season in prime time, *Top Cat* ran in syndication for several years afterward. In addition, amid a surge of movies based on classic cartoon characters that appeared in the 1970s and 1980s was *Top Cat and the Beverly Hills Cats* (1987), in which the gang travels to Beverly Hills after Benny seems on the verge of inheriting a fortune—a plot partly derived from that of the original series episode "The Missing Heir" (November 1, 1961). The series also inspired a comic book that began immediately after the premiere of the television show and continued to appear sporadically until 1973. The entire series is now available for home viewing on DVD. Thus, though Top Cat never became a first-level cartoon superstar like Fred Flintstone, he still remains a presence in American popular culture in the early twenty-first century.

The same can also be said for the major characters of *The Jetsons*, which was quite transparently conceived as another version of *The Flintstones*, this time transplanting the concerns of 1960s American society a hundred years or so into the future instead of into the distant past. As with the anachronistic appliances of *The Flintstones*, technological extrapolation is a major source of humor in *The Jetsons*, except that the technology of the 1960s is now replaced by a full array of futuristic gadgetry, including robots, flying cars, video phones, intelligent computers, and the Jetsons' own fully automated high-rise apartment of the future. In short, *The Jetsons* features many of the iconic images of its predecessors in science fiction, except that now these future technologies are treated humorously, intentionally exaggerated and with a self-conscious awareness of their status as science fiction clichés.

Like *The Flintstones*, however, *The Jetsons* is first and foremost an animated family sitcom. Indeed, in many ways George Jetson (voiced by George O'Hanlon) is a more typical American family man than Fred Flintstone, if only because he not only has a wife, Jane (Penny Singleton), but also a teenage daughter, Judy (Janet Waldo), and a preteen son, Elroy (Daws Butler).

In the early episodes the family is supplemented by the addition of the clunky, but devotedly nurturing robot maid, Rosey (Jean Vander Pyl, who also provided the voice of Wilma Flintstone), and the talking family dog, Astro (voiced by Don Messick, who supplied the barking and talking for any number of Hanna-Barbera dogs, including Bandit in *Jonny Quest* and, most importantly, Scooby-Doo).

In one episode, George himself describes this group as a "typical American-type TV family," suggesting the self-consciousness with which the Jetsons were modeled on the American family as established in the idealized sitcoms of the 1950s. The relations among the Jetson family members differ little from those in these sitcoms, and though the presence of children from the very beginning offers some plot opportunities that were not available in *The Flintstones*, family relationships in *The Jetsons* are in general less interesting than in *The Flintstones*. Jane Jetson is a particularly uninteresting character. Passive, insecure, and with little to do with her time (she has no job and can't even drive), Jane lacks the spunk of Wilma Flintstone. Meanwhile, the absence of any counterpart to Barney Rubble means that George lacks important friendships as well, leaving the futuristic setting itself to play a large role in *The Jetsons*. Nevertheless, the series often takes on an almost old-fashioned, nostalgic tone in which traditional human values are celebrated as more important than advanced technology. In the very first episode, "Rosey the Robot" (September 23, 1962), the Jetsons take on their robot maid (clearly based on the eponymous maid character played by Shirley Booth in the NBC series *Hazel*). Rosey is an obsolete model that technology has passed by, but the Jetsons decide to keep her because they develop a sentimental attachment to her. Similarly, in "The Coming of Astro" (October 21, 1962), the Jetsons have to choose between a stray mutt that follows Elroy home one day and a high-tech, low-maintenance robot dog purchased by George. They opt, of course, for the lovable and affectionate Astro, as opposed to the efficient, but emotionless robot. Astro then returns the sentimental favor in "Millionaire Astro" (January 6, 1962). Here, Astro is restored to his original owner, the fabulously wealthy J. P. Gottrocks. The dog finds, however, that his new life of luxury is no substitute for the love of the Jetsons, to whom he eventually returns.

Thanks to the presence of a teenage daughter in the title family, *The Jetsons* had ample opportunities to explore the youth culture of the future—which, of course, was pretty much the same as the emergent youth culture of the 1960s (or the prehistoric youth culture of *The Flintstones*). For example, "A Date with Jet Screamer" (September 20, 1962), the second episode aired, features the Elvis-inspired rock star Jet Screamer performing a couple of his snappy songs, accompanied by visuals that essentially make these sequences some of the first music videos. Judy is an adoring fan and is thrilled when she enters and wins a songwriting contest, the prize for which is a date with the rock star. Father George understandably views this development with considerable consternation, figuring that his impressionable daughter will be putty in the hands of the worldly rocker. So George tails the couple on their date, only to himself become a Jet Screamer fan when the singer lets him sit in on drums and even play a solo during a live performance that is part of the date.

This episode thus assures audiences that the rock music still viewed by many parents as a threat to the moral welfare of their children was in fact not so bad, after all. Television itself is a frequent topic of *The Jetsons*, as in "TV or Not TV" (February 24, 1963), a sort of remake of the "Naked Town" episode of *Top Cat*. Here, George and Astro unknowingly happen upon the scene of the filming of an episode of the television series *Naked Planet*. Thinking they have observed a real robbery, the two are terrified that the robbers will hunt them down as potential witnesses. They go into hiding after it becomes clear that they are indeed being pursued—by the TV production company, because George was accidentally caught on film and so must sign a release before the episode can air. This motif is then reversed in "Elroy's Mob" (March 3, 1963), when Elroy inadvertently becomes involved in a real robbery, thinking he is participating in the filming of a TV show.

The episode "Elroy's Pal" (December 23, 1962) focuses on Elroy as a fan of popular culture. Here, Elroy wins a contest sponsored by a cereal company to meet his favorite television star, "Nimbus the Great." Nimbus, however, doesn't show up, and Elroy is offered 200 boxes of cereal instead. Realizing Elroy's disappointment, George charges down to the TV station, where he discovers that the dashing and heroic Nimbus is actually a meek, diminutive actor, currently sidelined with a cold. Afraid that George's complaints will get him in trouble with the program's sponsor, the actor struggles into his Nimbus costume and visits Elroy after all, though the boy is surprised to find his hero so unimpressive in person. Meanwhile, not wanting Elroy to be disappointed, George dons a Nimbus costume and visits Elroy as well. Elroy knows it's George, but plays along. Afterward, when George returns as himself, the episode gets a warm and fuzzy ending as Elroy tells his father that he is the greatest guy in the universe, even greater than the fabulous Nimbus.

In "Elroy's Pal," television in the future seems pretty much like television in the 1960s, and the episode pokes gentle fun not only at contemporary children's programming, but at the cereal companies and others who sponsor them. Elroy himself gets a chance at television stardom in "Elroy's TV Show" (November 18, 1962). Here, however, in an obvious touch of irony that answers contemporary charges about the dumbing down of American culture by television, a television network is desperate because their programming has become so highbrow and educational that they are losing their audience. Jane Jetson herself exclaims in the episode that she has stopped watching television because it is over her head. In an attempt to resurrect the old-time entertainment value of television, the network decides to resurrect the old "boy and his dog" formula (specifically modeled, they note, on *Lassie*, though they can't quite remember the title of that show). When they spot Elroy and Astro playing, they immediately sign them up to play the lead roles (and draw large salaries), much to George's excitement—so much so that, in imitation of Fred Flintstone, he immediately quits his job with Spacely Space Sprockets. Meanwhile, George's old boss, Cosmo Spacely (Mel Blanc), grows jealous, while Spacely's nagging wife demands that he get their son into show business as well. George even lands a role in Elroy's show, though his overacting and constant interference nearly drive the show's director bonkers. In any case, Elroy soon tires of acting and wants to quit. All ends well, however, when Mr. Spacely's son and his dog are lined up as replacements, ending Spacely's jealousy of George's newfound showbiz career and causing him to give George his old job back.

George's job is constantly in play in *The Jetsons*, and George's work life is a far bigger part of the series than was Fred Flintstone's—despite the fact that George only has to work three hours a day and generally has little to do even then (except sleep or play cards with his work computer), thanks to the automation of almost everything. Yet he is constantly scheming to get off work, while at the same time dreaming of ascending from his lower-level management position to a vice presidency. A running gag in the series involves George's frequent promotions to vice president when he is in Spacely's momentary favor, generally followed almost immediately by a reversal that leaves Spacely furious and George, at least for the moment, unemployed.

The portrayal of the bullying, penny-pinching Spacely can be taken as a mild satire of American corporate culture, though Spacely also has a certain vulnerability—especially to his bossy wife—that prevents him from seeming quite as ruthless as he otherwise might. He also comes off better in the series because of his constant duels with rival magnate W. C. Cogswell (Daws Butler), head of Cogswell Cogs, because Cogswell is considerably more ruthless and vicious than is Spacely. Cogswell and Spacely are both intensely dedicated to the task of driving each other out of business, providing a commentary on the competitive nature of American capitalism. But it is generally Cogswell who appears the aggressor and Spacely the not-so-innocent victim, if only because his demise would be bad news for the Jetsons.

In "The Flying Suit" (November 4, 1962), for example, Cogswell's company develops a prototype flying suit that will make space cars (apparently the main application for space sprockets) obsolete. However, when Cogswell sends the suit to the cleaners prior to its first official demonstration, it gets mixed up with a suit that George had left at the same cleaners. George thus innocently comes home with the flying suit, which he dons just as Elroy, who is something of an amateur scientist, announces that he has developed a pill that, when swallowed, will allow people to fly. George swallows the pill in order to humor his son, only to discover that he can, indeed, now fly. When Spacely hears of the flying pills, he is convinced that he has at last obtained the advanced product he needs to be able to drive Cogswell out of business. Meanwhile, the demonstration of Cogswell's flying suit is a disaster, given that Cogswell now actually has George's suit. So Cogswell abandons that project, concluding that the suit doesn't actually work, while Spacely eventually learns that the flying pills don't work, either. The two companies—and their leaders—are left right back where they began.

A companion episode to "The Flying Suit" is "Astro's Top Secret" (December 9, 1962). Here, Cogswell and Spacely go golfing, but end up literally coming to blows—and vowing more than ever to destroy each other. Spacely assigns George to come up with an invention that will drive Cogswell out of business, while Cogswell assigns his groveling assistant Harlan to spy on Spacely. As George works at home, vainly trying to come up with a suitable product, Astro accidentally swallows Elroy's remote-controlled flying car, which naturally (in the world of *The Jetsons*, at least) lifts the huge dog and makes him fly under remote control as well. Harlan sees the flying dog and reports back to Cogswell that Jetson has invented an antigravity machine. The cold-blooded Cogswell immediately dognaps Astro to try to learn the secret of the device, but is unsuccessful. For a time, Spacely believes in the device as well, causing him to make George a vice president, but he soon learns the truth about Astro's flying after the dog coughs up the flying car, causing Spacely to fire George. Then, however, Astro swallows an "oral computer," and Spacely believes that the dog is actually reciting the intelligent-sounding information, which is actually nonsense, that comes from the device. Spacely believes George has found a way to supercharge the dog's brain and once again proclaims George a genius—and makes him a vice president.

In "Elroy's Mob," the obvious connection between *The Flintstones* and *The Jetsons* is acknowledged when one of Elroy's student is shown watching "the billionth rerun of *The Flintstones*" on his wristwatch TV. The direct link between *The Jetsons* and *The Flintstones* was also explicitly acknowledged in a 1987 made-for-TV film entitled *The Jetsons Meet the Flintstones*, featuring most of the original casts, except that Fred Flintstone was now voiced by Henry Corden in the wake of Alan Reed's death in 1977. Here, Elroy invents a time machine that takes the Jetsons back to prehistoric Bedrock, where they meet the Flintstones, who are subsequently propelled into the far future time of the Jetsons.

This film built on the renewed popularity of *The Jetsons* in the 1980s, when syndicated reruns of the 24 episodes of the original show were supplemented by the production of over 50 new episodes. The Jetsons themselves remained current enough in the American consciousness to star in their own theatrical film, *Jetsons: The Movie*, in 1990. The film was directed by Hanna and Barbera, and the major adult characters were voiced by the same actors as in the original series, though both O'Hanlon and Blanc died during production, forcing some of their lines to be supplied by imitators. Elroy and Judy were voiced by Patric Zimmerman and pop star Tiffany, who also performed several songs on the soundtrack. In the film Spacely attempts to counter falling profits for Spacely Sprockets by moving part of his operations into outer space, setting up a whole mining town around an orbiting asteroid. There, ore can be mined, processed, and turned into sprockets all in an essentially animated facility. It needs only a human manager to push the button to turn it on. Unfortunately, a series of such managers have already vacated the job in the wake of attacks on the plant by mysterious saboteurs. Desperate, Spacely tabs Jetson for the job, which also carries a corporate vice presidency. Excited that he has made it big at last, George moves his family to outer space over the objections of Judy, who, in an echo of "A Date with Jet Screamer" is forced to forego an upcoming date with rock star "Cosmic Cosmo."

George prepares to start up the plant, only to encounter more sabotage. Eventually, it turns out that the asteroid is inhabited by the "Grungies," small, cuddly, Ewok-like creatures, who are sabotaging the plant in order to attempt to prevent the destruction of their homes by the mining operation. Any potential anticapitalist or anticolonial messages that might arise from this scenario are muted, however, when George is able to arrange a deal so that the Grungies themselves will run the plant for Spacely Sprockets, overseeing the mining of the asteroid in such a way that their homes are protected. They get to keep their homes, Spacely gets to increase his profits, and the Jetsons return to earth to resume their former lives—except that George, at the insistence of the Grungies, is able to keep his VP title, though not his VP salary or duties.

The comeback of *The Jetsons* in the 1980s is a good illustration of the amazing staying power of the prime-time animated series of the 1960s. Even though these programs, with the exception of *The Flintstones*, failed to find a large audience in their initial prime-time runs, their continued showings on Saturday mornings and eventually in syndication in the 40 years since have made them among the best-known programs in American television history. On the other hand, that these programs often had more success on Saturday mornings and elsewhere than they had in prime time only served to cement the notion that animated programming simply could not succeed in prime time. This perception kept animated programming off of prime-time television for more than two decades. A single series, however, would change that perception, perhaps forever.

CHAPTER 3

Animation's New Age: Meet *The Simpsons*

When *The Tracey Ullman Show* began broadcasting in April 1987, it had the distinction of being the first program to be broadcast on the new Fox television network. A skit comedy program designed to showcase the considerable talents of its eponymous star, *The Tracey Ullman Show* was quite interesting in its own right. Ultimately, however, its most important legacy was the series of 48 brief cartoon segments that appeared on the program as bridges, or "bumpers" into and out of commercials, from 1987 to 1989. These segments featured a dysfunctional animated family known as the Simpsons, who would go on to become perhaps the most important TV family in American broadcasting history, while their self-titled series would become the most successful and longest-running animated program in the history of American prime-time television. At this writing, it is now in its seventeenth season in prime time on the Fox network—and going strong.

The "apprenticeship" on the Ullman showed served *The Simpsons* well, allowing the makers of the show to develop their characters and refine their distinctive animation style before the show began as a separate entity. That highly recognizable style (later transferred directly to the very different setting of the science fiction cartoon series *Futurama*) would become a staple of American popular culture, while those characters would become among the best known in American television history. Creator Matt Groening enlivened the series with the underground sensibility of his comic strip *Life in Hell*, while veteran producers James L. Brooks and Sam Simon helped to shape the program with their years of experience in the production of high-quality television programs such as *Taxi, Cheers, The Mary Tyler Moore Show,* and *Lou Grant.* Add a superb writing staff, and *The Simpsons* had, from the very beginning, just the right mix of ingredients to make it a popular television sitcom, while avoiding the banality and insipidity that have often marked that genre.

The Simpsons is justifiably famed for its satire of American suburban life and for its parodic engagement with American popular culture, especially the television culture of which it is itself a part. It is, however, first and foremost a family sitcom, and its most important satire and parody are aimed at that genre, which it has significantly revised, along with its fellow Fox program, the slapstick family sitcom *Married with Children* (1987–1997), and the edgy, working-class sitcom *Roseanne* (ABC, 1988–1997). *The Simpsons* mounts an all-out assault on the idealized representation of the American family in such classic sitcoms as *Leave It to Beaver* and *The Donna Reed Show.* Indeed, it is set in the fictional town of Springfield, which happens also to be the name of the hometown in the classic 1950s sitcom *Father Knows Best,* precisely the sort of idealized sitcom that *The Simpsons* is meant to unravel. In any case, *The Simpsons* enjoys the double distinction of being perhaps the most important animated program ever to air on American television as well as one of the most important sitcoms. These two aspects of the program reinforce each other: The success of *The Simpsons* as a sitcom has helped it to gain new audiences that would not previously have been interested in an animated program, while the show's animated status has helped it to break new ground and go where no sitcom had gone before.

Over the years, of course, *The Simpsons* would come to be renowned for its amusing use of material from any number of previous television shows as well as movies—such as *Citizen Kane* in the "Rosebud" episode (October 21, 1993)—and even literary classics such as *A Streetcar Named Desire*—in the episode "A Streetcar Name Marge" (October 1, 1992). This effective use of the vast storehouse of material that is American popular culture has helped to keep *The Simpsons* fresh year after year. Meanwhile, the Simpsons themselves have become beloved figures of this culture, and much of their success has come from the ways in which the travails of the Simpson clan appeal to a basic American yearning for family. While the dysfunctional Simpsons serve in obvious ways as a parody of idealized television sitcom families, they are still very much a family and typically come together (in their own way) in times of crisis. It is not for nothing that, in the show's signature opening sequence, the entire family rushes home to share a couch and watch television: Their lives may revolve around the television, but at least they revolve together.

The Simpsons also appeals to a yearning for stability in an uncertain and rapidly changing world. After all, the Simpsons have a unique sort of family stability in that, as animated characters, they all remain essentially the same age year after year, creating a sense of continuity that is rare in the rapidly changing landscape of American culture. The husband and father of the family and star of the show is Homer Simpson (brilliantly voiced by Dan Castellaneta), a fat, bald thirty-something who typically seems more devoted to drinking beer and eating doughnuts than to taking care of his family. Homer (whose middle name is Jay, in tribute to *Rocky and Bullwinkle* creator Jay Ward) is also ostentatiously lazy and stupid, a fact that makes his status as a nuclear-safety technician in the local power plant seriously problematic. Indeed, he frequently causes near-catastrophic crises at the plant, though things always somehow work out in the end. Yet Homer is at heart a good soul, oddly lovable, and given to doing the right thing in the final analysis, however grudgingly. He loves his wife and kids—though maybe not as much as beer and doughnuts—even if he doesn't always show it.

If anything, Homer tends to get more stupid and oafish as the series proceeds, though in the episode "HOMЯ" (January 7, 2001), we learn that he is naturally quite intelligent but was rendered stupid when he rammed a crayon up his nose and into his brain at age six (though there is no explanation of why he would do such a thing if he had been intelligent until that time). Scientists discover and remove the crayon, suddenly making Homer a brainiac, at least compared to the other denizens of the Springfield—a sort of microcosm of America that in some episodes seems to be a typical American small town and in others to be a big city. Actually, the episode stipulates that Homer's IQ has been raised 50 points to a whopping 105, but even this modest level of intelligence makes him unable to enjoy the pleasures of such things as watching Julia Roberts movies or shopping at the Disney store—suggesting that only idiots could enjoy such things. Homer's new intelligence also makes him highly unpopular among his former friends, with only daughter Lisa, the family brain, now being smart enough to understand him. Eventually, he opts to cram another crayon into his brain, thus returning to his former self.

Wife Marge (Julie Kavner) is the glue that holds the family together. Distinguished by her gravelly voice and towering blue hair, Marge is devoted to, though often frustrated by, her husband and children. Occasionally, however—as in the episode "Homer Alone" (February 26, 1992), when she has to go away to a spa to recover from a nervous breakdown—she reaches her limit. The stay-at-home mother of an infant, Marge frequently seeks projects outside the home in an effort to expand her horizons, though she usually has to do so without the cooperation of the rest of the family. She is also vaguely civic-minded, and occasionally becomes a political activist in the support of specific causes, though usually because those causes have a specific benefit for her family.

Ten-year-old son Bart (voiced by Nancy Cartwright, who does the voices of several of the other local children as well) is the family troublemaker. He embodies the most subversive energies of the series and is probably the character whose point of view is closest to that of creator Groening. Something of a chip off the old block who resembles his father in many ways, Bart is a terrible student who nevertheless has a genius for mischief. He particularly torments his father, despite, or perhaps because of, the fact that the two are actually much alike. He is also the bane of his teachers and sometimes even of the entire community, as in "Radio Bart" (January 9, 1992), when he fakes having fallen down a well (echoing the famous case of "Baby Jessica," who fell down a well in Midland, Texas, in 1987), mobilizing the entire town of Springfield to try, rather ineffectually, to get him out.

Eight-year-old Lisa (Yeardley Smith) is not only the brains of the family, but also the conscience. She makes straight A's in school but also becomes engaged in a variety of civic projects designed to help those less fortunate than herself. In both these senses, the saxophone-playing Lisa is somewhat out of place in the family, which may account for her occasional bouts of the blues and her sense of being alone in a world that doesn't understand her. On the other hand, she is not entirely free of the effects of her environment. Though an avid reader, she seems to enjoy watching television as much as anyone else in the family—and even shares much of Bart's and Homer's enjoyment of particularly lowbrow programming. Then again, her enjoyment of lowbrow television programming could also potentially be taken as a suggestion that watching such programming does not necessarily make one stupid. In fact, the incessant television viewing of Homer and Bart may not be responsible for their stupidity, either. In one episode, "Lisa the Simpson" (March 8, 1998), Lisa learns that there is apparently a "Simpson gene" that causes all Simpsons to turn stupid at about her age. She becomes terrified that she is about to follow suit. Luckily, however, it turns out that the gene affects only Simpson males, so she is able to retain her intelligence.

Baby Maggie is a relatively minor character, largely because (as a perpetual one-year-old) she cannot talk and has limited mobility. Distinguished by her ever-present pacifier and her constant falling down as she attempts to walk, Maggie nevertheless is at the forefront of several episodes. Like baby Sweet Pea of the classic *Popeye* cartoons, she has a knack for getting into danger, which is featured in episodes such as "Homer Alone" and "Moe Baby Blues" (May 18, 2003), in which she must repeatedly be saved by the bartender Moe Szyslak (Hank Azaria), one of the series' numerous important recurring characters. Maggie is also paradoxically a crack shot, showing off her marksmanship in such episodes as "Who Shot Mr. Burns?" (May 21, 1995, and September 17, 1995), the *Dallas*-inspired cliffhanger that ended season six and was resolved at the beginning of season seven—with Maggie revealed to be the shooter. Several flashforward episodes show Maggie at a later age, though these representations of her future are not necessarily consistent or even meaningful given that the Simpson children never actually age.

Many episodes of *The Simpsons* are devoted to an exploration of the family relationships among these various characters. In "There's No Disgrace Like Home" (January 28, 1990), the Simpsons attend a company picnic where Homer becomes disturbed by comparing his unruly family to an ideal family with perfectly loving, well-behaved children. When he sees an ad on TV for Dr. Marvin Monroe's Family Therapy Center, Homer decides to take his family there. He is, in fact, so dedicated to the proposition that he is willing to hock the family's beloved television set in order to get the cash to pay the doctor. Monroe is so confident in his ability to help anyone that he offers a double-your-money-back guarantee. The Simpsons, of course, thwart his best efforts. All is not lost, however. Monroe pays the refund, just to get rid of them, and they are able to use it to buy a new and better TV.

Numerous episodes explore the marriage of Homer and Marge, which is often troubled, though they always manage to stay together through every crisis. In "Life on the Fast Lane" (March 18, 1990), Homer takes a page from the book of his great predecessor Fred Flintstone and gives Marge a bowling ball (inscribed with his own name) for her birthday, assuming that she will simply hand it over to him. Instead, she decides to get revenge by taking up bowling herself, even though she has no real interest in the sport. When she goes to the lanes, leaving Homer home with the kids, she meets the suave Frenchman Jacques, who offers to give her bowling lessons—but really has seduction in mind. Marge starts going bowling every night, to the point that even the dim-witted Homer figures out that something is afoot. Bart and Lisa are convinced that their parents are headed for divorce. But then, on a crucial day when Jacques's attempts at seduction seem headed for success at last, Marge, driving to the Frenchman's apartment, at the last minute turns off and goes to the nuclear power plant to see Homer instead. With the romantic music of "Up Where We Belong" from the 1982 film *An Officer and a Gentleman* playing in the background, it is clear that the marriage has been saved.

Homer is also sometimes tempted to stray from the marriage, but always remains faithful in the end. In "Colonel Homer" (March 26, 1992), Homer becomes the manager of aspiring country singer Lurleen Lumpkin (voiced by Beverly D'Angelo), much in the mode of Elvis Presley's Colonel Tom Parker. His success in the role leads the singer to fall for him, but he ultimately remains true to the jealous Marge. Homer's sorest temptation probably occurs in "The Last Temptation of Homer" (December 9, 1993), in which he nearly falls for beautiful new co-worker Mindy Simmons (Michelle Pfeiffer), whose tastes and interests turn out to match his own almost exactly. The temptation is exacerbated when the two are sent away together on a business trip. The sexual tension mounts and Mindy comes to Homer's hotel room, making it clear that she is ready for love. At the last moment, Homer resists the temptation and opts instead to invite Marge to come join him for the rest of the trip.

In "The Way We Was" (January 31, 1991), Marge tells the story of how she and Homer started dating in high school. Then, in "I Married Marge" (December 26, 1991), Homer tells the kids how he and Marge first got together, including the groundbreaking (for a network sitcom) revelation that the two originally got married because Marge was pregnant with Bart, who was conceived in a moment of passion on a miniature golf course. The episode details in a rather sentimental fashion the early struggles of the irresponsible Homer to support his new family, which ultimately succeed when he lands a job at the nuclear power plant. Such background episodes add an extra dimension to the portrayal of the animated Simpson family, making them seem oddly real and adding weight to their status as a family with a long history together.

The Simpsons often veers into sentimentality in its depiction of the family as ultimately close-knit, despite the fact that they all seem to drive each other nuts. In "Home Sweet Homediddly-Dum-Doodily" (October 1, 1995), a series of events causes the Simpson children to be taken away from their parents and placed in a foster home—which turns out to be that of the next-door neighbors, the excessively wholesome Flanders family. Maggie is young enough that she adjusts well, but Bart and Lisa find that they miss their real parents greatly. The feeling is mutual, and there is a clear sense that the children have been saved when the family is ultimately reunited.

The series also includes extensive appearances by other members of both Homer's and Marge's families, especially Homer's father, Abraham Simpson (Castellaneta), and Marge's twin sisters, Patty and Selma Bouvier (Kavner). In addition, *The Simpsons* features a number of interesting recurring secondary characters, who actually carry a number of individual episodes, adding versatility to the show. This motif is significantly enhanced by the excellent talents of the actors who supply the voices of the various characters. Castellaneta, for example, voices numerous characters in addition to Homer Simpson, including Groundskeeper Willie, the surprisingly muscular Scottish maintenance man at Springfield Elementary School, and "Diamond" Joe Quimby, the modestly corrupt mayor of Springfield (voiced in imitation of John, Robert, and Teddy Kennedy). Particularly important here are Hank Azaria and Harry Shearer, who provide the voices of any number of important recurring characters. Azaria supplies the voices of the Indian Kwik-E-Mart clerk Apu, bartender Moe Szyslak, and the pig-snouted Police Chief Wiggum. Shearer, meanwhile, provides the voices for Homer's boss C. Montgomery Burns, Burns's toadying personal assistant Waylon Smithers, super-religious neighbor Ned Flanders, local news anchor Kent Brockman, the Reverend Lovejoy, and the much-embattled Principal Skinner. Numerous other excellent voice actors have made frequent appearances on *The Simpsons*, including Phil Hartman (who was a semi-regular on the show from 1991 until his death in 1998), Joe Mantegna, Kelsey Grammer, and Jon Lovitz (who appears as the voice of several characters, including Jay Sherman, spilling over from the animated series *The Critic*).

Burns is a particularly important character whose portrayal offers a number of opportunities for the show to satirize the greed of the rich. Burns, the owner of the Springfield Nuclear Power Plant, is ancient (he is at one point identified as being 104 years old), frail, and unceasingly vicious in his headlong pursuit of more and more wealth. He is perhaps at his most typical in the "Who Shot Mr. Burns?" two-parter, in which his greed is so rampant that virtually everyone in the town of Springfield wishes him dead, and in which even Smithers (whose sycophantic devotion to the old man becomes more and more homoerotic as the series proceeds) turns against him. Here, Willie strikes oil while digging a grave for a deceased gerbil in the basement of Springfield Elementary School. The school thus suddenly becomes rich, only to lose its wealth when the nefarious Burns taps their well by slant drilling, drawing off all the oil for himself and giving himself a full monopoly over the Springfield energy supply. The only energy source he doesn't own is the sun, so he constructs a device to block that out, making the city cold and dark—and creating even more of a market for the oil from his illicit well and the electricity from his power plant.

One of the most important secondary characters is Bart's TV hero, Krusty the Clown (voiced by Castellaneta), who is featured in a number of episodes, beginning with "Krusty Gets Busted" (April 29, 1990), in which the clown's much-abused TV sidekick, Sideshow Bob (Grammer) attempts to frame him for the armed robbery of Apu's Kwik-E-Mart. Bart, unable to believe that his hero could be guilty of such a crime, plays detective and ultimately exonerates Krusty, though not before the clown is humiliated in court by the revelation of his illiteracy. Krusty may be a clownish figure, but he actually has a great deal of depth. In addition to his illiteracy, we also learn that he was born Herschel Krustofski, the son of a rabbi. Krusty had long been estranged from his father, who did not approve of his son's choice of profession, but in "Like Father, Like Clown" (October 24, 1991), Bart, for once doing a good deed, effects a reconciliation between the two.

Krusty also adds significantly to the satire of television in *The Simpsons*, which may be more about television than anything else. Krusty's program itself parodies live-audience children's programming such as that pioneered by *Howdy Doody*, which ran on ABC from 1947 to 1960 and featured, in addition to the title puppet, a clown called Clarabell (played for the first couple of years by Bob Keeshan, who later played Captain Kangaroo for many years). Another important referent of the Krusty show is the *Bozo the Clown* show that was franchised to various local stations in the United States, running most prominently on Chicago television, where it was carried in various incarnations from 1960 to 2001, attracting a national audience when its Chicago station, WGN, went national during the cable explosion of the 1980s.

Among other things, Krusty the Clown is the kingpin of a vast merchandising empire that specializes in poor-quality merchandise, often dangerous to children. Thus, at the end of "Krusty Gets Busted" we see Bart going to bed between Krusty sheets with a Krusty bedspread and with a room entirely covered with Krusty toys and other merchandise. Perhaps the most critical depiction of Krusty's various business enterprises occurs in the episode "Kamp Krusty" (September 24, 1992), in which Lisa and Bart attend a summer camp endorsed by the clown, only to find that children are brutally mistreated at the rundown, dilapidated facility. The treatment of Krusty's merchandising in *The Simpsons* satirizes that phenomenon in general, though the most obvious referent here is *The Simpsons* itself, which has enjoyed some of the most successful and lucrative merchandising of any program in television history. The Simpsons, like the Flintstones, have also appeared in television commercials for a variety of products, most notably Butterfinger candy bars, Bart's favorite.

An important foil for Krusty and his lowbrow antics is the erudite Sideshow Bob, whose horror at Krusty's lack of cultural sophistication is matched only by the sheer malice of his hatred for popular culture, not to mention for both Krusty and Krusty's devoted fan Bart. That Krusty is perfectly willing to commit armed robbery and even murder in the interest of his cultural ends suggests that the high culture he so loves does not necessarily make one a good person. In "Sideshow Bob's Last Gleaming" (November 26, 1995), the cultured clown's hatred of the "chattering cyclops" of television finally boils over, causing him to escape from one of his many terms in prison—this time a minimum security facility where a fellow inmate is apparently Rupert Murdoch, the arch-conservative media mogul whose company owns the Fox network. Subsequently, Bob steals an atomic bomb and threatens to blow up Springfield if the town doesn't do away with television altogether. The town reluctantly complies, leaving only the Emergency Broadcasting System operational. Desperate to stay on the air, Krusty commandeers that channel, where his program can run nonstop, assured of a 100 percent share of the local viewing audience. Bob ignites the bomb, despite the efforts of Bart and Lisa to stop him, but it turns out to be a dud, having had a 1959 expiration date. After a spirited chase, Bob is captured and returned to prison, while Springfield television returns to its usual mindless fare.

Perhaps the most mindless fare of all is the ultraviolent *Itchy & Scratchy Show*, in which the sadistic mouse Itchy continually visits horrific cartoon violence on the dim-witted cat Scratchy (though Scratchy, in the tradition of Wile E. Coyote, is always able to bounce back for more). Bart and Lisa are both devoted viewers of the cartoon, which often appears as a segment on the *Krusty the Clown Show*. Snippets of *Itchy & Scratchy* cartoons appear in any number of *The Simpsons* episodes, while a number of episodes are centrally devoted to the cartoons of the cat-and-mouse duo. In "Itchy & Scratchy & Marge" (December 20, 1990), Marge is horrified when she realizes that the spectacular violence of the *Itchy & Scratchy Show* has apparently inspired baby Maggie to club Homer over the head with a mallet. Marge then launches an activist campaign that eventually forces such violence off the air in Springfield. As a result, the children of the city turn away from television, returning to a variety of wholesome, mostly outdoor activities of the type that might have been pursued by characters in the sitcoms of the 1950s. Then, however, Michelangelo's famous anatomically correct statue of David comes to Springfield in the

course of an American tour. Marge's former supporters in the antivio-
lence campaign now mount a protest against this "immoral" work of art,
causing Marge (who appreciates the greatness of the statue as a work of
art) to switch sides and to come out for freedom of expression rather than
self-righteous censorship. Marge wins the day, Itchy and Scratchy return
to television with their old style of cartoon violence, and all returns to
normal in Springfield.

"Itchy & Scratchy & Marge" is quite obviously a retort to those who
were already complaining that *The Simpsons* was not appropriate family
TV viewing—though it can also be taken as a general satire of attempts
by various special-interest groups to exert pressure to force television
programming to conform to their own particular standards. It can also be
taken as a commentary on the famous campaign launched by Michigan
housewife Terry Rakolta against their sister Fox program *Married with
Children*, beginning in 1989. This episode also anticipates controversies
over the potential negative impact on children of such programs as *Beavis
and Butt-head* and *South Park*, while looking back to complaints about the
violence in cartoons such as *Jonny Quest* in the 1960s. Meanwhile, *Itchy &
Scratchy* quite obviously derive from such predecessors as the *Tom and
Jerry* cartoons that gave William Hanna and Joseph Barbera their first big
success in animation back in the 1940s, reminding us that violence has
always been a part of the long and distinguished tradition of cartoons in
American culture.

Despite its departures, *The Simpsons* itself is self-consciously a part of
this tradition. For example, in drawing upon the family sitcom form, *The
Simpsons* followed directly in the footsteps of *The Flintstones*. Indeed, numerous episodes of *The Simpsons* have acknowledged the show's debt to this
prehistoric predecessor. In "Homer's Night Out" (March 25, 1990), Bart
snaps a photo of Homer dancing with a stripper, and the subsequent wide
distribution of the picture makes Homer something of a minor local celebrity. Thus, when Homer goes into a convenience store, he looks familiar
to the Indian clerk (Apu, who at this point had not been introduced as a
recurring character). When the clerk asks Homer if he's seen him on television or something, Homer responds, "Sorry, buddy. You've got me confused
with Fred Flintstone." In the opening of "Kamp Krusty," the Simpsons rush
home to watch TV, as they do at the beginning of every episode. This time,
however, they find their beloved couch already occupied—by Fred, Wilma,
and Pebbles Flintstone! And the opening of "Marge vs. the Monorail"
(January 14, 1993) mimics the famous opening of *The Flintstones* as the end
of Homer's workday is signaled by the five-o'clock whistle. He then shouts

"Yabba-Dabba-Doo!" and heads for his car. Driving home, he cheerfully sings (to the tune of the well-known *Flintstones* theme):

Simpson, Homer Simpson,
He's the greatest guy in history.
From the town of Springfield,
He's about to hit a chestnut tree!

The episode "HOM" spoofs the incongruity of the appearance of the alien Great Gazoo in *The Flintstones*. Here, the Simpsons attend an animation convention, where Lisa is puzzled by some of the nonsensical fare. Bart explains to her that "cartoons don't have to make sense," whereupon the Great Gazoo suddenly appears over his shoulder, noting, "He's right, you know." In addition to such direct references, numerous episodes of *The Simpsons* directly echo episodes of *The Flintstones*. For example, Homer's attempts to make it big by running his own business in episodes such as "Mr. Plow" (November 19, 1992) or inventing new products in episodes such as "Flaming Moe's" (November 21, 1991) or "The Wizard of Evergreen Terrace" (September 20, 1998) are reminiscent of any number of *Flintstones* episodes. Then again, it is a measure of just how far *The Simpsons* goes beyond *The Flintstones* that one of Homer's schemes to make money—in "There's Something about Marrying" (February 20, 2005)—involves becoming an ordained minister so he can perform same-sex marriages.

Homer also sometimes tries to make it in show business, despite his limited talents. In "Homerpalooza" (May 19, 1996), for example, he joins a traveling alternative rock festival—but only as a sideshow attraction in which he allows a cannon ball to be fired into his ample stomach. He enjoys stardom, and even Bart is finally impressed by his father, but he finally retires back to family life when he realizes that the repeated blows to the stomach are becoming a danger to his life. In the subplot (*Simpsons* episodes often contain more than one plot line) of "The Front" (April 15, 1993), Homer, who has long lived with the secret shame of not finishing high school, must return to school to complete his missing credit in remedial science, just as Fred Flintstone has to return briefly to Bedrock High School to get his diploma in "High School Fred" (December 7, 1962). And in "Deep Space Homer" (February 24, 1994), Homer becomes an astronaut, as did Fred and Barney in "The Astr'Nuts" (March 3, 1961). In fact, in this episode, Homer even shares his training with his own sidekick Barney—Barney Gumble (also voiced by Castellaneta), a hard-drinking patron of Moe's Tavern.

While not mentioning *The Flintstones* directly, "Deep Space Homer" is a classic *Simpsons* episode in its construction essentially as a series of pastiches of any number of other works of American popular culture. In the episode, Homer, the only employee at the nuclear plant who has never been named employee of the month, losing out even to an inanimate carbon rod, tires of never getting respect. Meanwhile, noting the popularity of shows such as *Home Improvement* and *Married with Children* that feature regular blue-collar slobs, officials at NASA decide to recruit such a person to be an astronaut in an effort to shore up flagging TV ratings for their space launches. So (naturally) they end up with Homer, who picks up the family and drives to Cape Canaveral in a heavily loaded truck à la *The Beverly Hillbillies*.

When Homer is introduced at a news conference, thoughts of his upcoming spaceflight remind him of the film *Planet of the Apes,* the ending of which he suddenly understands, dropping to the floor in imitation of Charlton Heston and crying out (Castellaneta's histrionics mimic Heston's own), "You maniacs! You blew it up! Damn you! Damn you all to hell!" During his training, Homer rides a centrifuge; the G-forces distort his face as in any number of SF films—except this time his face morphs into that of Popeye the Sailorman. The training also inexplicably includes *Star Trek*–style hand-to-hand combat, while we learn that Homer's fellow crewmembers on the spaceflight will be veteran astronaut Buzz Aldrin (voiced by himself) and one "Race Banyon," an obvious reference to Race Bannon from *Jonny Quest*. Meanwhile, Homer becomes increasingly terrified of the dangers of spaceflight, especially after he watches an episode of the *Itchy & Scratchy Show* set in outer space—an episode that itself contains riffs on of science fiction films such as *Star Trek, Alien, 2001: A Space Odyssey,* and *Total Recall.*

As the three astronauts prepare to enter their spacecraft, they walk forward in a pastiche of a scene from *The Right Stuff.* When the actual flight takes off, the G-forces morph Homer's face into that of Richard Nixon. Scenes from the actual mission then reference *2001: A Space Odyssey* again, combined with an appearance by James Taylor (voiced by himself), who sings to the astronauts from mission control. After Homer returns home a hero, Bart proudly writes the word "HERO" on the back of his father's head, then tosses his marker spinning into the air; it then transforms into a Fox telecommunications satellite in imitation of the famous cut early in *2001* in which an apeman's bone-club tossed into the air similarly becomes an orbiting spacecraft. In the final scene of the episode, we see the starchild from that film floating in his space bubble—though he now looks, oddly enough, exactly like Homer. Then the Fox satellite bonks the starchild Homer on the head, eliciting his trademark "Doh!" as the episode ends.

Several episodes of *The Simpsons* are designed as takeoffs on other specific television programs. For example, in "The Springfield Files" (January 12, 1997), Homer believes that he has spotted an alien in the woods near Springfield— to the accompaniment of the famous theme music from that other Sunday-night Fox hit, *The X-Files*. FBI agents Mulder and Scully, voiced by David Duchovny and Gillian Anderson (who play those characters in *The X-Files*), drop their other work and come to town to investigate the sighting. It all comes to nothing, however, when the glowing alien turns out simply to be Mr. Burns in the throes of his weekly rejuvenating treatments. Still, add in a guest appearance by Leonard Nimoy (who even sings), allusions to *E.T. the Extra-Terrestrial* and *Close Encounters of the Third Kind,* and a police lineup featuring a number of famous aliens from film and television (such as the robot Gort from *The Day the Earth Stood Still,* Chewbacca from *Star Wars,* and Marvin the Martian from *Duck Dodgers in the 24 1/2 Century*), and the episode makes for an entertaining romp through pop cultural science fiction. This episode also contains an example of the lampooning of the Fox Network that frequently appears in *The Simpsons.* When Bart and Homer prepare to go look for the alien, Homer declares that, if they can't find it, they'll "fake it and sell it to the Fox Network." "Yeah," says Bart in response to this reference to the notorious "alien autopsy" that aired on Fox in 1995, "They'll buy anything." When Homer replies that the people at Fox actually "do a lot of quality programming," he and Bart both break out in hysterics.

The title of "The Computer Wore Menace Shoes" (December 3, 2000) plays on that of the 1969 Disney film *The Computer Wore Tennis Shoes.* However, it has essentially nothing to do with that film. Instead, it draws extensively upon the classic British science fiction/espionage series *The Prisoner,* including a guest voice appearance by Patrick McGoohan, reprising his role as "Number 6" in that series. In the episode, Homer wins a Pulitzer Prize for the investigative reporting that appears on his personal website. Unfortunately, the fame that results from this award makes it impossible for him to gather any further information, so he simply starts making up stories. One of the stories, about a plot to lace flu shots with a mind-control drug, turns out to be true, causing the secret organization behind the plot to kidnap Homer and take him to the "Island," a secret location modeled on the "Village" of *The Prisoner.* By the end of the episode, the entire Simpson clan has been taken to the island, though we can be assured that they'll be back in Springfield in time for the next episode.

"Missionary Impossible" (February 20, 2000) satirizes any number of television phenomena. Here, Homer phones in a pledge of $10,000 to the local PBS station just so they will stop interrupting his favorite British lowbrow comedy with calls for pledges. He then becomes a missionary to a South Pacific island to avoid making good on the pledge, but teaches the natives to build a casino rather than bringing them to religion, meanwhile destroying their previously idyllic culture. This development can be taken as a strong critique of the destruction of indigenous cultures by missionaries, though the ultimate object of the satire in this episode is the Fox network itself. Eventually, the island is hit by a powerful earthquake, and Homer himself seems on the verge of being killed, when this program itself is interrupted by a Fox telethon calling for pledges, with figures such as Murdoch, Mulder and Scully from *The X-Files*, Hank Hill from *King of the Hill*, and Bender from *Futurama* taking calls. Fox needs pledges, hostess Betty White tells us, so crude, lowbrow television will be able to stay on the air. She then gestures to a television set showing the title logo of the *Family Guy* series. Bart quickly phones in a $10,000 pledge, at which Murdoch proclaims, "You've saved my network!" "It wouldn't be the first time," says Bart, sardonically.

Some episodes of *The Simpsons* satirize show business itself rather than specific programs. In "Radioactive Man" (September 24, 1995), Hollywood decides to make a film version of Bart's favorite superhero comic book, starring the Schwarzeneggeresque Rainer Wolfcastle (Shearer). They even decide to make the film in Springfield and to cast a local child as Fallout Boy, the superhero's youthful sidekick. Bart is convinced that he is perfect for the role, and then shocked when instead they cast his nerdy friend Milhouse. The entire city of Springfield mobilizes to try to cash in on the event, but the filming doesn't go well, and eventually the entire production is shut down when it goes broke after Mayor Quimby and the other small-town slickers of Springfield manage to bilk the poor yokels from Hollywood out of all their cash. So, in a masterpiece of irony, the chastened filmmakers flee back to Hollywood, where they know everyone will be honest, kind, and generous.

The Simpsons aims its satire at issues other than show business as well, becoming one of the few American sitcoms to have become actively engaged with politics. Politics has sometimes addressed *The Simpsons* as well, as when both the first lady and President George Bush (the first one) publicly took on the program, complaining that something as stupid as *The Simpsons* was so popular and was becoming an icon of American popular culture worldwide. In a short clip aired after the episode "Stark Raving Dad" (September 19, 1991), the program responded by showing the Simpsons watching an actual clip of Bush on TV as he vows to make American families "a lot more like the Waltons and lot less like the Simpsons." In a nice zinger that comments on the travails of the American economy under the Bush administration, Bart responds by saying, "Hey, we're just like the Waltons: We're praying for an end to the Depression, too." (Bart, like most in the audience, assumes that Bush is referring to the sentimental *Waltons* television program and not to the founding family of the Wal-Mart empire.) Then, in the episode "Two Bad Neighbors" (January 14, 1996), the Bushes, having retired from office (actually, having been booted out by the American voters), move to Springfield—right across the street from the Simpsons. A feud between the two clans predictably ensues, leading the Bushes to move out. Gerry Ford then moves in, and he and Homer become fast friends.

Other *Simpsons* episodes deal more with the internal politics of the world of Springfield, though they often comment on politics in a broader sense as well. In "Two Cars in Every Garage and Three Eyes on Every Fish" (November 1, 1990), a three-eyed fish is caught in the lake near the Springfield Nuclear Plant. When the mutation is attributed to pollution from the power plant, Mr. Burns runs for governor in an attempt to prevent the government from pressuring the plant to clean up its act. Aided by the best spin doctors money can buy, he seems on the verge of success. Then he has dinner with the Simpsons on live television in an attempt to demonstrate his affinity for the common man. His entire campaign then unravels when Marge serves him the three-eyed fish, and he is unable to eat it for fear of radiation poisoning.

In "Mr. Lisa Goes to Washington" (September 26, 1991), the whole Simpsons family gets a free trip to Washington, D.C., when Lisa becomes a finalist in a nationwide patriotic essay contest. The titles of *Simpsons* episodes are often based on those of well-known films, though the episodes often have little to do with those films. In this case, however, the episode bears a clear resemblance to the classic 1939 Frank Capra classic *Mr. Smith Goes to Washington*. Lisa, like Jimmy Stewart's Jefferson Smith, comes to the nation's capital brimming with patriotic enthusiasm; also like Jeff Smith, she is shocked when she observes evidence of corruption in government. But, just as all ends well in the film, Lisa's faith in the system is at least partly restored when her protests cause a crooked congressman to be arrested in a sting operation.

The much later "Mr. Spritz Goes to Washington" (May 9, 2003) is an even more direct takeoff on the Capra original—and contains even more satirical commentary on the American political system. Here the flight path for Springfield Airport is rerouted directly over the Simpsons' home, making it effectively unlivable. When they complain to their aged congressman, he gets so outraged that he drops dead on the spot. Then a local committee of Republican power brokers (headed, of course, by Mr. Burns) nominates Krusty as their candidate in a special election to replace the deceased congressman. Despite his flaws and bad habits, Krusty is entertaining, so he wins, suggesting the superficiality of the electoral process. Meanwhile, the Simpsons, having supported his campaign, convince him to crusade for a change in the flight paths. He actually attempts to follow through, but finds (as did Capra's Jeff Smith) that no one in Congress is interested in doing the right thing. He is thus blocked at every turn, while more senior congressmen see their pet projects fly through. Luckily, a savvy janitor (who looks suspiciously like Walter Mondale) helps the Simpsons pull a few behind-the-scenes strings, and Krusty's bill manages to pass. The Simpsons return home, where all has returned to its former quiet state. Bart blissfully proclaims victory: "At last those planes are flying where they belong." "That's right," says Homer. "Over the homes of poor people."

The Simpsons also deals with a number of other political issues at various times, ranging from the xenophobic fear of immigrants, to homophobia, to the shortcomings of the American educational system. In "The Cartridge Family" (November 2, 1997), the series takes on the issue of gun control. Here, civil unrest in Springfield leads Homer to seek to buy a gun at the Bloodbath & Beyond Gun Shop for home protection. The ease with which he does so, despite his checkered past, serves as a commentary on the ineffectiveness of current gun-control legislation (he is judged "potentially dangerous," so is limited to buying a maximum of three handguns). Moreover, once Homer gets the gun, it takes over his life. He joins the National Rifle Association (though he appears to think "NRA" stands for Nachos, Rifles, Alcohol) and becomes so gun crazy that Marge and the kids move into a cheap sleazy motel for their own safety. In the end, Homer finds that he loves his family even more than his gun, so he convinces them to come home by giving the gun to Marge so she can dispose of it. Unfortunately, she then becomes seduced by the gun and pops it into her purse, fantasizing herself the next Mrs. Emma Peel, as music from *The Avengers* sounds in the background.

"Last Exit to Springfield" (March 11, 1993) deals with the important issue of labor politics, even if in a way that ultimately fails to move beyond clichéd representations of both labor and management as greedy and corrupt. As the episode begins, the union president at the Springfield Nuclear Power Plant has mysteriously disappeared (apparently murdered) after promising to clean up the union. Meanwhile, Burns vows to take back concessions that had earlier been made to the union, concentrating on the dental plan that they won in the strike of 1988. Unfortunately, the cancellation of the dental plan occurs just as it turns out that Lisa needs braces, so she has to get horrible-looking, cut-rate antique ones. When Homer thus speaks out against giving up the dental plan at a union meeting, he is made the new union president. The bumbling Homer turns out (inadvertently) to be an unexpectedly tough negotiator, and the workers at the plant go out on strike to protest the loss of their dental plan. Buoyed by Lisa's inspiring folk singing, the workers show strong solidarity, even when Burns shuts down the plant and deprives the entire town of Springfield of electricity. Ultimately, Burns gives in and reinstates the dental plan, but only on the condition that Homer resign as union president.

Local Springfield politics is an issue in several episodes of *The Simpsons,* as in "Sideshow Bob Roberts" (October 9, 1994), which comments on the dirtiness and corruption of local politics, while suggesting that conservative candidates (especially Republicans) may tend to be just a bit more unscrupulous than their liberal opponents, a point also made by the film *Bob Roberts* (1992), from which the episode takes its title. Here, a Rush Limbaughesque talk-show host manages to get Sideshow Bob (Kelsey Grammer) released from prison, where he had been serving a sentence for the attempted murder of Marge's sister Selma in the episode "Black Widower" (April 9, 1992). The town's Republicans, impressed by Sideshow Bob's right-wing views, decide to run him for mayor in an attempt to unseat Quimby, a Democrat. Sideshow Bob wins the election, but only by being more corrupt than Quimby. Lisa, in fact, discovers that he won the election by falsifying the votes of a large number of deceased voters. She and Bart (despite having been warned that no child ever crossed the Republican Party and lived) then trick the conservative candidate into admitting his cheating in front of the whole town, and Quimby is restored to his position as mayor.

In "A Tale of Two Springfields" (November 5, 2000), Springfield becomes so large that the phone company decides to divide the city into two different area codes. Incensed that his side of town (the poor side, of course) is the one forced to change its area code, Homer incites a protest that leads his side of town to secede and declare itself to be the town of New Springfield, with Homer as mayor. The subsequent feud between New Springfield and Olde Springfield eventually causes Homer to have a wall constructed to separate the two cities, but everyone except the Simpsons deserts New Springfield and moves back to the more affluent side of the city. Then, when the rock band The Who are about to play a big concert in Olde Springfield, Homer convinces them to move the concert to New Springfield to try to lure people back there. Ultimately, the band mediates the dispute, and their loud music even breaks down the wall, leading to the reunification of the city. This seemingly silly episode may be more about Homer than about urban politics in America, but it does comment on the large gap between the rich and the poor that can be found in any number of American cities.

Similarly, the poor judgment of the people and governmental officials of Springfield can be taken as a comment on the management of cities in general. A classic episode in this regard is "Marge vs. the Monorail," in which Mr. Burns is caught dumping radioactive toxic waste in a Springfield park. He is forced to pay a $3 million fine (which to him is pocket change), which leaves the people of Springfield to decide how to spend the money. A town hall meeting ensues, at which slick con man Lyle Lanley (voiced by Phil Hartman in a scene that recalls the film *The Music Man*) convinces the citizenry to spend the money to build a new monorail—despite the fact that they have no need for it and that the town's existing infrastructure is in a sad state of disrepair. The monorail is built and looks impressive, though it may not be a good sign that Homer, always looking for an easy gig, manages to land the job as the "conductor" of the high-tech train. It also doesn't look good when Homer discovers a family of possums living in a compartment of the train. Suspicious, Marge travels to the town of North Haverbrook, where Lanley built his last monorail. When she learns that the project was dangerously unsafe and never actually worked, she rushes back to Springfield to try to save Homer. Amid great media hoopla, the Springfield Monorail is launched on its maiden voyage, with passengers including such notables as Krusty the Clown and *Star Trek*'s Leonard Nimoy (who serves as grand marshal of the opening ceremonies, at which Mayor Quimby mistakes him for one of the Little Rascals). Homer, with Bart at his side, cranks up the train, which promptly goes out of control and seems unstoppable. All aboard seem doomed, until Homer manages to stop the train through the ludicrous expedient of dropping an anchor that lodges in a giant doughnut that serves as the sign for a local doughnut shop.

While such episodes seem rather innocuous, *The Simpsons* has sometimes veered into controversial territory. For example, the irreverence of the satire in *The Simpsons* has often brought the program in for criticism from the Christian right. Thus, many felt that the episode "There's Something About Marrying"—in which Marge's sister Patty admits to being a lesbian and announces her intention to marry a lesbian pro golfer (who turns out secretly to be a man, much to Patty's chagrin)—endorsed lesbianism and same-sex marriage. The Christian right has also frequently complained about the representation of religion in *The Simpsons*, one of the few network programs that has dared to tackle that topic, perhaps the most sensitive in American culture. Religion is, in fact, a bigger part of the lives of the Simpsons than of virtually any other family on network television. For example, the Simpsons regularly go to church, even if they aren't really all that into it. In "Homer the Heretic" (October 8, 1992), Homer discovers how relaxing it is to stay home on Sundays when the rest of the family has gone to church. So he decides to found his own religion, which requires him to stay home and wallow in sloth every Sunday. Even God (a conventional, deep-voiced, white-bearded man who comes to Homer in a dream) admits that this lifestyle has a certain attraction. Then Homer's house catches fire while he is napping on one of his restful Sundays and he is saved only by the intervention of his Christian neighbor Flanders, causing him to return to the fold. In "Simpsons Bible Stories" (April 4, 1999), the Simpsons all fall asleep in church and then have dreams that are fractured versions of well-known biblical tales. They then emerge from the church, relieved to find that it had all been a dream. Unfortunately, they inexplicably emerge into the apocalypse. The Flanders family ascends to heaven, while the Simpsons trudge down a stairway to hell. The apocalypse doesn't hold, of course, and Springfield is back to normal in the next episode.

In general, *The Simpsons* is quite moderate in its treatment of religion, never quite daring the kind of biting religious satire that would eventually mark such animated series as *South Park* and *Family Guy*. Nevertheless, the program does sometimes explore potentially dangerous territory. For example, the big problem with the Flanders family in "Home Sweet Homediddly-Dum-Doodily" (and elsewhere) is their excessive religiosity. Thus, as the episode draws to its mock-dramatic close, Homer must rush to the Springfield river to rescue Bart and Lisa from being baptized in the river by the overzealous Flanders—the baptism being treated as a horrifying event. The very next week, in the episode "Bart Sells His Soul" (October 8, 1995), the Reverend Lovejoy attempts to terrorize the local children by making them recite a graphic litany of the torments their souls will suffer in hell if they misbehave. Later, Bart assures Milhouse that there is no such thing as a soul, to which Milhouse responds by asking what religions would have to gain by lying about such things. The episode then cuts immediately to a scene of Rev. Lovejoy counting his cash. The implication that religions fabricate their mythologies in order to extort money from believers could not be more clear. On the other hand, as the episode proceeds, Bart mockingly sells his soul to Milhouse, and then discovers that his life suddenly feels empty and incomplete, suggesting either that the soul is real or that it is at least a useful fiction.

Other episodes are even more skeptical about religion. In "НОМЯ," the momentarily intelligent Homer constructs an ironclad proof that God doesn't exist. He presents his findings to Flanders, who examines them carefully, admits that Homer's work is irrefutable, and then quickly burns the evidence to prevent the fall of Christianity. In "Lisa the Skeptic" (November 23, 1997),

Lisa discovers the skeleton of what the whole town of Springfield concludes is an angel. The sensible Lisa works, however, to disprove that theory and is ultimately vindicated when the skeleton turns out to have been planted as part of a publicity stunt for the opening of a new mall. In "The Joy of Sect" (February 8, 1998), virtually everyone in town falls prey to a cult that is really nothing more than a colossal scam. Marge, however, escapes from the cult camp (to the music of *The Prisoner,* while being pursued by a large balloon-like ball similar to the "Rover" that captured attempted escapees from the village of that series) and manages to mount an anticult campaign that eventually ends with the leader of the cult exposed as a con artist.

The Simpsons was already satirizing religion in the *Tracey Ullman* shorts, but the program's ability to continually get away with its rather irreverent treatment of religion may be attributable to the fact that, while never taking itself overly seriously, the program has over the years become an American cultural institution in its own right. The list of prominent figures who have appeared as guest voices on the program, often playing themselves, reads like a who's who of contemporary popular culture. This list includes such figures as Nimoy, Aldrin, The Who, and Taylor as mentioned above, as well as such well-known actors and comedians as Mel Brooks, Bob Hope, Paul Newman, Richard Gere, Ian McKellen, Brooke Shields, Mel Gibson, James Woods, and Pierce Brosnan. Other actors, such as Duchovny, Anderson, and McGoohan as noted above, appear on *The Simpsons* as the voices of characters they play on other well-known television series. *The Simpsons* has been particularly rich in appearances by figures from the world of popular music. Three of the Beatles have appeared at various times, as have Mick Jagger and Keith Richards from the Rolling Stones. Little Richard, Lenny Kravitz, Elvis Costello, Elton John, Sting, Tom Jones, Linda Ronstadt, Tony Bennett, Peter Frampton, and James Brown have also appeared, as have such groups as U2, R.E.M., Smashing Pumpkins, the Red Hot Chili Peppers, and Aerosmith.

The Simpsons has featured appearances by numerous talk-show and game-show hosts, including *Jeopardy*'s Alex Trebek, Johnny Carson, Jay Leno, Steve Allen, Larry King, Charlie Rose, and Conan O'Brien, who had been a writer for the program before becoming the host of *Late Night with Conan O'Brien.* Moving beyond show-business proper into the culture at large, a number of famous athletes, including baseball, football, basketball, and tennis players, have appeared as themselves on *The Simpsons.* Other prominent figures as diverse as physicist Stephen Hawking and *Playboy* magnate Hugh Hefner have also appeared. The program has even featured appearances by prominent authors, such as Amy Tan, Stephen King, and even the notoriously reclusive Thomas Pynchon. In fact, Pynchon briefly appears in two episodes. In "Diatribe of a Mad Housewife" (January 25, 2004), his animated character appears with a bag over his head to emphasize his reclusiveness—though he also wears a signboard that identifies him and lives in a house decorated with neon signs that identify its owner. In "All's Fair in Oven War" (November 14, 2004), he again wears the bag when he attends a church pot-luck supper at which he samples the products of Marge's elaborate new kitchen.

The institutional nature of *The Simpsons* can also be seen in the success of its holiday episodes, which make the program a part of the holiday season. Indeed, the very first episode of *The Simpsons* was a Christmas special (in which Homer anticipates the 2003 film *Bad Santa* by playing a highly unconventional department-store Santa to try to get Christmas money for the family). Since that time the program has made a tradition of unconventional and irreverent holiday episodes, though these episodes generally have happy, family-oriented endings. The exception—and by far the most successful of the holiday episodes of *The Simpsons*—is the sequence of "Treehouse of Horror" episodes that have appeared in conjunction with every Halloween since the second season of the program. (The first season did not begin in time for a Halloween episode.) Halloween, of course, is by its nature an irreverent holiday, so it is perfect for the particular *Simpsons* brand of humor. The first "Treehouse of Horror" episode (October 25, 1990) is preceded by an on-screen announcement that the following program is far too scary to be appropriate for children. That announcement, of course, only made the program more attractive to children who were in the Halloween mood. The program itself then consists of a series of three spooky stories swapped by Bart and Lisa as they try to scare each other in their treehouse at night. In the first story, the Simpsons move into a haunted house, built, as was the house in the 1982 film *Poltergeist*, on the site of an ancient Indian burial ground. The house, however, ends up destroying itself just to escape from occupation by the Simpsons, who refuse to move out. In the second story, the Simpsons are abducted by aliens, who beam them up to their flying saucer (though Homer is so fat that it takes two beams to lift him). The aliens treat the Simpsons royally as they head with them back to their home planet, but become insulted and return the family to earth after the Simpsons wrongly begin to suspect, after finding a suspicious cookbook, that the aliens plan to eat them. The referent here is the 1962 *Twilight Zone* episode "To Serve Man," in which aliens who ostensibly seek to aid humankind actually hope to serve them as food, as is revealed when the humans finally manage to translate a cookbook that the aliens have brought with them. The final episode is a comic rendering of Edgar Allan Poe's "The Raven," featuring Bart as the ominous bird, given to saying things like "Eat my shorts," instead of "Nevermore."

The ongoing popularity of the "Treehouse of Horror" episodes is indicative of the extent to which *The Simpsons* has become an integral part of the cultural landscape of contemporary America—to a greater extent than perhaps any other single television series. Meanwhile, the popularity of the series as a whole has helped to trigger a renaissance in prime-time television animation, including the science fiction spoof *Futurama*, a sort of *Simpsons* spin-off featuring the same animation style and much of the same creative team. Many of the programs to appear in the wake of *The Simpsons* have been family sitcoms, of which some of the most important (including *King of the Hill*, *Family Guy*, and *American Dad*) have also appeared on the Fox network. In addition, the irreverent satire of *The Simpsons* has opened the way for such outrageous programs as *South Park*, which has in turn inspired several subsequent programs. This explosion of prime-time animation in the 1990s and beyond is the subject of the remaining chapters in this volume.

CHAPTER 4

Family Guys from *King of the Hill* to *American Dad*

In "The Italian Bob" (December 11, 2005), an episode of *The Simpsons*, the Simpson clan travels to Italy (with, of course, near-disastrous results). There, they encounter Bart's old nemesis Sideshow Bob, now living as the mayor of a village in Tuscany. When the Simpsons reveal Bob's true identity, the local police whip out their handbook of American criminals. Sure enough Bob is in there, identified as a multiple attempted murderer. But the handbook also features a large picture of *Family Guy*'s Peter Griffin, with the label "Plagiarismo," followed by a picture of *American Dad*'s Stan Smith, with the label "Plagiarismo di Plagiarismo." This good-natured suggestion that Griffin might have a little bit too much in common with Homer Simpson (and that *American Dad* is basically just *Family Guy* warmed over) is all in fun, but it does indicate the extent to which the explosion of prime-time animation in the 1990s and beyond is indebted to *The Simpsons*. Of course, given the importance of *The Simpsons* as the founding text of the current Golden Age in prime-time animation, it is not surprising that so many of the animated programs that have appeared in prime time have used the same basic family sitcom format. Such programs include not only *Family Guy* and *American Dad*, but also the long-running *King of the Hill*, all of which appeared on the Fox network. Other, less-successful animated family sitcoms have included such unusual entries as *God, the Devil, and Bob* and *The Oblongs*, indicating an additional versatility in the genre.

Of the numerous animated family sitcoms to appear on prime-time television in the wake of the success of *The Simpsons, King of the Hill* is clearly the one that attempts the most realistic depiction of suburban life in America at the end of the twentieth and beginning of the twenty-first century. Co-created by Mike Judge, who had earlier created the groundbreaking MTV animated program *Beavis and Butt-head,* and Greg Daniels, who had been a writer for *The Simpsons, King of the Hill* focuses on the day-to-day life of Hank Hill (voiced by Judge). Hill is a salesman of "propane and propane accessories" who lives with his family in the fictional small town of Arlen, Texas, which seems to be somewhere near Dallas, though at times it also seems to be within easy driving distance of Houston or of the Mexican border. In many ways, the tone of *King of the Hill* is set by a scene in the pilot episode (January 12, 1997) in which Hank stares at the engine of his pickup truck, accompanied by his three neighbors and lifelong friends, Dale Gribble (Johnny Hardwick), Bill Dauterive (Stephen Root), and Jeff Boomhauer (Judge). The four stand around the engine, sipping beers, taking turns saying "yep," and occasionally quoting (or misquoting, in Dale's case) automotive diagnostic clichés. Then the conversation suddenly turns to the *Seinfeld* series, one of the most successful sitcoms in television history. All four, somewhat surprisingly, seem to be fans, and Boomhauer seems to understand the gist of the show perfectly. "Them dang ole New York boys," he says with his trademark fast-paced mumble. "Just a show about nothing." To a large extent, *King of the Hill* is a sort of down-home counterpart to *Seinfeld,* a show about dang ole Texas boys (though Hank, we—and he, much to his chagrin—learn in the fifth season, was actually born in New York City) engaged largely in the trivialities of day-to-day existence. However, the series does address a number of important and potentially controversial issues that impact the daily lives of ordinary Americans, including sex education, racism, religious intolerance, alcohol and drug abuse, and (perhaps most centrally) changing gender roles.

Crucial to the treatment of gender is Hank's wife, the bespectacled Peggy Hill (Kathy Najimy), who works as a substitute teacher of Spanish in the Arlen schools. Peggy is intelligent and thoughtful, though she aspires to being considerably more of an intellectual than she really is. She is a loyal and faithful wife, though she is also a strong woman who is perfectly willing and able to stand up to her husband and to let him know in no uncertain terms when she thinks he is in the wrong. If anything, however, Peggy is less sensible than Hank. She, indeed, is the one who tends to get carried away with things and then have to be brought back to earth by her husband, which runs counter to the usual animated sitcom formula of the out-of-control husband stabilized by the sensible wife.

Having grown up the son of a father who was the ultimate male sexist pig (Cotton Hill, voiced by Toby Huss), Hank attempts to treat Peggy with the respect he knows she deserves, and he is generally successful, though in the process he also struggles mightily with his own masculinity. Central to these struggles is their son Bobby (Pamela Segall Adlon), a chubby 12- to 13-year-old who is a failure at most sports and whose interests are far from those that might have traditionally been expected of a young Texas male. He dreams of being a stand-up "prop comic," or perhaps even a clown, and he enjoys bubble baths and other pastimes that Hank, a former high-school football star, finds highly unmasculine. Yet Hank is intensely devoted to his son and learns to appreciate him for who he is, even if he isn't who Hank might have hoped he would be.

Bobby, of course, is at an impressionable age, so his interests and attitudes can change considerably from one episode to another. In one key early episode related to the treatment of gender—"Shins of the Father" (March 23, 1997)—he falls under the influence of his sexist grandfather. The diminutive Cotton (who has extra-short legs because his shins were shot off by the Japanese in World War II) comes to visit for Bobby's birthday (presumably his twelfth), bringing along his new 39-year-old wife, Didi (Ashley Gardner)—though "parts of her are much younger," as Peggy cattily remarks in reference to Didi's new breast implants, for which Cotton got a discount because they are both "lefties." Hank thus has to come to grips with the fact that his father, who is divorced from his mother, is now married to a woman Hank's own age—in fact, Hank and Didi were kindergarten classmates. Peggy, however, has even more to deal with. In addition to the fact that Cotton brings Bobby a real shotgun for his birthday, Peggy also has to cope with Cotton's ultrasexist attitudes, including his oafish domination of the slow-witted Didi and his far less successful attempts to boss around Peggy herself. Things come to a head when Bobby begins to mimic his grandfather's behavior. When Bobby orders his mother to bring him his dinner, then slaps her on the behind, Peggy has had enough. She demands that Hank stand up to his father, but he backs off when Cotton pleads for sympathy on the basis of his war wounds. Finally, when Bobby gets sent home from school for starting a sexist riot, then accompanies Cotton to a hotel to look for prostitutes (though they find only a convention of woman lawyers), Hanks stands up to his father and sends him packing. Hank then tries to explain to Bobby that he should respect Peggy and other women. "Women were not put on this earth to serve you and me," he tells the boy.

Then they go off to a drive-in for ice cream—where they are, of course, served by a woman.

Much of the success of *King of the Hill* comes from its focus on such family moments. Indeed, despite the importance of its satire of suburban American life and of American masculinity, the show's real strength is the development of its characters and the relationships among them. In this sense, Hank, Peggy, and (to a lesser extent) Bobby provide an anchor of normalcy, while the other characters tend to be a bit more exaggerated. The Hill household is completed by Luanne Platter (Brittany Murphy), the eighteenish daughter of Peggy's brother and an abusive, alcoholic mother now in prison for attempting to murder Luanne's father with a fork. Luanne has come to live briefly with the Hills until she can find a permanent home after the disintegration of her own nightmarish family. However, she ends up staying essentially permanently after she rents, with roommates, another house in the same neighborhood, but later returns. Hank is horrified, especially given her tendency to wander about the house in a partial state of undress. On the other hand, she does have her virtues—she is, for example, a talented auto mechanic—and Hank gradually grows fond of her, despite her longtime occupation of his personal den.

Dale, Bill, and Boomhauer are also crucial to the series. The latter is a womanizing bachelor who figures less prominently than the first two. Bill, whose wife has left him, is a lonely figure who adds a touch of pathos to the humor of *King of the Hill*, which is often bittersweet. A career army man (he is a sergeant who works as a barber on the local army base), the bald, portly Bill lives a mostly empty life, dreaming someday of finding a woman to love him. He does occasionally have his moments, however, as when he has a fling with ex–Texas governor Ann Richards (voiced by herself) in "Hank and the Great Glass Elevator" (February 11, 2001). Dale is in some ways an even more pitiful figure, though he is also funnier, so much over the top that it is hard to take his problems seriously. An intense paranoid who is convinced that a variety of forces (including the U.S. government and the United Nations) are plotting to get him, he attempts to avoid participation in official society as much as possible. He refuses, for example, to sign any forms issued by the government. He also refuses to file tax returns, so he is forced to work as a self-employed exterminator, a job at which he brings in virtually no income. The family is actually supported by his wife, Nancy Hicks Gribble (Gardner), the beautiful blonde weather girl (and sometime feature reporter) on a local television station. One of the running jokes of the series is that Nancy has been having an affair with local Native American New Age healer John Redcorn (voiced by Jonathan Joss except in the first season) since the start of her marriage to Dale. It is obvious, given the boy's appearance, that Redcorn is, in fact, the father of Bobby's young friend and classmate, Joseph Gribble (voiced in the first four seasons by Brittany Murphy, then by Breckin Meyer after the onset of puberty causes his voice to change). Obvious, that is, to everyone but Dale, who doesn't seem to notice anything suspicious about the fact that "his" son is the spitting image of Redcorn or that Nancy spends most of her time with Redcorn. (Dale thinks the healer is treating her for the headaches that make her unable to have sex with Dale except on Christmas and his birthday.)

The cast of wacky neighbors in *King of the Hill* is rounded out by the presence of the Laotian Souphanousinphone family, including father Kahn (Huss), mother Minh (Lauren Tom), and their daughter (also voiced by Tom), who is named Kahn Jr. because her father wanted a boy. Kahn Jr., generally referred to as Connie, becomes Bobby's first girlfriend, but Kahn and Minh quickly become the nemeses of Hank and Peggy, respectively. Importantly, however, any animosity felt by the Hills toward the Souphanousinphones has nothing to do with the ethnicity of the latter, but simply has to do with personality clashes. If anything, it is the Laotians, insisting that the Hills are "rednecks," who are the bigots in this relationship. Both Kahn and Minh are grasping, competitive, and materialistic, and their crass attitudes clash sharply with the more old-fashioned values of the Hills.

King of the Hill satirizes a number of the foibles of the Hills and their neighbors, as well as American society as a whole. Perhaps the most consistent object of satire is the Wal-Mart discount store chain, represented in the series by the Mega Lo Mart. Hank frequently finds himself forced to shop there despite the fact that he regards it as an anti-American embodiment of pure evil because of its tendency to drive smaller and more specialized businesses with more knowledgeable employees out of business. Hank's battles with Mega Lo Mart come to a particular head at the end of the second season in "Propane Boom" (May 17, 1998), when Mega Lo Mart starts selling propane, causing Hank's branch of Strickland Propane to shut down and leaving Hank out of a job. Hank is then forced to swallow his pride and go to work for Mega Lo Mart, where his experience is made even more humiliating by the fact that his supervisor in the propane department is Buckley (David Herman), Luanne's dim-witted teenage boyfriend. Ultimately, Buckley's incompetence causes a propane explosion that destroys the entire store, leaving us to wonder if Hank himself has been killed. This season-ending cliffhanger is then continued in "Death of a Propane Salesman" (September 15, 1998), where Hank turns out to be okay, though Buckley is killed and Luanne has all her hair burned off, causing her to become a political activist in the mold of Sinead O'Connor.

Meanwhile, Hank's near death by propane explosion causes him to develop a fear of the gas, though he is finally able to overcome his anxieties and return to the work that he loves.

However, while the Hills are conservative, God-fearing Texans, they are not caricatures. Neither are they racists, religious fanatics, or rednecks. As Hank himself explains in "A Rover Runs Through It" (November 7, 2004), "I am not some redneck, and I'm not a Hollywood jerk. I'm something else entirely. I'm complicated." In this sense, the program challenges a number of negative stereotypes about conservative suburbanites, though the program does sometimes oppose the Hills to stereotypical versions of outsiders, typically Northerners, Californians, or intellectuals. In the pilot episode, for example, Hank is accused of abusing Bobby by a well-meaning but incompetent social worker from Los Angeles whose ignorance of Texas culture leads to a sequence of misinterpretations and misunderstandings. Meanwhile, in "The Arrowhead" (October 19, 1997), a self-serving, unscrupulous anthropology professor not only destroys Hank's beloved lawn digging for Indian artifacts, but seems to be making a move on Peggy until Hank puts him in his place.

The satire of such figures is part of a larger (and actually quite cynical) tendency of the show to depict almost all authority figures in a negative light. Hank, a bit gullible and naïve, tends to believe virtually every facet of the rhetoric of the American dream, especially in its particular Texas inflection. As part of this attitude, he consistently expects the best from authority figures. He is, however, consistently disappointed, especially by politicians and government officials, who almost invariably turn out to be corrupt, or at least incompetent. Even his political hero, George W. Bush, disappoints him when he turns out to have a damp, limp handshake in "The Perils of Polling" (October 1, 2000). In fact, Hank is so distraught over Bush's weak handshake that he decides to give up voting altogether, and even flees to Mexico on election day—though he of course returns just in time to vote.

Perhaps the authority figure who disappoints Hank most (other than his disastrous father) is his boss, Buck Strickland (Root), for whom Hank has worked throughout his career. Hank is intensely devoted to his work in the propane industry, which he pursues with great zeal, but also with great integrity. He expects Strickland, his professional hero, to do the same, but then continually finds his boss engaged in immoral, unethical, or illegal practices as the series proceeds. Strickland also frequently fails to appreciate Hank's contributions to the company. Thus, in the episode "Snow Job" (February 1, 1998), Strickland suffers a heart attack but chooses a business school graduate over Hank to run the company while he recuperates. Hank, meanwhile, is given the job of feeding Strickland's dogs. To make matters worse, when he goes to Strickland's home to perform this task, Hank discovers that Strickland has an electric stove. Shocked to find that his hero lacks his own loyalty to propane, Hank considers leaving the propane business to open a general store where he can provide personal service to his customers. Ultimately, however, he returns to the gas that he loves.

Perhaps the key Buck Strickland episode is the two-parter that ran on February 6 and February 13, 2000. In the first episode, "Hanky Panky," Strickland's wife, Miz Liz Strickland (Kathleen Turner) files for divorce after discovering that her husband his having an affair with one of his office employees, Debbie Grund (Reese Witherspoon). As part of the subsequent legal wrangle, Miz Liz takes over Strickland Propane, promotes Hank to manager, and attempts to make him her boy toy. Then Debbie, attracted to the power of his new position as manager, makes a move on Hank as well. Hank, of course, fends off all the advances, but matters become more serious in the second episode, "High Anxiety," after Debbie is found dead in a dumpster, shot in an apparent murder. Hank emerges as the prime suspect in the subsequent investigation, especially after Strickland (who thinks Miz Liz is the killer) plants evidence in an attempt to frame Hank. Hank, meanwhile, has an alibi, but is too embarrassed to use it: He was inadvertently, in a hilarious scene, smoking pot with Debbie's hippie roommate. Hank is cleared in the end, as it turns out that Debbie accidentally shot herself, but Hank returns to work all the more disillusioned about the values of his boss.

The murder mystery plot of these two episodes is indicative of the way in which *King of the Hill*, over the years, has supplemented its core focus on *Seinfeld*-like trivialities to include more outrageous plots, almost in the mode of *The Simpsons*. In addition to the cliffhanger that ended season two, season three also ended on a cliffhanger, "As Old as the Hills" (May 18, 1999). Here, Hank and Peggy, feeling old, decide to celebrate their twentieth wedding anniversary by going skydiving, but Peggy falls to earth from a plane when her parachute fails to open. Then, at the beginning of the fourth season, in "Peggy Hill: The Decline and Fall" (September 26, 1999), we learn that Peggy survived, thanks to landing on soft, marshy ground. However, as opposed to the cartoon tradition in which characters can survive such falls without a scratch, she is badly hurt and must undergo an extensive process of recuperation and rehabilitation, indicating the tendency of *King of the Hill* toward greater realism than virtually any other animated series, even in the episodes with extreme plots.

Many of these episodes center on the naiveté of both Hank and Peggy, which often gets them into spectacular trouble. In the classic "Jumpin'

Crack Bass" (November 2, 1997), Hank nearly lands in prison when he buys crack cocaine, thinking it is a new kind of fishing bait. Similarly, Peggy gets into trouble in "Death and Texas" (April 27, 1999) when she inadvertently smuggles cocaine into a prison for a prisoner who claims (falsely) to be a former student of hers. And Peggy briefly becomes an Internet porn star in "Transnational Amusements Presents: Peggy's Magic Sex Feet" (May 14, 2000) when she models her amazingly big feet for a photographer who then secretly posts the photos on a foot fetish site. Then, in "Ho Yeah!" (February 25, 2001), both Hank and Peggy are unaware that a young woman they invite into their home as a house guest is a prostitute (voiced by Renée Zellwegger). Hank, however, has one of his periodic heroic moments when he faces down her pimp (Snoop Dogg) so that he and Peggy can help her to go straight.

The Hills sometimes get to interact with famous people, as in the episode "Peggy's Fan Fair" (May 21, 2000). Here, Peggy, dreaming of a career as a songwriter, sends one of her songs ("This Is Just the Way God Made Me," about her gigantic feet) to virtually every major country music star. She receives only one reply—a rejection letter from Randy Travis's law firm—but even that is enough to convince her that she has a bright future in the business. She then convinces her church to go to the Country Music Fan Fair Nashville for their annual bus trip. The whole Hill family, along with the neighborhood gang, accompanies Peggy on the trip, where they encounter a number of country music stars (all providing their own voices). Clint Black and Lisa Hartman Black, Terri Clark, Charlie Daniels, Wynonna Judd, and Martina McBride make brief appearances as themselves, while Vince Gill provides the voice of Assistant Pastor Larry, who leads the bus trip, and becomes convinced in the process that Peggy is a dangerous lunatic. Peggy's real troubles on the trip start when, standing in line for an autograph, she discovers that Travis, who appears as the comic villain of the episode in a particularly good-natured turn, has apparently recorded her song without giving her credit. Infuriated, she slugs Travis, though he later tries to convince her, and does convince Hank, that the similarity between the two songs is purely coincidental. Then, at a live performance of "This Is Just the Way God Made Me," Travis explains the story behind the song—which also seems to have been stolen from Peggy, making her even more incensed.

At the fair, country duo Kix Brooks and Ronnie Dunn befriend Bobby and Luanne, so the two younger Hills take them an Apple Brown Betty baked by Peggy. Unfortunately, they drop it in horse manure on the way, which apparently enhances the taste but also makes Brooks so sick when he eats it that he has to be hospitalized. Meanwhile, Bill and Boomhauer help Peggy toilet paper Randy Travis's trailer, during which they inadvertently dump it in the lake, with Travis (unbeknownst to them, because Dale is supposedly keeping an eye on him elsewhere) trapped inside. The heroic Hank swims out to the submerged trailer and saves the singer, but even he wonders if Peggy might have attempted to drown Travis on purpose. He also wonders if she intentionally poisoned Brooks and if she is trying to do the same to Travis when she brings him an Apple Brown Betty as well (to apologize for the trailer incident). Police are on the verge of taking Peggy away in cuffs when Hank shows his ultimate faith in his wife by tasting the pie to prove that it isn't poisoned. Then, when Travis again takes the stage, the singer tells the story of how *he* saved *Hank* from drowning—apparently Travis will steal anything that isn't nailed down. This time Hank volunteers to punch the singer, but Peggy concludes that there's no point.

As of this writing, *King of the Hill*, now in its tenth season, has become a fixture on the Fox network on Sunday nights. It also runs extensively in syndication on both Fox and Fox's subsidiary cable channel, FX. The series has thus joined *The Simpsons* as a longtime institution of American popular culture, a fact that can be seen in its ability to attract some of America's finest and best-known actors to provide guest voice talent. In addition to those mentioned above, some of the actors who have appeared on the series include Ed Asner, Laura Dern, Will Ferrell, Brendan Fraser, Sarah Michelle Gellar, Jeff Goldblum, Dennis Hopper, Milla Jovovich, Lucy Liu, Burt Reynolds, Chris Rock, Meryl Streep, Billy Bob Thornton, and Henry Winkler. Public figures such as James Carville have also appeared, as have a number of athletes and musicians, especially country music stars.

Though *King of the Hill* was able to replicate at least some of the success of *The Simpsons*, not all animated family sitcoms have been so well received. *God, the Devil, and Bob*, for example, debuted on NBC in March 2000, but was pulled from the air after only three episodes because of cries of outrage from religious groups who saw the series as blasphemous because of its comic treatment of sacred motifs. (In all, 13 episodes were made. All were broadcast on British television and all are now available on DVD.) The show was, if anything, pro-Christian and certainly pro-family. And the religious issues are treated with a very light touch and all in fun—but apparently some things are not supposed to be fun. In particular, the depiction of God as an all-too-human, beer-swilling ex-hippie who looks suspiciously like Jerry Garcia of the Grateful Dead was a bit too much for some.

The basic premise of the show (somewhat similar to that of Bertolt Brecht's classic 1943 play *The Good Person of Sezuan*) is that God (voiced in a congenial, down-to-earth manner by James Garner) has grown frustrated with the fallen state of his creation and is thus tempted to wipe it all out and start over. However, this is not the furious God of the Old Testament, so God seeks a reason to preserve humanity. Ultimately, drinking in a bar in Detroit with his rather friendly—and emotionally fragile—antagonist, the Devil (Alan Cumming), God decides to make a wager. He will allow the Devil to choose one human; if that human shows an ability to make the world a better place through his actions, humanity will be saved. If not, they will be annihilated.

The human chosen by the Devil is the allegorically named Everyman, Bob Allman (French Stewart), who happens to be drinking in the bar at the time. Bob is an embattled family man who works in an auto plant. He drinks too much and has a fondness for porn, but he really isn't a bad sort. In fact, as the series proceeds, Bob and God become fast chums, much to the frustration of the Devil, whose attempts to sabotage Bob's efforts continually fail. Much of the action has to do with Bob's family and with the way his experiences with God help him to be a better husband and father. Wife Donna (Laurie Metcalf) is frustrated by Bob's excessive drinking and wants him to help more around the house, but she still loves him. Daughter Megan (Nancy Cartwright) is a 15-year-old who, being a teenager, has issues with both her parents. Son Andy (Kath Soucie) is still young, but seems to be the most intelligent of the group. In the brief course of the series, Bob gets to know them all much better and learns to appreciate them for who they are.

God, the Devil, and Bob can sometimes be amusingly satirical, though most of its satire is not really aimed at religion. Typical in this regard is the episode "There's Too Much Sex on Television" (not broadcast in the original U.S. run). Here, God charges Bob with the task of getting the amount of sex on television reduced to a more acceptable level—though he assures Bob that he has nothing against sex per se—he did, after all, invent it. Alarmed at the project, Smeck, the Devil's toadying assistant (Jeff Doucette), exclaims to his boss, "Oh no, we're losing television! The one thing we love, the one thing you're good at!" Bob starts with the mundane expedient of writing a letter to the networks asking them to show less sex on TV. When that doesn't work, he heads for Hollywood to attack the problem at its source, with the Devil and Smeck hot on his heels.

In Hollywood, Bob runs into a famous, but unnamed, actress (voiced by Sarah Michelle Gellar) who happens to be living at his seedy motel and who claims to want to help him with his project—but who is actually working for the Devil, who has promised to help her with her acting career. Bob goes to the programming department of the Network, but discovers, in another satirical swipe, that it is nothing more than a satanic cult. Horrified by that discovery and by the actress's attempts to seduce him (with God looking on disapprovingly), Bob heads back home, defeated. When he arrives in Detroit, he goes straight to his favorite bar, where he discovers that the local news channel is airing a special on gratuitous television sex. Realizing that the special is just a ploy for ratings, Bob decides to resume his quest and take direct action. He rushes back home and rummages through his videotapes (most of which are apparently porn), but finally finds a tape labeled "Heidi." He goes to the TV station and substitutes the tape for that of the special on TV sex. Unfortunately, the movie *Heidi* has been taped over—with a private sex tape of Bob and Donna that she allowed him to make on his birthday. The sex tape is broadcast all over Detroit, and people all over town start to throw their TV sets out the window, screaming in horror at the sight of Bob and Donna having sex. Bob is mortified, of course, but God is pleased. With their sets destroyed, people all over town are not only exposed to less gratuitous sex, but are also forced to spend more time with their families, just to pass the time.

One of the most unusual of all animated family sitcoms to air in prime time was *The Oblongs*, which began a brief run of eight episodes on the WB in the spring of 2001, then returned for five more episodes in the fall of 2002. Based on the picture book *Creepy Susie & 13 Other Tragic Tales for Troubled Children*, by Angus Oblong, the series features a bizarre family of deformed misfits, all of whom have contracted their various disabilities and deformations as a result of exposure to toxic and radioactive waste that runs down into their low-lying poor neighborhood from a nearby factory (run by Globocide, Inc., which specializes in the manufacture of poisons, pesticides, and other chemicals, which they of course test on animals). The pollution in the valley is also made worse by the runoff from the lavish and wasteful lifestyles of the wealthy denizens of "The Hills," which tower over the valley. This basic premise obviously offers a number of possibilities for satire aimed at such targets as the arrogant rich and exploitative, environmentally irresponsible corporations. Ultimately, however, the show is very much about the Oblong family and their relationships with one another.

The family patriarch is Bob Oblong (voiced by Will Ferrell), who lacks arms and legs but actually gets by just fine, holding down a job at the Globocide factory and generally doing what TV fathers do. In fact, except for his lack of limbs, the pipe-smoking, sweater-wearing Oblong might have stepped straight out of a 1950s sitcom. His wife, Pickles Oblong (Jean Smart), is originally from the Hills and thus has no congenital deformities, though she is an alcoholic and a chain smoker. In addition, since falling in love with Bob and moving to the valley to be with him, she has lost all of her hair due to the toxic environment there. Seventeen-year-old Chip and Biff (Randy and Jason Sklar) are conjoined twins, attached at the waist, sharing three legs and three butt cheeks. Eight-year-old Milo (*King of the Hill*'s Pamela Segall Adlon) is relatively normal physically, though he is afflicted with a variety of disorders, including diabetes and attention deficit disorder, that force him to take a massive amount of medication. Four-year-old Beth (Jeannie Elias) has a large, pickle-shaped tumor growing out of her head, but otherwise seems relatively normal.

The other residents of the valley tend to suffer from the same sorts of ailments as the Oblongs, though we see relatively little of them except for a gang of neighborhood children who are Milo's friends and hang out with him in his clubhouse. These include Jawless Peggy Weggy the Mutant (Becky Thyre), a girl with no lower jaw and only one breast; the toadlike, ever-hungry Helga Phugly (Lea Delarea); Mikey Butts (Jeannie Elias), whose pendulous butt cheeks sag down below his knees; and Creepy Susie (Elias), a morbid goth girl who dresses in black and unaccountably speaks with a French accent. Meanwhile, the healthy, well-to-do Hill children are represented primarily by the "Debbies," a group of beautiful, interchangeable high-school girls (mostly voiced by Segall Adlon, though Debbie Klimer, the daughter of Bob's boss, is voiced by Thyre). The pretentiousness of the Debbies is matched only by their conformist zeal to be fashionable and their contempt for those less fortunate than themselves.

The Oblongs is presented in a consistently light, upbeat spirit, which perhaps makes its dark subject matter a bit more palatable. The lightness of the series, however, tends to water down its potentially powerful political satire, suggesting that its condemnation of corporate ruthlessness and class-based inequality is merely a joke and should not be taken seriously. Thus, the program can make radical anticapitalist statements, yet seem innocuous. For example, in "My Name Is Robbie" (October 6, 2002), the Oblongs visit a Globocide-owned amusement park, "Old Globocide Village," that not only spoofs Disneyland and Disneyworld, but also the corporate culture of which Disney and its products are principal advocates worldwide. As the episode begins, the Oblongs watch a television commercial for the park in which a cowboy on horseback rides through the streets of the park, welcoming visitors and announcing that the park will "show you the fun side of a soulless corporate future." Always gullible and eager to embrace the corporate culture that has so mangled their lives, the Oblongs rush to the park, especially after the ever-cheerful Bob gleefully announces that "as a company employee I get a 10 percent surcharge!" At the park, they observe a factory of the future, which suggests that Bob's job at the real factory will soon be taken over by robots, "eliminating the need for moronic human workers." "Super!" declares Bob. Then they see a variety of rides, all based on rides at the Disney parks, but tweaked to satirize the corporate culture that lies behind the rides. These include the "Trickle-Down Log Flume," "The Downsizer," "Corporate Pirates of the Cayman Islands," and "It's a Third World' (where canned music based on the well-known Disney theme "It's a Small World" happily proclaims the joys of working in the Third-World factories of transnational corporations). Impressed, Milo proclaims that he wants to work in a sneaker factory, but his mother explains that he's too old.

In "The Golden Child" (May 6, 2001), however, Milo does find work when he invents his own sports energy drink so that he can make money for playing video games in the local arcade. His drink, which he calls "Manic," is really just sugar water, but it seems to have an unaccountable effect on its drinkers, living up to its name. The drink becomes an instant success, causing Globocide quickly to move not only to acquire the rights to the drink, but to Milo himself (who thus becomes just another commodity). In fact, they proclaim Milo to be the long-awaited "Corporate Messiah." Globocide executives immediately begin training the boy in the tactics of unscrupulous corporate manipulation, but when the Manic drink goes into mass production with his formula, the new product unaccountably lacks the kick of the original. As it turns out (perhaps in a comment on the cocaine content of the original Coca-Cola), Milo had been packaging his drink in morphine bottles garnered from a medical waste dump, but had not cleaned the bottles, leaving morphine residue in the drink. Without the morphine, Manic really is just sugar water. Milo's corporate career is thus cut short, and he is returned to his family, discarded when he is no longer considered a valuable asset.

The Oblongs may have been just a bit too odd, and too potentially offensive, politically and otherwise, to draw a large audience. On the other hand, by the time it was aired, programs such as *South Park* had demonstrated that offensiveness in an animated program could actually attract certain audiences, especially the much-coveted (by advertisers) young adult male demographic. *Family Guy* went for much of this same market, but broadened its appeal by sticking much more closely to the formula that had made *The Simpsons* such a big hit (thus the tongue-in-cheek charge of plagiarism noted earlier). Still, *Family Guy* consistently goes well beyond *The Simpsons* in many important respects, taking many aspects of that great predecessor to new heights—or depths, as the case may be. As a result, *Family Guy* has never had the broad appeal of *The Simpsons* and has always been steeped in controversies, yet has a core viewer base that is more devoted to the show than are most fans of *The Simpsons*.

Family Guy was the brain child of young Seth McFarlane, growing out of a cartoon about a middle-aged wastrel and his talking dog he had created as a student project while enrolled at the Rhode Island School of Design. When the first episode of *Family Guy* aired on Fox on January 31, 1999 (right after Super Bowl XXXIII), McFarlane was still only 25 years old, though he had already worked short stints for both Hanna-Barbera and Walt Disney Studios before coming to Fox. That first episode includes an allusion to the Super Bowl (in which Peter Griffin dumps a load of cash into the stadium during the game, causing pandemonium), thus indicating early on the extent to which *Family Guy* would carry on a dialogue with the television and pop cultural context in which it appears.

After an abbreviated first season of seven episodes, the show began its first full season on Fox in the fall of 1999, though it quickly lost its regular slot and was frequently moved around to different days and times during that season, often opposing other networks' top-rated programs. As a result, ratings for *Family Guy* suffered, and Fox announced that the show was being canceled at the end of the second season. Viewer outcries and changes of personnel at Fox led to the show being brought back for a third season after all. Fox still failed to give the show a regular time slot, however, and it was canceled "for good" at the end of the third season. *Family Guy*, however, proved to be hard to kill, and the support of devoted fans remained strong, even after the show's cancellation on Fox. *Family Guy* went on to become a bulwark of the Adult Swim programming block on the Cartoon Network, consistently coming in as the top-rated program in that block. DVD releases of the first three seasons (the first two were combined into a single release) were huge sellers, topping the sales of single-season DVD packages even of such popular programs as *Sex in the City* or *Friends*. As a result, Fox, always struggling to find viewers, gave the show new life, and a fourth season began broadcasting on May 1, 2005. Since that time, the show has had a stable Sunday-night time slot and seems to be on the road to joining *The Simpsons* and *King of the Hill* as a Sunday-night staple.

The Griffin family of *Family Guy* has much in common with the Simpsons, especially in the way its fat, obnoxious, dim-witted father, Peter (voiced by McFarlane), resembles Homer Simpson. The 42-year-old Peter initially works for (or at least is employed by) the Happy-Go-Lucky Toy Company, which is probably appropriate given his consistently immature behavior. Ultimately, however, he becomes essentially unemployed, trying his hand at an array of jobs. Peter is even better than Homer Simpson at getting into trouble, and his outrageous conduct (or misconduct) gets him into a variety of spectacular jams. For example, in "E Peterbus Unum" (July 12, 2000), he secedes from the United States and founds his own country, then subsequently annexes his neighbor's swimming pool, which is still part of the United States, leading to all-out war between "Petoria" and the U.S. army.

Peter's wife, Lois (Alex Borstein), is a 40-year-old stay-at-home mother, though she works part-time as a piano teacher and has numerous other activities that take her out of the home as well. She is also an attractive redhead, in this sense more in the mold of Wilma Flintstone than Marge Simpson. Indeed, when Peter and Lois are stranded in Cuba after being taken there aboard a hijacked plane—in the Stewie-in-love episode "Dammit Janet" (June 13, 2000)—televised news reports of the event describe the couple involved as including "a fat man who is inexplicably married to an attractive redhead," then show an artist's rendering of what the couple might look like—a drawing of Fred and Wilma Flintstone. Lois in some ways provides the family with a conscience and common sense, but she has a wild side and is anything but a conventional, conservative suburban housewife. She is also the daughter of fabulously wealthy parents from Newport—Carter and Barbara Pewterschmidt—who greatly resent her marriage to the lowly Peter (whom she met when he was working as a towel boy at her country club). Conversely, Francis Griffin, Peter's fanatically Catholic father, hates Lois because she is a Protestant.

Like the Simpsons, the Griffins have three children. However, the two elder Griffin children, 16-year-old Meg (voiced by Mila Kunis, except in the brief first season) and 13-year-old Chris (Seth Green) are somewhat older than Bart and Lisa Simpson, which offers a number of new plot opportunities as the two teenage Griffins struggle to deal with puberty and the pressures of adolescence. Meg, who owes her birth to the fact that an antibiotic interfered with her mother's birth control pills, seems relatively intelligent, but is bespectacled, plump, and generally unpopular in her school, James Woods Regional High School (named for the actor, one of the few Hollywood stars to have grown up in Rhode Island). Chris is a student at Buddy Cianci Junior High School, which is named for the controversial, longtime mayor of Providence, who was sentenced to a federal prison for conspiracy in 2002. Chris, who owes his birth to a broken condom, leading to a lawsuit whose proceeds paid for the family home, is stupid and obese, following very much in the footsteps of his father.

What really sets *Family Guy* apart from *The Simpsons* is the portrayal of the two remaining family members. The family dog, Brian (McFarlane), talks and acts like a human being. A former attendee of Brown University, he is highly cultured and intelligent, given to sipping martinis while listening to classical music. He is a complex and interesting character, so much so that he is actually the central character in numerous episodes—as in the season three two-parter "The Thin White Line" (July 11, 2001) and "Brian Does Hollywood" (July 18, 2001), in which a bored Brian seeks fulfillment by becoming a drug-sniffing police dog, which leads to a cocaine habit that he then breaks in a rehab center. Still unhappy with his life in Quahog, he heads to Hollywood to try to make it in show business and ends up becoming an award-winning director of adult films.

If Brian thus has dimensions that go far beyond those of the family dogs in *The Flintstones, The Jetsons, King of the Hill*, or *The Simpsons*, the abilities of Baby Stewie (McFarlane) are just as remarkable. The Griffin baby is about the same age as Maggie Simpson, but there the similarities end. Stewie (whose middle name is Gilligan, indicating his parents' devotion to TV) is, in fact, the real star of *Family Guy*, despite the fact that Peter is ostensibly the title character. Stewie, at least in the beginning, is a diabolical genius bent on world domination—or at least on killing Lois, whom he despises with misogynistic zeal. Distinguished by his striking, football-shaped head and his snide, British intonation, Stewie is constantly concocting evil schemes and designing super weapons, somewhat in the mold of a Bond villain. He even drew a map of Europe and began planning conquest of the continent while still in the womb.

Such unrealistic, exaggerated characters as Brian and Stewie have numerous cartoon precedents, of course, though their completely over-the-top portrayal takes them well beyond any of the characters in *The Simpsons*. However, the true secret to the success of both of these characters is that they still retain realistic components. He may like reading the *Wall Street Journal* and watching PBS, but Brian also likes to sniff other dogs' butts and is sometimes unable to resist dragging his ass across the carpet or peeing on the rug. Stewie, however diabolical and ingenious, still wears diapers, needs to be burped, and finds certain elements of infant culture (like watching *The Teletubbies* on television) absolutely irresistible. Thus, Brian is in many ways a normal dog and Stewie a normal infant, which combines with their otherwise over-the-top portrayals to create a tremendous space for irony and incongruity.

Family Guy gains additional richness from the fact that it features a large cast of characters in addition to the Griffins, many of whom play important roles in episodes of the series. For example, the show's extensive satire of the media includes frequent references to the programming of Quahog's local station, channel 5, especially the local news, featuring co-anchors Tom Tucker (McFarlane) and Dianne Simmons (Lori Alan), supported by the on-the-scene reporting of "Asian reporter Tricia Takanawa" (Borstein). Tucker and Simmons frequently appear off the air as well, though they are most notable for their on-the-air antics. The other men of the Griffins' neighborhood are also important characters, somewhat in the vein of *King of the Hill.* Much risqué humor is gained, for example, from the appearances of bachelor neighbor Glenn Quagmire (McFarlane), an over-the-top sex maniac who works as a pilot but devotes his life to the pursuit of sex—the kinkier the better. Something of a low-key foil to the hyperactive Quagmire is Cleveland Brown (Mike Henry), an African American delicatessen owner who sometimes provides the show with a voice of reason—or at least calm. He is so calm in fact, that he sometimes seems almost catatonic, while his slow, monotone speaking style does not signal a lack of intelligence so much as a lack of emotional energy. Cleveland and Quagmire are often at odds, no more so than in "The Cleveland-Loretta Quagmire" (June 12, 2005), in which Peter catches Quagmire having sex with Cleveland's wife Loretta (Borstein), then virtually has to jump-start Cleveland to get him angry about it—eventually leading to the Browns' divorce.

The other important neighbor is he-man paraplegic Joe Swanson (Patrick Warburton), a policeman injured in the line of duty when he fell after a rooftop battle in which he attempted to prevent the Grinch from stealing Christmas. Despite having lost the use of his legs and being confined to a wheelchair, Swanson is a highly capable macho man whose wife Bonnie (Jennifer Tilly), in an apparent allusion to the unchanging nature of characters in animated programs, is perpetually pregnant without ever actually giving birth. Indeed, Swanson is so capable and so much admired for having overcome his disability that Peter envies him greatly. In "A Hero Sits Next Door" (May 2, 1999), when the Swansons first move into the neighborhood, Peter doesn't realize that Joe is crippled and recruits him for his company softball team. But Joe comes through, winning the game wheelchair and all. Eventually, Peter grows so jealous of Joe's hero status that he tries to foil a bank robbery so that he can compete—but then of course Joe ends up having to save Peter from the bank robbers.

Joe's prowess, like the intellects of Brian and Stewie, seems incongruous, but then incongruity is a key source of humor in *Family Guy,* which features numerous scenes in which the dialogue is inappropriate to the action or an allusion to some other cultural product is completely inconsistent with the nature of that product itself. For example, in "Let's Go to the Hop" (June 6, 2000), Peter and Lois prepare for bed, discussing their children (in this case, the threat of drugs to their children) in dialogue that would be perfectly at home in any number of more conventional sitcoms. However, this stock sitcom scene comes off very differently in *Family Guy* because, as they have this conversation, Peter and Lois are in the process of donning elaborate S&M gear to prepare for a bout of rough sex. Another typical kind of incongruous scene occurs in "Blind Ambition" (May 15, 2005), as Peter and the neighborhood men are confronted by Lois and the neighborhood women, who want Quagmire removed from the neighborhood after he is caught voyeuristically peeping at Lois inside a stall in a bowling alley restroom. Suddenly, a giant rooster appears—out of nowhere and for no reason, though the rooster and Peter had also battled in "Da Boom" (December 26, 1999)—and attacks Peter. The ensuing battle leads to an extended action-movie sequence (lasting almost two-and-one-half minutes) in which the two go through a spectacular fistfight involving explosions, car crashes, a battle atop a moving train, a fall off a cliff and through the glass ceiling of a cruise ship dining room, a crash of the ship into Quahog pier, and finally a last round on the runway of Providence Airport, where the rooster is apparently ground up in an airplane propeller, though he seems to be still alive and potentially dangerous. Peter then returns to Quahog and resumes the initial conversation as if nothing had happened.

Despite such absurdities, *Family Guy* is in some ways actually more realistic than most cartoons. For example, as opposed to the generic Springfield setting of *The Simpsons*, *Family Guy* is set in the more specific Quahog, Rhode Island, a fictional suburb of Providence. In fact, the skyline of Providence can be seen in most of the series' establishing shots of the Griffin home. Far from being a limitation, however, this specific setting adds richness to the show, which gains considerable texture from its overt immersion in Rhode Island culture. As the naming of the two schools in the show indicates, *Family Guy* takes every opportunity to allude to places in or people from Rhode Island, and many elements of the culture of Quahog (such as frequent references to clams) are authentic reflections of the culture of Rhode Island. Though Quahog itself is a fictional town, its name is taken from a type of clam that is, in fact, is the official state shellfish. And the annual clam festival that is a key part of the local culture of Quahog is based on the International Quahog Festival held every year in Rhode Island.

Peter, despite being a buffoon, also has a realistic side and an odd charm, sometimes becoming a genuine object of sympathy as he attempts to cope with the failures of his life. For example, in "Blind Ambition," when even Quagmire becomes a hero after he resuscitates a woman who collapses in a mall dressing room (though he was apparently simply trying to molest her while she was unconscious), Peter is left as the only man he knows who's never done anything memorable. So he comes up with a plan to become famous by setting a new world record for eating nickels. Unfortunately, he then contracts nickel poisoning, which causes him to go blind. All works out in the end, however. When God inadvertently sets fire to the Drunken Clam while trying to impress a woman by lighting her cigarette with lightning, Peter, not realizing the bar is on fire, wanders in and ends up saving the bartender, thus becoming a genuine hero. In the final scene, he accepts a medal from Quahog mayor Adam West (yes, the Adam West of *Batman* fame, voiced by himself), bestowed on him in a ceremony that is modeled on the famous ending ceremony of *Star Wars* (1977). Chewbacca, C-3PO, and R2-D2 are even in attendance. The closing credits and music of the episode then mimic those of the film.

The *Star Wars* riff at the end of "Blind Ambition" is a blatant tie-in to the Fox film *Star Wars: Revenge of the Sith*, which opened in the United States four days after the airing of the episode. However, it is less a promotion for the film than another self-referential sign of *Family Guy*'s consciousness of its status as a work of American popular culture, surrounded by a sea of other such works. *Family Guy* addresses its troubled relations with the Fox network particularly directly, especially in "North by North Quahog" (May 1, 2005), the first episode aired when the program came back from "permanent" cancellation. The episode opens as Peter sadly explains to the family that they've been canceled because Fox just has no room for them on the programming schedule. After all, he notes, Fox has such "terrific" shows as *Dark Angel, Titus, Undeclared, Action, That Eighties Show, Wonderfalls, Fastlane, Andy Richter Controls the Universe, Skin, Girls Club, Cracking Up, The Pitts, Firefly, Get Real, FreakyLinks, Wanda at Large, Costello, The Lone Gunmen, A Minute with Stan Hooper, Normal Ohio, Pasadena, Harsh Realm, Keen Eddie, The Street, American Embassy, Cedric the Entertainer, The Tick, Louie,* and *Greg the Bunny.* In response to this list, Lois asks, "Is there no hope?" "Well," says Peter, "I suppose if all those shows go down the tubes we might have a shot." All those shows did, of course, go down the tubes on Fox after the cancellation of *Family Guy.* This in-your-face, I-told-you-so rejoinder to the Fox brass that canceled them in the first place is then followed by one of the most outrageous *Family Guy* shows ever, as if McFarlane and the other makers of the show wanted to signal to their loyal fans that they weren't going to be chastened by their original cancellation.

The episode begins with Peter watching Mel Gibson's *The Passion of the Christ* on TV, complaining to Brian that Christ is a wimp for taking all that punishment without fighting back. Then the Griffins, with their sex life going stale, decide to go on a second honeymoon. On the way to Cape Cod, Peter crashes the car because he is trying to drive while reading a *Jughead* comic book. They spend all their money to fix the car and are about to head home when they see a TV news report (from Tricia Takanawa, of course) about the luxurious new Park Barrington Hotel in Manhattan, where "Christian enthusiast Mel Gibson" keeps a permanent room that he hardly even uses. So Peter decides to pose as Gibson (claiming to have gained weight for an upcoming movie role) and check into the room, which features toilet paper made from real money, a gold crucifix over the bed, and a variety of Nazi paraphernalia, in a reference to widespread charges of anti-Semitism in *The Passion of the Christ*. The suite also features a secret screening room, in which the Griffins discover an advance cut of *Passion of the Christ II: Crucify This*, an action-comedy sequel to the original, with Chris Tucker as Jesus' sidekick and with the tag line, "Let he who is without sin kick the first ass." Peter, horrified, decides to try to spare America from more "Mel Gibson Jesus mumbo jumbo" by stealing the film. "We've gotta get rid of this thing for the sake of Jesus and Snoopy and all the other beloved children's characters," he proclaims. They leave the hotel, pursued by two ninja priests, leading to a high-action car-chase sequence, morphing into an extended pastiche of Hitchcock's *North by Northwest*, beginning with the famous crop-duster scene. Ultimately, the priests kidnap Lois and demand that Peter bring the film to Mount Rushmore in order to get her back. Gibson himself holds Lois hostage, and Peter's attempt to rescue Lois leads to a chase across the presidential heads on the mountain, then finally to Gibson's careless fall from the monument, which occurs, according to Peter, because "Christians don't believe in gravity." Peter and Lois then have sex atop the monument, the spark once again restored to their marriage.

All of this, by the way, is only one of two plots in this episode, the other involving the attempts of Brian and Stewie to babysit for Chris and Meg while their parents are away. That subplot is itself quite rich in comedy (including one hilarious scene in which Tom Tucker insults Brian by calling him "Benjy," to which Brian responds by dragging his ass around on Tucker's carpet). This episode is thus typical of the amazing comic density of *Family Guy*, each episode of which is typically packed with as many one-liners, sight gags, and amusing references to other works of popular culture as can possibly be crammed in. Extra comic bits are sometimes even inserted in the closing credits or before the signature opening song sequence, and that sequence itself is sometimes replaced by alternative openings that lampoon the openings of other well-known programs.

In fact, as a whole, *Family Guy* produces some of its funniest moments not in the actual plots of individual episodes but in the numerous brief comedy bits that are inserted into each episode, generally having little or nothing to do with the actual plot, and often making reference to films or other television series. These inserts are of several different sorts. For example, the action of *Family Guy* is frequently interrupted by musical numbers in which various characters suddenly and inexplicably burst into song—just as they do in movie musicals. Music is, in fact, an unusually large part of *Family Guy*, starting with the signature opening sequence that begins, in the mode of the beginning of *All in the Family*, with Peter and Lois singing while she plays piano, then leads into an elaborate production number featuring an array of Rockette-style dancers (and lyrics that ironically apotheosize precisely the kind of old-fashioned values that *Family Guy* overtly flouts). Many of the moments that occur within episodes refer to specific moments from musical film, as in "Road to Rhode Island" (May 30, 2000), when Brian and Stewie, trying to make their way back home by hopping a train, suddenly launch into a duet in the mode of Bob Hope and Bing Crosby in their "road" films. Perhaps the greatest musical moment in *Family Guy* occurs in the very next episode, "Let's Go to the Hop." Here, in a superb episode that lampoons any number of films about high-school life (with a plot taken most directly from the 1958 exploitation classic *High School Confidential!*), Peter goes underground to return to high school as cool kid Lando Griffin, hoping to help stamp out the new drug craze (licking South American toads) that is sweeping the school. He delivers his main anti-drug message in a hilarious and elaborate musical production number ("Better Give It Up") that recreates the John Travolta-Olivia Newton John duet "You're the One that I Want" from *Grease* (1978), complete with Travolta-like dance moves on the part of the corpulent Peter. As the song ends, one of Lando's fellow students admiringly proclaims, "You're the coolest, Lando!" Then another student agrees, at the same time indicating the show's self-conscious awareness of the unrealistic nature of the sudden musical numbers that punctuate the show (and movie musicals): "Yeah. We never spontaneously broke into song and dance before!"

Other inserted bits of comedy involve snippets of programs that the Griffins, who are as devoted to watching television as are the Simpsons, watch on television. Many of these are mock commercials, somewhat in the mode of the mock commercials often featured on *Saturday Night Live*. Most commonly they are fractured versions of various movies or movie genres or classic television programs from the past, many of them family sitcoms, including *The Brady Bunch*, *Eight Is Enough*, and *Happy Days*, though cartoons such as *The Flintstones, The Jetsons, Rocky and Bullwinkle,* and *The Roadrunner* and programs such as *Star Trek, Little House on the Prairie,* and even *The Dukes of Hazzard* are spoofed in these scenes as well. In a variation of this theme, scenes in *Family Guy* itself sometimes suddenly morph into scenes from other programs. Thus, a mock scene from the *Dilbert* cartoon suddenly appears in the middle of "Mr. Griffin Goes to Washington" (July 25, 2001), while, in "One If By Clam, Two if By Sea" (August 1, 2001), the guys boycott the Drunken Clam after it is converted into a British-style pub. Then they are suddenly seen standing (or, in Joe's case, sitting) in an alley in front of a privacy fence, sipping beers and taking turns saying "Yep," mimicking the signature scene of *King of the Hill.*

There are also moments in which the narrative of *Family Guy* momentarily swerves off into strange (usually allusive) directions. For example, in "A Hero Sits Next Door," as Peter prepares to go off to try to capture a gang of bank robbers, he suddenly yells "To the Batcave!" Then he exits through a secret door in the Griffin home and slides down a Batpole into a dark Batcave. There, he is viciously set upon by a swarm of ravenous bats, from which there seems to be no escape. Then the program cuts back to the main action, with no explanation of how Peter got out of the cave.

The final major form of inserts that punctuate the program are flashbacks, usually nonsensical memories of bizarre past events that are either completely disconnected from or inconsistent with the overall narrative of the program. For example, in "North by North Quahog," Peter recalls the time he experimented with gene splicing and ended up with the head of a moose on his body. In "A Very Special *Family Guy* Freakin' Christmas" (December 21, 2001), Peter remembers the time he was taping *Monday Night Football* without the express written permission of the National Football League, and an FBI swat team burst into his house, riddling his VCR with bullets. Finally, in "When You Wish Upon a Weinstein," Peter recalls having been eaten by big-mouthed self-help guru Tony Robbins at a book signing.

Despite such interruptions, the episodes of *Family Guy* do have main narratives, which are often reminiscent of episodes of *The Simpsons* or even *The Flintstones,* though generally going well beyond such predecessors in outrageousness. Thus, there are the requisite attempts to get into show business, to garner greater financial success, or to avoid the temptations of marital infidelity. There are also film parodies, and some of the best episodes of *Family Guy* involve extended parodies of specific films or film genres. For example, most of the episode "Wasted Talent" (July 25, 2000) is a takeoff on the well-known film *Willy Wonka and the Chocolate Factory* (1971), except that the Wonka Chocolate Factory is replaced by the Pawtucket Patriot Brewery.

Here, Peter drinks case after case of Pawtucket Patriot Beer and finally finds one of the four silver scrolls hidden in random beers that allow the bearer to enter the mysterious brewery for a private tour conducted by the reclusive Pawtucket Pat himself. (Joe is one of the winners as well, though he is unable to enter the brewery because it doesn't have wheelchair access.) The tour then echoes that of the chocolate factory in the film, complete with singing Chumba Wumbas (instead of Oompa Loompas). Unfortunately, Peter and Brian get ejected from the factory for excessive farting after drinking permanently carbonated beer, echoing the belching scene of the original. All is not lost, however. Peter comes home drunk and discovers that, when inebriated, he is a piano prodigy—which allows him to win an important piano contest and allows Lois, as his teacher, to defeat her longtime rival, Alex Radcliffe. Unfortunately, the amount of drinking required to win the contest kills all of his brain cells but one. The episode then ends with a typical *Family Guy* extra comic bit: The single brain cell is delighted at last to have quiet time alone to read, but then drops and breaks its glasses and is unable to read at all—just like Burgess Meredith's Henry Bemis in the classic *Twilight Zone* episode "Time Enough at Last" (November 20, 1959).

"Da Boom," like all other episodes of *Family Guy,* is chock full of pop cultural references, though it gets outside the normal family sitcom framework and suddenly makes the program into a riff on postapocalyptic science fiction. Here, Peter gets Y2K fever (though he at first thinks Y2K is "some kind of sex jelly") and becomes convinced that the upcoming New Year will bring an apocalyptic end to civilization as we know it. He stocks up on food and water and prepares to take refuge in the family basement, while his friends and family members scoff at his concerns. He manages to lure the family into the basement anyway (though he has to throw Lois down the stairs), which helps them to survive the all-out chaos that occurs as midnight arrives. They emerge into a grim, postapocalyptic landscape, with Peter gleefully gloating that his fears were justified. The family is also healthy and mutation free—as opposed to the neighbors, who suffer a variety of bizarre maladies; for example, Joe has been fused to his driveway, while Cleveland and Quagmire have been fused to each other.

The family also has food, unlike anyone else in Quahog. Tom Tucker and Dianne Simmons, for example, are forced to devour Asian reporter Trish Takanawa in order to stay alive, at which Peter quips that eating her is useless because they'll just be hungry again in an hour. On the other hand, Peter devours the entire year's worth of dehydrated meals that he has stowed away in the basement and then nearly explodes when he takes a drink of water, forcing the Griffin clan to go on the road to look for more food. Peter knows of a Twinkee [sic] factory in nearby Natick, Massachusetts, so they head there, assuming that Twinkees can survive almost anything. On the way, they encounter a variety of dangers, including a *Road Warrior*-style gang of bandits and (even worse) Randy Newman singing and playing piano. Eventually, they reach the factory and start to devour the remaining Twinkees, dreaming of building a utopian New Quahog around the bounty of the factory—with Peter as mayor for life. Unfortunately, radioactive contamination in the area turns Stewie into a weird purple octopus creature, which then gives birth to hundreds of identical octopus babies. Meanwhile, Peter's sudden determination to use the utopian community's metal resources to manufacture guns causes the entire Griffin family to be ejected from New Quahog. As they walk sadly away, Peter admits he was wrong and that no one needs guns—just as Stewie's babies attack and destroy the town, which has now been made defenseless by burning the guns manufactured by Peter. Not to worry, however. As the episode ends (with the Griffins headed for Framingham to look for a Carvel factory), we cut to a live-action shot of a sleeping Victoria Principal (as Pamela Barnes Ewing), who suddenly awakes. It was all her dream, of course—just as the death of Bobby Ewing and the entire 1985–1986 season of *Dallas* were revealed to have been Pamela's dream at the notorious beginning of that program's 1986–1987 season. Indeed, in the *Family Guy* episode, Pamela gets up and goes to the bathroom, where she finds Bobby (Patrick Duffy) showering, as in the *Dallas* episode. She falls into his arms, weeping that she has just dreamed the weirdest episode of *Family Guy* ever. "What's *Family Guy*?" he responds. They both look into the camera, looking stunned and puzzled.

This irreverent treatment of the Y2K scare (only days before many truly felt that disaster was looming) is typical of the brash satire of *Family Guy*, just as the send-up of the genre of postapocalyptic science fiction is typical of its parodic treatment of popular culture. Science fiction is, in fact, a favorite target, as when Peter seizes control (from Lois) of the Quahog Players and, seeking bigger box office, turns their production of *The King and I* into a science fiction action thriller in "The King is Dead" (March 28, 2000). Peter is a devoted fan of *Star Trek*, which shows up in several episodes. In "I Never Met the Dead Man" (April 11, 1999), Peter and William Shatner become friends, but then Meg, practicing to get her driver's license, accidentally runs over and kills Shatner. Stewie's inventions also add an element of science fiction to *Family Guy*. In "Emission Impossible" (November 8, 2001), he builds a high-tech ship and then shrinks it (and himself) down to microscopic size so that he can go inside Peter's body and try to destroy all his sperm before he can impregnate Lois with still another baby. This motif clearly recalls the classic science fiction film *Fantastic Voyage* (1966), though the voice of the talking computer that helps control Stewie's ship is supplied by none other than Majel Barrett (widow of *Star Trek* creator Gene Roddenberry), who had played Nurse Chapel on the original *Star Trek* series and who supplied the voices of the ship's computers in several of the *Star Trek* films and in the *Deep Space Nine* and *Voyager* television series.

Family Guy treats more sensitive issues, such as politics and religion, just as irreverently as it treats popular culture, though the various categories tend to run together in the series. Many episodes, though, are specifically devoted to politics or religion. Like the Simpsons and the Hills, the Griffins sometimes get involved in local politics, as when Peter and Lois both run for election to the Quahog school board in "Running Mates" (April 11, 2000). Peter wins, but only by employing dirty tactics, including accusing Lois of being a slut and displaying on television a naughty picture he once took of her. His preposterous policies while on the board (such as replacing hall monitors with killer robots based on the ED-209 "bad" robot from the *Robocop* film) are then cut short when he is driven from the board after it is discovered that he has supplied Chris with girlie magazines, which Chris has subsequently circulated around his school.

"Mr. Griffin Goes to Washington" is *Family Guy*'s contribution to the genre of cartoon episodes based on *Mr. Smith Goes to Washington,* though it of course goes well beyond the episodes of *The Simpsons* based on this film. Here, Peter is sent to Washington to lobby for the tobacco industry (because he's an idiot, like everyone in Washington) after the El Dorado Cigarette Company takes over Happy-Go-Lucky Toys and then promptly starts to produce toys—such as "Baby Smokes-a-Lot"—designed to encourage children to smoke. In Washington, Peter takes a group of politicians (including both Al Gore and George W. Bush) to a strip club, where a senator accidentally kills a stripper. Peter then wins the politicians over to the side of the tobacco industry by helping to cover up the death. But when Peter's success in promoting tobacco causes even little Stewie to start smoking, Peter changes course and speaks out against cigarettes in Congress, convincing that august body to come down hard on El Dorado Cigarettes, fining them into bankruptcy. The episode then ends with a mock public service announcement in which Peter makes a statement, not against smoking, but against killing strippers.

In "Mr. Griffin Goes to Washington," the executives of the tobacco company are so evil that they are shown using live puppies as targets to practice skeet shooting. Most network programming might have shied away from showing such a scene, but *Family Guy* revels in such images. The show features considerable violence against animals and at least one major instance of bestiality—when Lois's father impregnates his beloved racing dog in "Screwed the Pooch" (November 29, 2001). This outrageous motif actually echoes an earlier scene from *South Park; Family Guy*, in fact, often resembles *South Park* in the way that virtually no topic is considered out of bounds by the program, which is peppered with jokes about Hitler and the Holocaust, violent death, rape, child abuse, drug use, and other topics generally avoided by network television comedies. Again echoing *South Park*, it is the outrageously irreverent treatment of religion (in which the program seems to go out of its way to be offensive) that is probably the most controversial aspect of *Family Guy*. Jesus and God both frequently appear as characters in the series, as when God performs various stunts (such as pouring beer with no hands) in order to try to pick up chicks, or when Jesus appears as a cheap parlor magician. Even Christmas isn't sacred, as in "A Very Special *Family Guy* Freakin' Christmas," the third-season Christmas special, in which Peter begins a nativity pageant by announcing that Christmas is "that mystical time of year, when the ghost of Jesus rises from the grave to feed on the flesh of the living—so we all sing Christmas carols to lull him back to sleep." Then, in a slap at the show's critics, an outraged audience member is told there's nothing he can do about such jokes, so he concludes, "Well, I guess I'll just have to develop a sense of humor." Then, in the pageant itself, the ever-pregnant Bonnie Swanson, playing the mother of Jesus, announces "I am the virgin Mary—that's my story and I'm sticking to it."

The Griffins do seem to go to (Catholic) church regularly, though they are considerably less pious even than the Simpsons. In the pilot, "Death Has a Shadow" (January 31, 1999), Peter gets drunk on the communion wine and makes a spectacle of himself by proclaiming that, if this is really the blood of Christ, then "that guy must have been wasted 24 hours a day!" Actually, though this scene appears in the DVD version of this episode, it was cut by Fox censors when the episode was originally aired. The same gag did, however, appear in the broadcast version of a later episode, "Fifteen Minutes of Shame" (April 25, 2000).

A typically irreverent treatment of organized religion is the episode "Holy Crap" (September 30, 1999), in which Peter's fanatically Catholic father, newly retired from his work in a mill, comes for a visit, terrorizing the entire family, except Stewie—who greatly enjoys the bedtime stories of Biblical violence, proclaiming, "I love God! He's so deliciously evil!" To keep the old man occupied, Peter gets him a job in the toy factory, where his efficient work quickly wins him the position of shop foreman, in which capacity he mercilessly drives the men working under him. The other workers convince

Peter to complain about their mistreatment, at which point Francis fires him. When the pope comes to Boston for a visit, Peter hijacks the popemobile and brings the pontiff to Quahog, then eventually gets rid of Francis by sending him off to serve as the pope's roadie. Meanwhile, Francis returns in "The Father, the Son, and the Holy Fonz" (December 18, 2005), again trying to force the Griffins into his brand of militant Catholicism. (Among other things, he gives Stewie a serious disease by attempting to baptize him in contaminated holy water.) When Lois convinces Peter to assert his religious independence from his father, he responds by founding his own religion, "The Church of the Fonz," devoted to the worship of Fonzie from *Happy Days*. The church is a big success, but Francis isn't impressed. "What I saw today wasn't religion," he complains after attending the church. "It was just a bunch of sheep singing songs and listening to ridiculous tall tales." Brian, however, quickly sets him straight. "Actually," he says, "that *is* religion."

One of the most controversial episodes of *Family Guy* was the third-season "When You Wish Upon a Weinstein," which Fox refused to air because their censors judged the entire episode to be too offensive. Perhaps anticipating the furor, Peter at one point in the episode lectures Cleveland for not knowing the difference between edgy and offensive—a lesson the Fox censors apparently failed to heed. Virtually the entirely episode is devoted to satirizing Jewish stereotypes (and, by extension, stereotypes in general), though the real target of the satire seems to be self-serious people who have no sense of humor. Peter, concerned about his own inability to handle the family finances, concludes that he needs to hire a Jewish accountant, given that Jews are so notoriously good with money. He even bursts into a full-length musical number (sung vaguely to the tune of the beloved Disney children's classic "When You Wish Upon a Star"), ending with the stanza

Though by many they're abhorred,
Hebrew people I've adored.
Even though they killed my lord,
I need a Jew!

Peter finds his Jewish accountant in the person of one Max Weinstein, who turns out to be just as efficient as Peter had hoped. Impressed, Peter decides to convert Chris to Judaism so that he will have a greater chance for financial success. When the local rabbi (voiced by Ben Stein) understandably balks at Peter's request to declare Chris an immediate Jew without the requisite study or preparation, Peter and Chris head for Las Vegas, where they figure they can get a quickie Bar Mitzvah. And they almost do, but

Lois arrives at the last minute to intercede in a scene that pastiches the interrupted wedding scene of *The Graduate* (1967)—except that Lois fights off the enraged onlookers and then bars the synagogue door with a star of David rather than a cross. The Griffins then catch a bus to make their escape—but on the bus they are set upon by an enraged gang of ruler-toting nuns, incensed that Peter has denied his Catholic heritage in trying to make his son a Jew.

Given the general emphasis on risqué and politically incorrect humor in *Family Guy,* it is a bit difficult to see what all the fuss was about concerning the "Weinstein" episode. Meanwhile, the program seems to have settled in as part of the Fox Sunday-night lineup—though this scheduling pits it directly opposite the ABC megahit *Desperate Housewives,* a fact to which the program sometimes alludes, as in "The Father, the Son, and the Holy Fonz," when Stewie dares viewers to turn to *Housewives* for just five seconds, just to be reminded of how old and horrible-looking the supposedly hot women on it really are. Stewie, of course, might not be the best judge of feminine beauty, but this sort of direct challenge to a mighty competitor indicates the new-found confidence with which the show seemed to be proceeding by the end of 2005. Add in the long list of cameo appearances by famous figures from country star Waylon Jennings, to porn legend Ron Jeremy, to *Jeopardy*'s Alex Trebek, to Kelly Ripa and Regis Philbin (often in bits in which the humor is at their own expense, as when Ripa is revealed to be a hideous man-eating alien off camera with her makeup removed), and *Family Guy* seems to be well on its way to becoming an American TV institution in its own right.

Indeed, *Family Guy* as a cultural force extends well beyond its newly steady Sunday-night appearances on the Fox network. The show continues to be a hit in syndication on Adult Swim and to be a DVD favorite—a set of the first episodes from the fourth season appeared in late fall of 2005, even while the season was still going on! That same fall also saw the release of a made-for-DVD movie, *Stewie Griffin: The Untold Story* (2005), a feature-length film that differs very little, except in length, from an episode of the TV series. Here, the typical self-consciousness of the series is emphasized by an opening sequence in which the Griffins and other notables are shown arriving for the premiere of the new film entitled (of course) *Stewie Griffin: The Untold Story.* Then, we are shown this film within a film, in which we follow Stewie in a science fiction narrative in which he travels into the future and discovers that his 35-year-old self is a timid loser, having long given up his former plans for world domination. He lives in a crappy apartment, works at a lousy job, is still a virgin, and (apparently most horrifying of all) reads *Parade* magazine. Stewie's attempts to straighten out his older self only lead to disaster, but luckily the infant Stewie manages to return to the past and prevent the traumatic event that set him on the road to failure in the first place (thus reopening the possibility of future world domination). The film then ends back in the world of the opening sequence, an after-party in which the Griffins are welcomed back onto the air and Peter promises to bring serious, quality content to *Family Guy*—then loudly farts.

In one scene of *Stewie Griffin: The Untold Story*, Stewie works as a gate attendant as the cast of *Jonny Quest* boards a plane. All are allowed to board the plane without incident except the turban-wearing Hadji, who is of course immediately identified as a suspicious character and stopped for further examination. This satirical commentary on the persecution of individuals who look like they might be of Arab descent in post-9/11 America is actually unusually political for *Family Guy*. It is, however, quite typical of the humor of *American Dad*, the series co-created by McFarlane that began a regular run on Fox on May 1, 2005, immediately after the return episode of *Family Guy*. (The pilot of *American Dad* had aired on February 6, 2005.)

American Dad features the same style of outrageous humor as *Family Guy*, though in this case the satire typically engages more with politics and less with popular culture. The title character is Stan Smith (voiced by McFarlane), a fanatically right-wing CIA agent, devoted to battling what he perceives to be the enemies of the American way of life, which in his case includes women, gays, minorities, Democrats, and anyone else in the world who doesn't entirely accept his own paranoid agenda. Meanwhile, he is so prudish that he has never masturbated in his life—until the episode "A Smith in the Hand" (September 18, 2005), when he becomes a compulsive masturbator after an injury, suffered while trying to teach his son about the evils of masturbation, forces him to start applying ointment to his penis. All is well, however: Stan is able to blame his new obsession on the general moral decay brought about by television, a favorite target of the religious right. Smith's extreme views, which turn out not to be all that different from those of his employers in the Bush administration—or McFarlane's employers at Fox—offer ample opportunity for political satire. Indeed, Stan is sometimes linked directly to the Bush agenda, as in the episode "Deacon Stan, Jesus Man" (June 19, 2005), when Stan manages to get elected the new deacon of his church thanks to the help of campaign manager Karl Rove, who also engineered much of the political success of George W. Bush. In a motif the implications of which are clear, Rove is depicted as a figure of supernatural evil, emanating from hell and looking like the Grim Reaper.

Stan is at his paranoid best (and *American Dad* at its satirical best) when he is essentially acting out the ideology of the Bush administration, or at least of the Christian right. For example, the episode "Homeland Insecurity" (June 12, 2005) spoofs the extremities of the Patriot Act as Stan discovers that his new neighbors, the Memaris, are of Iranian descent—and therefore surely must be terrorists. Stan quickly invokes the Patriot Act and converts his back yard into a terrorist detainment camp so that he can lock the Memaris up in it. When the other neighbors complain, he locks them up as well. Then Steve accidentally blows up a transformer and knocks out power to the neighborhood, inadvertently leaving behind evidence that points to Stan as the culprit. Always quick to act, Stan arrests himself as a suspected terrorist, then begins to beat and torture himself to try to make himself confess. The episode ends as his wife Francine (Wendy Schaal) intercedes and gets a neighbor to snap a photo of her comically pointing to Stan, in underwear with a bag over his head—a clear reference to one of the notorious abusive photos taken by American soldiers of Iraqi prisoners in Abu Ghraib prison.

The rest of the Smith family parallels the Griffins of *Family Guy* in numerous ways—though it is supplemented by a talking goldfish (instead of a talking dog) and Roger the lonely, sarcastic gray alien (instead of Stewie the diabolical baby). Francine is, like Lois Griffin, a housewife with occasional ambitions outside the home, though in her case the pursuit of those ambitions is made considerably more difficult by Stan's sexist insistence on keeping her within the domestic sphere. Thus, when in the episode "Threat Levels" (May 1, 2005) Francine becomes a successful real estate agent (and even makes more money than Stan), he responds with extreme measures due to the perceived threat to his masculinity. The motif is reinforced by a sight gag in which one of his fellow CIA agents drops his pants to show the results of his own wife's growing independence—he now has no genitals whatsoever. Francine is a former wild child and rock groupie who has now largely accepted her husband's right-wing beliefs and accepts his domination of her with surprising good humor—though he does sometimes cross the line, forcing her to stand up for herself. After all, as she herself points out, "I may be blonde and have great cans, but I'm pretty smart when I've had my eight hours."

Stan's main political antagonist is his teenage daughter Hayley (Rachael McFarlane, Seth's sister), a student at Groff Community College and a devotee of various liberal causes who scoffs at Christianity as a farcical con game. Understandably, Hayley and Stan are constantly at odds, as in the episode "Stan Knows Best" (May 8, 2005), in which Hayley dyes her hair green to show her solidarity with the Green Party, prompting Stan to cut it off in her sleep, leaving her entirely bald. A furious Hayley moves out of the house, then ends up working as a stripper to support herself. She does well, but her new career goes awry when the patrons of the club where she works discover her bald head: "That's the one place where you want them to have hair," one of them explains. In the end, Hayley is reconciled with her family and comes back home, though the usual tensions remain.

Hayley's younger brother, Steve (Scott Grimes), is a student at Pearl Bailey High School. A hopeless nerd, Steve is basically apolitical, devoted to role-playing games, computers, *Star Trek,* and other geeky pursuits, though his real dream (which seems unlikely to be realized) is actually to score with a member of the opposite sex. Stan, of course, is constantly frustrated by Steve's lack of manliness, though it occasionally comes in handy, as in "All About Steve" (September 25, 2005), when Steve's geeky knowledge of *Lord of the Rings* helps Stan capture a dangerous cyber-terrorist. Steve has other moments as well, as in "Star Trek" (November 27, 2005), when he becomes a rich and famous author after writing a children's book about Roger. His fame goes to his head, of course, and he divorces his parents to live alone in his new mansion. However, he reconciles with them after they help him dispose of the body of an actor slated to play him in a movie, whom Roger mistakenly murders (having intended to murder Steve) to get revenge for his depiction in the book.

The final two members of the Smith household are Klaus (Dee Bradley Baker), the Germanic talking goldfish into whose body a CIA experiment has apparently transferred a human mind, and the flitting, effeminate Roger (voiced by Seth McFarlane in imitation of Paul Lynde). Klaus, to date, has never quite developed as a character, though his smart-aleck remarks and his ongoing lust for Francine can be quite humorous at times. Roger is typically a comic background character as well, though he sometimes plays a more major role and even dominates some episodes. In "Roger Codger" (June 5, 2005), for example, we get the background story of how he first came to live with the Smiths. As it turns out, Stan and other agents were attempting to keep the alien from escaping from captivity in Area 51, in the course of which he ended up saving Stan's life, forcing Stan to take him in out of gratitude.

In the main plot of "Roger Codger," Roger goes into a stress-induced hibernation cycle, causing the Smiths to think he is dead. Stan leaves the body in a garbage dump just to get rid of it, but then Roger awakes. Insulted at being left in the garbage, he strikes out on his own and is nearly captured by the CIA. The Smiths mobilize to save him, however, and even Stan (who first plans to kill Roger to keep him from revealing that the

Smiths have been harboring him) realizes that he has become fond of the alien, despite the fact that, earlier in the episode, he had declared to Steve that "feelings are what women have—they come from their ovaries." In the end, Roger returns to the Smith household, now essentially a full member of the family.

"Roger Codger" also marked the first major appearance (he had appeared briefly in one previous episode) by former *Star Trek: The Next Generation* star Patrick Stewart as the voice of Avery Bullock, Deputy Director of the CIA and Stan's boss. Stewart is hilarious in the role and features in other episodes as well, including "Bullocks to Stan" (September 11, 2005), in which Steve finds Dick Cheney's Blackberry and discovers that it contains the numbers of key contacts such as "the secret White House bunker," "the secret Halliburton bunker," and Satan. Steve and Roger then use the numbers in the device to make crank calls to various dignitaries around the world. Meanwhile, Bullock admits that the CIA invented crack and introduced it to the inner city, just before Hayley arrives and insults him. Stan, who is angling for a promotion, sides with Bullock and is furious with his daughter, then heads for Bullock's home to kiss up—only to find his boss shacked up with Hayley, who has just broken up with her boyfriend Jeff. Stan freaks out, but calms down when Bullock agrees to the promotion. Unfortunately, Hayley decides to go back to Jeff, so Bullock orders Stan to kill Jeff. Things spiral out of control from there until Stan nearly kills Bullock for insulting Hayley, but Bullock (in a bravura performance by Stewart) gets him to back off by convincing him that the whole elaborate plot was just a test to make sure Stan had the proper mettle for the promotion.

The appearances by Stewart (a distinguished Shakespearean actor in addition to his well-known roles in *Star Trek* and the *X-Men* films) add a certain weight to the already excellent voice cast, as do occasional appearances by longtime comedy stalwart Martin Mull and talented voice artist Stephen Root. In addition, the series in its brief run has already featured guest appearances by the likes of Beau Bridges, Elias Koteas, Molly Shannon, Matthew Lillard, Sarah Silverman, Zooey Deschanel, Gina Gershon, Richard Kind, and Carmen Electra. The show has yet to find the devoted followings of *The Simpsons* and *Family Guy*, and its political content keeps it on the edge of controversy. But it has scored some early success and seems to have a chance to become another of the recent long-running prime-time animation success stories. After all, *American Dad* is certainly no more controversial than *South Park*, which entered its ninth season on Comedy Central as *American Dad* was in its first. However, the political subject matter of *American Dad* does take it a bit out of the family sitcom format and, with the exception of *South Park*, prime-time animated programs that have deviated from that format have struggled to find an audience. Some of the most important of those programs are discussed in the next chapter.

CHAPTER 5

Beyond the Family Sitcom: Prime-Time Animation Seeks New Formats

If the success of *The Simpsons* opened the way for a number of other animated family sitcoms on prime-time television, it also made it easier for other kinds of animated programs to find their way onto the air in prime time. Several of these series, in fact, were created by writers who had worked on *The Simpsons*, while others showed a clear *Simpsons* influence. None of these series matched the success and longevity of *The Simpsons*, though some, including *Dr. Katz: Professional Therapist* and *Futurama*, did have considerable runs. Indeed, *South Park*, another non–family sitcom animated program, is probably the most successful prime-time animated program other than *The Simpsons* in television history.

The first major non–family sitcom animated program to appear in prime time was *The Critic*, which premiered on ABC on January 26, 1994, but was canceled after a single 13-episode season. It was picked up by Fox beginning with the episode "Sherman, Woman, and Child" (March 5, 1995), but lasted only 10 additional episodes before cancellation in late May 1995. It features film critic Jay Sherman (voiced by Jon Lovitz), who hosts a televised review show entitled *Coming Attractions*. Short, fat, and bald, Sherman does not seem well suited for success on television, though he can be an insightful critic, as witnessed by his two Pulitzer Prizes for criticism. It also doesn't help that he is perceived as cold, mean-spirited, and elitist—to the point that a poll shows he is less popular even than Adolf Hitler. In addition to his negative personal image, Sherman's taste in film is completely out of step with that of his television audience. He likes only highbrow foreign films and finds most Hollywood fare intolerable. He particularly hates almost all popular films, summing up his reaction to each of them with his trademark, "It stinks!"

Coming Attractions appears on the Phillips Broadcasting cable network, owned by the vaguely Ted Turneresque Duke Phillips (Charles Napier), a wealthy sportsman who owns several other cable networks as well. Phillips constantly exhorts Sherman to try to attract a larger audience for his show, but the critic manages to foil all of his efforts to give the show a warmer and more human feel. Apparently, The Critic itself had some of the same problems as Coming Attractions, and audiences never quite warmed up to Sherman and his surrounding cast of characters, perhaps because relationships among those characters typically lacked warmth as well. Sherman has virtually no luck with women in the first season, though he does get a girlfriend in the second season in Alice Tompkins (Park Overall), who comes to New York from Knoxville, Tennessee, and lands a job as Sherman's assistant. Sherman is divorced, with an ex-wife who detests him and constantly hounds him for more alimony. He does, however, have a good relationship with his son Marty (Christine Cavanaugh), who resembles him greatly. The same cannot be said for Sherman and his own fabulously wealthy adoptive parents. His father, Franklin (Gerrit Graham), is a former governor of New York and was once an important member of the Republican Party. However, he is now totally insane—perhaps from excessive drinking, and especially from once drinking some punch that was spiked by Ted Kennedy—and generally has little idea what is going on around him. Jay's mother, Eleanor née Wigglesworth (voiced by Judith Ivey in imitation of Katharine Hepburn), is a former debutante who is much concerned with keeping up appearances proper for such a prominent family. She is entirely ruthless and has no sympathy for those less fortunate than herself, among whose number her adoptive son can definitely be included. The final member of the Sherman clan is his 16-year-old sister Margo, who gets on well with Jay but espouses liberal social and political views that keep her at constant odds with her mother.

Episodes of The Critic often deal primarily with Jay Sherman's private life, but his position as a critic offers numerous opportunities for the show to satirize the film industry, establishing a dialogue with popular culture of the kind that had already played a big role in the success of The Simpsons. For example, the show also includes portions of Coming Attractions, including clips from warped versions of well-known, mostly recent films, as well as Sherman's usually negative reviews of the films. Films lampooned in this way include Godzilla (1954), Willy Wonka and the Chocolate Factory

(1971), *Robocop* (1987), *The Silence of the Lambs* (1991), *Scent of a Woman* (1992), and *Jurassic Park* (1993). *The Critic* also has a great deal of fun at the expense of well-known celebrities, sometimes in ways that seem a bit mean-spirited, as in its frequent fat jokes at the expense of Orson Welles and Marlon Brando.

Scenes of *The Critic* itself are sometimes based on specific films; indeed, the entire plot of the episode "Dukerella" (May 14, 1995) is based on the classic Cinderella story, especially as presented in the 1950 Disney film, with liberal dashes of *A Streetcar Named Desire* (1951) thrown in for good measure. Similarly, "Miserable" (February 16, 1994) spoofs the Stephen King film *Misery* (1990). Here, in an episode with clear undertones of sadomasochism and bondage, a film projectionist obsessed with Sherman seduces him, then lures him to her apartment and holds him captive, keeping him tied up and repeatedly drugging him.

In "L. A. Jay" (June 22, 1994), Sherman decides to break into the movie business himself, hoping to inject some quality into the industry. Taking a leave of absence from his job as a critic, he takes a script he has written to Hollywood. The script is apparently quite good, so much so that the ironically named Quality Studios buys it for $100,000 just so they can bury it, wanting to keep quality *out* of the industry. But when Sherman still wants to get into the business, the studio hires him to write the script for *Ghostchasers III*, the sequel to two other films that Sherman has already panned as a critic. This time the studio head hates the script, but the studio nevertheless manages to make the film, which of course stinks, at least according to Sherman, who reviews it on *Coming Attractions* after returning to the show.

The Critic often comments on television (Fox is a favorite target in the ABC season; ABC in the Fox season) as well as film. For example, the episode "Dr. Jay" (June 29, 1994) takes a shot at Ted Turner's project of "colorizing" classic black-and-white films for airing on his cable channels. Here Phillips comes up with a process called "Phillipsvision" that modifies classic movies to make them more attractive to a contemporary audience, usually by inserting computer-generated happy endings. Sherman, a lover of film purity, is understandably horrified by the process, which also inserts commercials for other Phillips products into the films. By the end of the episode, however, Sherman has come up with an experimental cure for a deadly disease contracted by Phillips, who expresses his gratitude by withdrawing the Phillipsvision process.

The Critic also features occasional appearances by well-known real-world film critics, such as Rex Reed and Gene Shalit, who provide their own voices in these appearances. In the episode "Siskel & Ebert & Jay & Alice"

(March 12, 1995), prominent TV film critics Gene Siskel and Roger Ebert (again voiced by themselves) are actually major characters. Here, the long-time duo decides to split up, and each decides to try to hire Sherman as his new partner. However, Sherman, despite his excitement at this opportunity, soon realizes that the two are really meant to be together, and so he engineers a reunion, returning to his old job at Phillips Broadcasting.

The Critic was created by *Simpsons* writers Al Jean and Mike Reiss, who also served as the show's executive producers, along with James L. Brooks, co-developer and executive producer of *The Simpsons*. In addition, *The Critic* was produced by Columbia Pictures in association with Brooks's Gracie Films, best known as the production company of *The Simpsons*. The show's animation was produced by Film Roman, the company that also does the animation for *The Simpsons, King of the Hill,* and *Family Guy,* among others. And it was co-produced and sometimes written by former *Tonight Show* writer Patric Verrone, who also wrote and produced for both *The Simpsons* and *Futurama*. Such links are acknowledged in the episode "Dukerella" (May 14, 1995), in which Jay and Alice attend a costume ball dressed as Homer and Marge Simpson. In the episode "Dial 'M' for Mother" (February 9, 1994), a family is shown viewing *Coming Attractions;* growing confused by Sherman's highbrow commentary, they hastily switch the channel—to *The Simpsons,* just as Bart proclaims his trademark, "Ay Carumba!" "Now," says the father, "that I can understand!" This suggestion that *The Simpsons* is relatively lowbrow (a jab that *The Simpsons* itself would later take at *Family Guy*) may partly account for the fact that *Simpsons* creator Matt Groening was reportedly highly upset when Jay Sherman (still voiced by Lovitz) appeared in *The Simpsons* episode "A Star Is Burns" (March 5, 1995). On the other hand, Sherman also appears in "Hurricane Neddy" (December 29, 1996), while Lovitz provided the voices of several other characters in *Simpsons* episodes as well, most prominently that of unscrupulous businessman Artie Ziff.

If Sherman's job as a film critic made it difficult for him to become a beloved Everyman character in the mode of Homer Simpson, the same might also be said for the profession of the central character of *Dr. Katz: Professional Therapist*. However, this program ran on Comedy Central from May 28, 1995, to December 24, 1999, for a total of 78 episodes, though three additional unaired episodes were made. It can thus legitimately claim to be the first truly successful prime-time animated program that was not primarily based on the family sitcom format. Created by comedian Jonathan Katz and animator Tom Snyder (not the former TV talk-show host), *Dr. Katz* was technically inventive, employing a style of computer animation known as "Squigglevision," in which characters and foregrounded objects appear in color with constantly wavering outlines, while the roughly drawn black-and-white background remains stable. Many viewers found this style highly annoying, but it gave the show a distinctive look, though Snyder did use the same technique on other programs, including the Saturday-morning show *Squigglevision* and the later prime-time series *Home Movies*.

Of the successful animated programs of the 1990s, *Dr. Katz* may be the one that owes the least to *The Simpsons*, growing instead out of the stand-up comedy of Katz and a long list of other comedians who brought their routines to the show. In this, of course, it participated in a wave of 1990s sitcoms that were inspired by stand-up comedy and comedians, beginning with *Roseanne* (1988–1997 on ABC) and including *Seinfeld* (1990–1998 on NBC), *Grace Under Fire* (1993–1998 on ABC), *Ellen* (1994–1998 on ABC), *The Drew Carey Show* (1995–2004 on ABC), and *Everybody Loves Raymond* (1996–2005 on CBS). Of these, *Dr. Katz* came up with the most effective format for bringing stand-up directly to the sitcom: It featured Katz as a psychotherapist of the same name, while most of his patients were other stand-up comedians who basically did their stand-up acts (while sitting down) during therapy sessions. Incidentally, one of Katz's most frequent guest patients, though he appeared mostly in the first two seasons, was Ray Romano, whose comedy provided the basis for *Everybody Loves Raymond*. Other prominent comics who appeared as guests on the show included Dom Irrera, Joy Behar, Dave Attell, Fred Stoller, Rita Rudner, Laura Kightlinger, Steven Wright, Janeane Garofalo, Gary Shandling, Richard Jeni, Kathy Griffin, Jon Stewart, Rodney Dangerfield, Sandra Bernhard, Dave Chappelle, and Elayne Boosler. Other guests included Winona Ryder, Julia Louis-Dreyfuss, Jeff Goldblum, David Duchovny, and David Mamet.

The therapy sessions involving these guest stars remained the heart of the show throughout its six-season run. However, the ongoing stories of Katz and those around him gradually evolved into important and interesting parts of the show as well. Katz is 48 years old and seems not to have had a serious romantic relationship since the breakup of his marriage 10 years earlier, though his occasional forays into dating do constitute an ongoing element of the show. Katz's most important relationship is with his 24-year-old son, Benjamin (H. Jon Benjamin), who still lives at home and is having definite trouble finding a direction in life. In that sense, *Dr. Katz* is a sort of animated family sitcom, reminding us that families come in a variety of configurations. Benjamin has lived with his father since the breakup of his parents' marriage, and Katz treats the lazy, overweight slacker with remarkable patience and good humor, partly because he seems to feel guilty that

Ben was left motherless after the breakup. In the course of the show, Ben tries (or at least considers trying) a variety of jobs—from raising pot-bellied pigs, to running his own limo service, to radio broadcasting—but never really finds anything that suits him. He and his father get on well and seem to share a similar sense of humor, especially about their relationship itself, which both of them continually compare to a marriage, with Ben as the stay-at-home wife. In fact, this aspect of their relationship verges on the pathological. Ben is very possessive of his father and, in the one case where he suspects that Katz is developing a serious romantic attachment—in "Ball and Chain" (December 24, 1999)—he becomes furiously jealous of his father's new girlfriend. It turns out, however, that Katz has no real interest in the woman: She may be a brilliant doctor and best-selling author, but she has virtually no chin.

The day-to-day lives of Katz and Ben, which are mostly filled with realistic trivialities of the kind that might actually occur to anyone in their situation, are central to the plots of most episodes. Generally (*Seinfeld* is again an important predecessor), very little happens in these episodes, which have very much the texture of the real Katz's low-key stand-up routines. Thus, episodes revolve around events such as Katz getting a new pair of glasses, Katz buying a new electric-powered bicycle, Katz throwing out a beloved stuffed animal from Ben's childhood, Katz buying a fanny pack to carry his growing collection of electronic gadgets, or Ben getting his wisdom teeth pulled. Occasionally, the plots of individual episodes contain slightly more significant events that make them begin to resemble the plots of ordinary sitcoms, as in "Thanksgiving" (November 23, 1998), when Ben's mother Roz (Carrie Fisher) happens to be in town and comes over for Thanksgiving dinner with a very nervous Ben and Katz. Ben cooks, with disastrous results, but all ends amiably, though it is clear that Roz now has no real connection with either her son or her ex-husband.

Dr. Katz often discusses his various dilemmas with his friend Stanley (Will Le Bow), with whom he regularly drinks in Jacky's bar, where the two also develop a friendship with their barmaid Julie (Julianne Shapiro). Apart from his father, Ben has few friends—though in the last season he does develop a sort of relationship with the clerk at the video store where he rents movies—and no girlfriends, and he seems content to spend his time sitting at home snacking and watching TV, though he does conduct a persistent, if inept and unsuccessful, campaign to get a date with his father's beautiful, but bored, world-weary, and incompetent receptionist Laura (Laura Silverman). Laura is a nightmare employee who insults Katz's patients, bungles his filing, and generally ignores his instructions in favor of the pursuit of her own agenda. Yet Katz lacks the assertiveness to put his foot down or fire her, so she continues in this vein throughout the run of the series. Nevertheless, Laura also has an odd sort of charm, though we never learn much about her life away from the office—partly because she herself is very guarded about her personal life and shares very little information with Ben or Dr. Katz. She does, however, attend the Thanksgiving dinner with Roz (Ben does nothing to correct mother's assumption that Laura is his girlfriend), because she would have otherwise spent the holiday alone. There are, in fact, several hints that Laura leads a fairly lonely existence, though in "Movies" (July 6, 1998), Ben and Dr. Katz, who both show signs of jealousy—though Ben is particularly disturbed—observe her on a date with another man. Indeed, in the unaired episode "Uncle Nothing," Laura actually becomes engaged, but quickly cancels the engagement, much to the relief of the still-hopeful Ben.

With its clever use of stand-up comedy, *Dr. Katz: Professional Therapist* was a perfect fit for Comedy Central, where it gained a following that helped to put the fledgling network on the map. The success of *Dr. Katz* also helped to open the way for more animated programming on Comedy Central, especially the wildly successful *South Park*, which premiered on that same network in 1997. Indeed, the comparatively greater success of *South Park* might have helped to push *Dr. Katz* off the air by the end of 1999, when the series went out with a bang as the last nine episodes to air were shown as a continuous marathon on Christmas Eve. There was, however, at least one instance of crossover between the two series when Dr. Katz (still voiced by Jonathan Katz) himself appeared as the psychotherapist of Mr. Garrison in the *South Park* episode "Summer Sucks" (June 24, 1998). Here, Katz was again shown in Squigglevision, though the other characters remained in the standard *South Park* style.

Oddly enough, *Dr. Katz* was canceled just as prime-time animated programming as a whole was beginning to get hot. *The Simpsons* and *King of the Hill* were still going strong, *South Park* was building a growing audience, and *Family Guy* was in its first full season. Several other prime-time animated series premiered in 1999 and 2000 as well. For example, based on the extremely popular Scott Adams comic strip and book series of the same title, the animated television series *Dilbert* premiered in January 1999 on UPN. Thirteen episodes ran during the 1999 spring season, and the series returned for a second season beginning in November 1999 and running through July 2000, with a three-month hiatus between February and May 2000. The series never quite gained the following of the original *Dilbert* comics (which has run in newspapers since 1989), though its exploration of life in the workplace did break new ground in television animation.

Dilbert focuses on the professional life of its eponymous protagonist (voiced by Daniel Stern), a highly competent engineer who works for a highly dysfunctional company that constantly changes its name. The company is plagued by the inefficiencies of its management style, which makes it virtually impossible for Dilbert and the engineers who work with him to do their jobs properly. The series also gives us glimpses into the home life of Dilbert, a bachelor who lives with his highly intelligent and articulate (but somewhat sadistic) canine Dogbert (Chris Elliott) in a suburban home where Dilbert tries out various inventions intended to make his life easier and more convenient. Due to his particular genius, Dogbert is sometimes called in as a consultant for Dilbert's company. He is also a financial wizard who seems to command an extensive business empire of his own, though the vast income from his various enterprises never seems to affect his lifestyle.

In a true departure for animated television, much of the first season of *Dilbert* was essentially devoted to a single continuous plot line, centering on the production of a new product, the Gruntmaster 6000, by Dilbert's company. There are, however, numerous digressions, as in "The Takeover" (February 15, 1999), when Dilbert and Wally use Dogbert's investment advice to momentarily become majority stockholders in the company. Meanwhile, Dilbert heads the team that designs and develops the Gruntmaster (a super-high-tech exercise machine), aided by fellow engineers Wally (Gordon Hunt) and Alice (an uncredited Kathy Griffin). Dilbert, of course, is devoted to producing a good product, though he finds that his efforts are constantly jeopardized by the fact that his company is interested less in the quality of the product than in following established corporate procedures to the letter. It also doesn't help that Dilbert's Pointy-Haired Boss (Larry Miller) tries to micromanage the development of the Gruntmaster 6000, even though he is not a competent engineer and has no idea what he is doing. In addition, along the way Dilbert nearly triggers a revolution in the underdeveloped country in which the product is to be manufactured in a sweatshop, the company headquarters develops sick-building syndrome, and Dilbert has to head the company's efforts to deal with the Y2K crisis.

As the first season ends, in "The Infomercial" (May 24, 1999), the Gruntmaster 6000 is still in the testing stage. Nevertheless, the Pointy-Haired Boss goes ahead with the production of an infomercial to market the product starring himself and a bikini-clad model. Meanwhile, he arranges to have Dilbert's prototype sent off to a redneck family (whose mother is given to threatening her children that the Baby Jesus will come down and do terrible things to them if they don't behave) in Squiddler's Patch, Texas. Unfortunately, a flaw in the unit's Graviton generator causes it to form a black hole when activated, leading to near-disastrous results. Luckily, however, Dilbert is able to go into the black hole and travel back in time so that he is able to prevent the prototype from leaving his design lab in the first place.

Dilbert often veers into the absurd in this way, as in "Little People" (April 5, 1999), when it is discovered that company employees terminated due to downsizing are actually still secretly inhabiting the company headquarters, but have now been literally downsized to tiny dimensions. Such absurdities reinforce the show's presentation of corporate bureaucracy as absurd. However, they also add a comic surreal element that ultimately softens *Dilbert*'s critique of the corporate business world. Indeed, the show's satire is more like good-natured ribbing than genuine critique, and its inability to attract a large audience was due less to its anticapitalist implications than to the fact that a mass audience was unable to identity with the show's engineer protagonist.

Mission Hill was even less successful: It ran for 2 episodes on the WB in the fall of 1999, then was pulled until the summer of 2000, when 4 more episodes were aired, though a total of 13 episodes were made. All episodes eventually aired on Adult Swim, where the program seemed to be a better fit with the network's young adult target audience. Created by former *Simpsons* writers and executive producers Bill Oakley and Josh Weinstein, *Mission Hill* featured aspiring cartoonist Andy French (voiced by Wallace Langham) as its protagonist, which created numerous opportunities for self-referential commentary on the cartoon genre, though it was most notable for its exploration of unusually adult subject matter, especially involving sexuality. Set in the Mission Hill district of the city of Cosmopolis, a fictional locale that nevertheless has much in common with the Wicker Park neighborhood in Chicago, *Mission Hill* focuses on the somewhat-halfhearted attempts of 24-year-old Andy to make it as a cartoonist, while meanwhile working in a water bed store and attempting to cope with life in general. This life includes being the guardian of his teenage brother Kevin (Scott Menville), left with Andy to finish high school in the city when their parents move to Wyoming in the series pilot. Andy and Kevin share an apartment with Jim Kuback (Brian Posehn), a bearded hipster computer jockey, and Posey Tyler (Vicki Lewis), a New Age airhead who grows organic vegetables on the roof of their building. Other residents of the building who figure prominently in the show include the gay couple Gus and Wally (Nick Jameson and Tom Kenny) and the married couple Carlos Hernandez-Leibowitz (Herbert Siguenza) and Natalie Leibowitz-Hernandez (Lewis).

Unusually realistic for an animated series, *Mission Hill* captured a series of slices of urban Generation X life, again almost in the mode of *Seinfeld*, but with younger protagonists. It is also unusually frank sexually. In the episode "Kevin's Problem (or Porno for Pyro)" (October 8, 1999), Kevin is clerking in a neighborhood market when he goes into the bathroom to masturbate to a girlie magazine, leaving the store untended. Two local delinquents decide to rob the store and end up locking Kevin in the bathroom after catching him in the act. He panics and tries to burn the magazine so he won't get caught with it; but he ends up setting fire to the store and is nearly killed. Ultimately, he is forced to confess to "manipulating" himself in order to prevent the delinquents from going to prison for arson and attempted murder.

Mission Hill is also distinctive for its depiction of the gay couple buying condoms, though it is important that Gus and Wally, though comical characters (Gus is a bald, gruff, tough-guy type; Wally a dowdy, bow-tie type), are not caricatures. Nor is their relationship treated as bizarre or preposterous. *Mission Hill* won an award from GLAAD for its straightforward depiction of them as a normal couple, and the show's depiction of the Gus-Wally relationship can, in fact, be quite romantic, as in the episode "Planet 9 from Mission Hill (or I Married a Gay Guy from Outer Space)" (not originally aired), which tells the touching story of how they got together. Here we learn that Wally had once, back in the 1950s, been a promising young filmmaker, tapped to make an ambitious and thoughtful science fiction film that was to be an allegory about the Cold War arms race. Then Wally met Gus, who was working as a teamster on the set. Instant love ensued, and Wally insisted on making Gus the star of the film, which eventually spiraled downward into *The Man from Pluto*, perhaps the worst film ever made, transforming what was to have been *The Day the Earth Stood Still* into what was essentially *Plan 9 from Outer Space*. His career sacrificed for love, Wally was driven out of the film business, so he left Hollywood for Mission Hill, where he and Gus have lived together ever since.

Mission Hill is at its satirical best (even if it takes a conservative turn) in the second installment of the two-part episode "Unemployment," though, in a telling commentary on the lack of support for the series by the WB, only the first of the two parts was originally aired. In that part, Andy loses his job at Waterbed World when his abusive boss Ron (Jameson) is sent away to prison. The first episode of the two-parter focuses on Kevin's misadventures after he gains ownership of Ron's expensive foreign sports car as part of Ron's attempts to hide his assets from the IRS. It is, however, in the second episode when the results of Andy's unemployment are really explored. Here, Andy becomes more and more of a lazy slob, content to live on unemployment and thinking that he is making a sort of political statement about his generation's rejection of the rat race. Then he discovers to his amazement that Jim, seemingly a slacker like himself, is actually a highly paid executive at an advertising agency, where he provides crucial insights into the tastes and inclinations of young adult males like himself. Indeed, once he looks around, Andy realizes that others of his generation are beginning to get on with successful careers as well. So Andy resigns himself to going back to work, getting a job at the ad agency thanks to the good offices of Jim, who seems to have a tremendous amount of clout there.

If *Mission Hill* thus ultimately rejects slackerdom, the animated series *Clerks*, based on the 1994 Kevin Smith film of the same title, is a sort of celebration of that lifestyle—which may account for the fact that it was canceled even more quickly than *Mission Hill*. Six episodes were made, but only two aired on ABC in the spring of 2000 before the series was abruptly canceled. All six episodes are now available in a DVD set, which also restores scenes cut by ABC censors from the two episodes that did air. This set has sold well, presumably thanks to the cult following of the original Smith film. The series built upon the same premise as the film, with the same major characters, voiced by the same actors who played them in the film. These include Quick Stop convenience store clerk Dante Hicks (Brian O'Halloran) and RST Video Store clerk Randal Graves (Jeff Anderson). Also important are the two slackers who hang around outside their stores, Jay and Silent Bob (Jason Mewes and Kevin Smith)—who, by the time the series aired (or didn't), had appeared in several Smith-directed films, becoming minor American cultural icons.

The series premiered on May 31, 2000, with a strong episode in which Jay slips on some soda spilled on the floor of the Quick Stop by the clerks. He then decides to sue Dante and the Quick Stop for big bucks, leading to a ludicrous legal battle with actor Judge Reinhold (voiced by himself) as the judge and Randal as Dante's preposterously incompetent lawyer. This episode was actually intended to be the fourth aired, but was substituted for the original pilot when that episode fared poorly with test audiences. The second episode aired was a clip show of the kind that often appears in long-running sitcoms—the joke being that this show, which was meant to follow the pilot, was only the second of the entire series. Unfortunately, the only episode thus available to flash back to was the original pilot, but these flashbacks made little sense because the pilot had never aired. After that, the series was canceled, never really having had a chance to develop or find an audience.

While the film version of *Clerks* presented scenes from the everyday lives of these characters, the animated series adds a number of important new elements, made possible by the resources of animation. For example, in the would-be pilot episode (which was never aired), the evil Leonardo Leonardo (voiced by Alec Baldwin) returns to the town of Leonardo, New Jersey, where the series is set and which his family founded generations earlier. Leonardo promptly builds a Quicker Stop convenience mall in the town, which threatens to put Dante and Randal's block of stores out of business. Ultimately, Leonardo plans to enslave the town's population, forcing them to work underground while he converts the entire town itself into a pleasure dome for the rich. He is foiled, however, when Jay and Silent Bob blow up the Quicker Stop while playing with fireworks.

In another unaired episode, the block of stores is enclosed in a hermetically sealed dome after Leonardo Leonardo falls ill from eating bad burritos, causing Randal (working under the influence of the film *Outbreak*) to conclude that he has been bitten by an infected monkey from the new pet store that just opened in the block. The final two episodes indicated a potential for self-referentiality and engagement with popular culture that the show never had a chance to fulfill. Episode five is essentially a string of movie parodies, including riffs on *The Bad News Bears* (1976), *The Last Starfighter* (1984), and *Indiana Jones and the Temple of Doom* (1984). Here, in action that moves far away from the original *Clerks* film, Randal saves the world. In episode six, which serves almost as a response to episode five, Dante and Randal attend a comic convention, where fans complain that the animated series has strayed from the original film. They promise to get back to the format that originally made them famous, but of course they had no chance to do so, given that the show was canceled well before this episode had a chance to air.

Clerks was never a good fit for the Disney-owned ABC, though the network apparently promised a considerable amount of support to Smith and his partners, support that was never delivered. Then again, the quick demise of *Clerks* was typical of many of the animated series that debuted around the turn of the century. On the other hand, Fox (the dominant force in prime-time animation) did score a moderate success at this time with the animated series *Futurama*, which premiered in March 1999. *Futurama* is a sort of science fiction sitcom that in some ways looks back to predecessors such as *The Jetsons*, but that builds most importantly upon *The Simpsons*, whose creator, Matt Groenig, also created *Futurama*. Using very much the same distinctive animation style as *The Simpsons*, *Futurama* features many of the same kinds of in-jokes and hip pop cultural references that helped to make *The Simpsons* so successful. In addition, just as *The Simpsons* derived much of its humor from its irreverent treatment of the sitcom tradition, so too did *Futurama*, from the very beginning, rely heavily on parodic references to the entire tradition of science fiction television, which has sometimes suffered from a certain self-seriousness. *Star Trek*, as the central work of TV science fiction, is crucial to the allusive texture of *Futurama*, as when, in the first episode, we find that the head of Leonard Nimoy has been preserved in a jar in a "head museum" as one of the crucial figures in the history of the future world of the series.

Set in the year 3000, *Futurama* focuses on Philip J. Fry (voiced by Billy West), a 25-year-old New York pizza delivery boy from the late twentieth century who is accidentally frozen on New Year's Eve, 1999, in a suspended animation machine (*Futurama* doesn't worry much about technological verisimilitude) only to awake exactly 1,000 years into the future. Once he arrives in this astounding new world of technological marvels, he resumes his life as a somewhat dim-witted slacker and even continues his career as a delivery boy—only this time he makes deliveries to various points in outer space as an employee of Planet Express Delivery Service, an enterprise run by his nephew many generations removed, Professor Hubert J. Farnsworth (also West), the world's oldest living scientist (named for Philo Farnsworth, one of the inventors of television). Indeed, despite the high-tech nature of the future society of *Futurama*, in most ways very little has changed since Fry left his own world in 1999. Thus, the satire of the series is clearly aimed at our own contemporary world, and *Futurama* has no particular interest in imagining what the future might actually be like—indeed, it projects a future designed specifically to satirize our own present. This satire is often quite reminiscent of that in *The Simpsons*. However, *Futurama* is typical of much science fiction, despite its comic and parodic elements. After all, the best science fiction typically uses its settings in distant times or on distant planets to provide a fresh perspective on the here and now.

Fry's *Futurama* delivery crew is captained by his would-be love interest, Turanga Leela (Katey Sagal), a mutant (though through most of the series she appears to be an alien) woman with a talent for martial arts who is also quite beautiful—if you can only get past the fact that she has only one large eye in the middle of her forehead, which, unfortunately, most people in the year 3000 can't. Leela, in fact, is the only one-eyed "alien" on earth, just as Fry is the only person in the year 3000 who is from the twentieth century. To that extent, they are two of a kind, and the series continually hints that they are meant for each other, though Leela is much more intelligent and capable than Fry—and is constantly having to get him out of trouble.

Perhaps the central comic figure in the series is the foul-mouthed, ill-tempered, kleptomaniacal robot, Bender Bending Rodriguez (John DiMaggio), who guzzles alcohol and chomps cigars and generally makes a nuisance of himself, all the while somehow remaining lovable—in a despicable sort of way. The crew is frequently joined by a young intern, Amy Wong (Lauren Tom), the cute but none-too-bright daughter of a fabulously wealthy Martian Chinese family. The crew is sometimes also accompanied by the voracious company physician, Dr. John Zoidberg (West), a lobster-like alien from the planet Decapod 10—whose understanding of human anatomy is spotty at best. Meanwhile, back on earth, Planet Express Delivery Service is managed by the Jamaican Hermes Conrad (Phil LaMarr). A workaholic bureaucrat and stickler for efficiency, Hermes occasionally shows a lighter side. In fact, we learn that he is anal only 78.36 percent of the time. He is also a former Olympic limbo champion who turned away from that sport after a young boy was horribly injured trying to imitate his back-bending technique.

Numerous other recurring characters add significant comic energy to the series as well. Probably the most important of these is Zapp Brannigan (West), a sort of sleazy, swaggering, overweight version of *Star Trek*'s Captain Kirk. Brannigan is patiently accompanied by his loyal, long-suffering, and frequently exasperated aide, the green alien Kif Kroker (Maurice LaMarche), who tries his best to keep the lame-brained Brannigan out of trouble. Brannigan, meanwhile, is a would-be womanizer who actually gets nowhere with the ladies, though he does make it with Leela in "Love's Labours Lost in Space" (April 13, 1999), a fact that Leela spends the rest of the series trying to live down. At times, Brannigan is identified merely as a ship's captain; at other times he seems more important and is described as a "25-star general" who commands the entire military force of the Democratic Order of Planets (doop), quite specifically identified in the series as analogous to *Star Trek*'s Federation of Planets. Brannigan claims to be the originator of the doop directive (modeled on the "Prime Directive" of *Star Trek*) that forbids interference with undeveloped planets. He, in fact, calls this directive "Brannigan's Law," but he seems to have no compunction about engaging in battle with weaker foes and seems to have made his military reputation by winning battles against groups such as pacifists and the elderly.

Of course, the future setting of *Futurama* is also a crucial element of the show—as it had been in *The Jetsons*, clearly an important predecessor. Many of the future technologies on display in *Futurama*'s world of 3000 are clearly designed either to spoof the science fiction tradition or to provide satirical opportunities to comment on our own world. Of these, perhaps the most important is the "head museum" technology that was introduced in the first episode. This technology was invented, we learn in "A Big Piece of Garbage" (May 11, 1999), by pop inventor Ron Popeil, who provides the voice for his own head in the episode. It also allows Richard Nixon—in "A Head in the Polls" (December 12, 1999)—to be elected president of earth in 3000, thanks to carrying the robot vote after attaching his preserved head to the body of a giant killerbot. (Nixon, voiced by West, is a recurring character in the show.) This head-preservation technology is crucial to *Futurama*'s dialogue with twentieth- and twenty-first-century popular culture by allowing many prominent figures from the past to make appearances (as jarred heads) in the world of the year 3000. It also provides opportunities for numerous celebrity guest stars to voice their own heads, following in the footsteps of *The Simpsons*, the clout of which gave *Futurama* immediate credibility and helped them to attract such guests. The very first *Futurama* episode featured both Nimoy and Dick Clark, whose head hosts "New Year's Rockin' Eve" in 2999. Even Vice President Al Gore provided the voice for his head in two episodes, while other celebrity voice artists have included the likes of Pamela Anderson, Jonathan Frakes, John Goodman, Lucy Liu, Conan O'Brien, and William Shatner. Most of the major players in *The Simpsons* have made guest appearances as well, including two bravura appearances by Dan Castellaneta (the voice of Homer Simpson) as the Robot Devil.

These appearances provide numerous opportunities for amusing references to popular culture from the show's own era, which are supplemented by a variety of other sight gags and brief allusions to genres or specific works of twentieth-century popular culture. For example, in "A Bicyclops Built for Two" (March 19, 2000), Leela suddenly appears dressed as Peg Bundy, the role played by Sagal from 1987 to 1997 on Fox's *Married with Children*. "A Head in the Polls," meanwhile, begins with a brief skit that is a takeoff on the classic *Twilight Zone* episode "Time Enough at Last," while "A Fishful of Dollars" (April 27, 1999) shows Bender in the kitchen, sporting an apron that says "To Serve Man," in reference to the 1962 *Twilight Zone* episode of that title (also spoofed in *The Simpsons* first "Treehouse of Horror" episode back in 1990). In addition, numerous entire episodes of *Futurama* are constructed largely as pastiches of specific well-known films or other works of popular culture. For example, "A Flight to Remember" (September 26, 1999) is based on the James Cameron megahit *Titanic* (1997). Here, the Planet Express crew vacations on a space cruise ship (called the *Titanic*); love (almost) blooms between Fry and Leela and between Bender and an aristocratic lady robot, until the ship crashes into a black hole (thanks to

Brannigan's incompetence as its captain), rather than an iceberg. Similarly, "Mars University" (October 3, 1999) draws significantly on *Animal House* (1978), while "Fry and the Slurm Factory" (November 14, 1999) lampoons *Willy Wonka and the Chocolate Factory* (1971)—thus predating the *Family Guy* takeoff on that film by eight months.

Not surprisingly, many of the films spoofed by *Futurama* come from the realm of science fiction. "A Big Piece of Garbage" is largely a parody of the film *Armageddon* (1998), with that film's earth-threatening asteroid replaced by a giant ball of garbage, long ago launched into space but now falling back to earth and headed straight for its origination point in New New York. Similarly, "When Aliens Attack" (November 7, 1999) is a takeoff on *Independence Day* (1996), featuring a fleet of enraged aliens who come to earth to protest the interruption of the broadcast of a crucial episode of their favorite earth TV program, *Single Female Lawyer* (modeled on Fox's *Ally McBeal*, still at the height of its popularity when the *Futurama* episode was originally broadcast). It turns out that the broadcast was interrupted back in 1999 when Fry spilled beer on a console while delivering pizza to the Fox studios in New York. The aliens demand to see the rest of the show or else they will destroy the earth—as they have already destroyed the White House and various other monuments—in imitation of *Independence Day*. As luck would have it, most videotapes on earth were destroyed during the second coming of Christ in 2443 (apparently the apocalypse was limited to the destruction of videotapes), including all tapes of *Single Female Lawyer*. Fortunately, though, all humans pretty much look alike to the aliens, so Fry and the crew are able to save the day, and the Earth, by filming their own version of the episode and screening it for the aliens.

Futurama also includes frequent passing allusions to *Star Trek*, *Star Wars*, *Doctor Who*, and other well-known works of science fiction film and television. Indeed, the references to SF in the series go well beyond the obvious nods toward *Star Trek* and other well-known predecessors. They include a variety of more complex and sometimes esoteric allusions, as in the episode "Fear of a Bot Planet," when the three heroes travel to the planet "Chapek 9," which is inhabited entirely by androphobic robots. Only science fiction fans would be likely to realize that the name of this planet derives from that of Karel Čapek, the Czech science fiction writer who is credited with coining the term "robot" in his 1920 play *R.U.R.* Perhaps more fans, however, would recognize that the title of the episode refers to the classic 1990 hip-hop album *Fear of a Black Planet*, by the group Public Enemy, a connection that reinforces the status of this episode as a satire (albeit a light-hearted one) on racism.

The episode begins as several of the principals attend a "blernsball" game, a sort of jazzed-up, high-tech version of baseball. Sitting in the crowd, Bender complains that robots are not allowed in the game, but only work in the stadium in various menial tasks. Further, he argues that the major league players they are watching couldn't hold a candle to the best players of the old "robot leagues" (such as "Wireless Joe Jackson"). This obvious reference to the longtime segregation of the game of baseball, in which African American players were banned from the majors and forced to play in the separate "Negro League," introduces the topic of racism that will be central to the remainder of the episode.

In the main plot of the episode, Leela, Fry, and Bender have the task of delivering an important package to Chapek 9, the robot inhabitants of which despise humans to the point where they kill them on sight. Thus, Bender is tabbed to make the actual delivery, though Fry and Leela end up on the planet as well to try to save Bender after he (predictably) gets into trouble. They disguise themselves as robots and go down to the surface, only to find that Bender has now become an important figure on the planet by proclaiming a virulent hatred of humans that goes beyond the norm even on Chapek 9. The unreasonable hatred of humans, informed by a variety of lurid stereotypes about human behavior, that drives the robot inhabitants of Chapek 9 clearly echoes racist attitudes on twentieth-century Earth. In addition, much of the antihuman paranoia of the robots echoes the anti-communist hysteria of the 1950s, a point that is emphasized by a scene in a 3-D theater in which an audience of identical-looking robots watches *It Came from Planet Earth* while wearing 3-D glasses—which of course don't work on the one-eyed Leela—thus providing a pastiche of one of the iconic images of 1950s culture on earth. Ultimately, Leela and Fry are detected as humans but escape with Bender in tow—and even win the affection of the Chapek 9 robots when it is discovered that they have delivered a crate of much-needed lug nuts to the planet.

Many episodes of *Futurama* play with standard science fiction conceits rather than specific predecessor works of science fiction. Such episodes include "Roswell That Ends Well" (December 9, 2001), which won the 2002 Emmy Award for Outstanding Animated Program (for programming less than one hour)—the only such award won by *Futurama* in a category dominated by *The Simpsons*, which has won it eight times. No other series has, at this writing, won more than once. This episode has much in common with the hilarious *Star Trek: Deep Space Nine* episode "Little Green Men" (November 6, 1995), in which the Ferengi Quark, brother Rom, and nephew Nog accidentally enter a time warp and crash their ship at Roswell, New Mexico, in 1947. However, the *Futurama* episode does not appear to have been based on the *Star Trek* episode so much as the time-travel genre in general. Here, the Planet Express ship is accidentally hurled back in time by an exploding supernova. They land (of course) in Roswell in 1947, thus becoming not only an important part of UFO lore, but also triggering a whole string of time-travel paradoxes. For example, the so-called Grandfather Paradox has long been central to speculations on the possibility of time travel: If a time traveler went back in time and killed his own grandfather before the conception of his father, then that time traveler would never be born—and couldn't go back to kill his grandfather, in which case he could still be born and go back to kill his grandfather, and so on, ad infinitum. Here, Fry accidentally causes his own putative grandfather to be killed (in a nuclear bomb test) before the conception of his father. Never fear, though. Fry solves the paradox (sort of) by sleeping with and impregnating his grandmother, thus becoming his own grandfather.

The original *Star Trek* series is far and away the most important source of science fictional material for *Futurama*. In addition to a variety of running motifs that recall *Star Trek*, several individual episodes are specifically devoted to *Star Trek* parodies. In "Why Must I Be a Crustacean in Love" (February 6, 2000), Zoidberg is overcome by the periodic mating lust that characterizes his species and must return to his home planet to participate in a mating frenzy. The referent here, of course, is the classic *Star Trek* episode "Amok Time" (September 15, 1967), in which Spock must return to Vulcan to mate. The entire *Futurama* episode parodies the *Star Trek* original (complete with a fight to the death between Fry and Zoidberg, paralleling the famous battle between Kirk and Spock), with a dash of *Cyrano de Bergerac* thrown in for good measure. Other episodes are only vaguely related to *Star Trek* predecessors, as when "The Problem with Popplers" (May 7, 2000) draws material from *Star Trek*'s "The Trouble with Tribbles" (December 29, 1967). In "Where No Fan Has Gone Before" (April 21, 2002), however, *Futurama* pulls out all the stops to acknowledge its *Star Trek* predecessor.

This episode not only draws upon the plots of numerous *Star Trek* episodes but features guest voice performances by most of the original *Star Trek* cast, including William Shatner, Leonard Nimoy, George Takei, Nichelle Nichols, and Walter Koenig—and even a brief appearance by Jonathan Frakes of *Star Trek: The Next Generation*. In a plot based on the *Star Trek* episode "The Menagerie" (a two-parter from November, 1966), we learn that Fry is being court-martialed, apparently for merely uttering the forbidden words "Star Trek," while the bulk of "Where No Fan Has Gone Before" consists of flashbacks deriving from the testimony at his trial. Among other things, we learn from this testimony how devoted Fry had been to the original *Star Trek* series in his own time. We also learn why such devotion is now forbidden: By the twenty-third century *Star Trek* fandom had become a religion (identified as the "sci-fi religion that doesn't take all your money," as opposed to Scientology) so powerful that it threatened the authority of all the world's governments. The governments responded by banning the new religion, executing most of its adherents by throwing them into volcanoes, the "method most suitable for virgins." *Star Trek*'s sacred texts (tapes of the show's episodes and the first six *Star Trek* movies) were then dumped on the forbidden planet of Omega 3, presumably never to be seen again. A few hundred years later, however, the heads of the original *Star Trek* stars traveled from earth to Omega 3 to join the tapes (except Nimoy, who couldn't get out of the lease of his apartment, and James Doohan, who dropped out of the cast when they started doing musical reunion specials in the twenty-third century). There, they were taken over by a powerful energy being that had become a zealous fan of the show by watching the exiled tapes. The being, Melllvar, restored their bodies, constructed sets of the various episodes, and then used the actors essentially as action figures to play out its fantasies regarding the show. The Planet Express team travels (with Nimoy's head) to Omega 3 to try to retrieve the tapes, then runs afoul of Melllvar, who ends up pitting the *Enterprise* crew and the Planet Express crew in combat against one another, as in *Star Trek* episodes such as "Arena" (January 19, 1967). Eventually, the Planet Express crew and *Star Trek* crew, now once again reduced to heads in jars to cut down on weight, escape together from Omega 3, with Melllvar in hot pursuit. Melllvar ultimately turns out, like the superbeing in the *Star Trek* episode "The Squire of Gothos" (January 12, 1967), to be a mere child (or at least an immature 34-year-old who still lives in his parents' basement), despite his power, but he calls off the pursuit of his TV idols when Fry convinces him to get a life and stop living within the fantasy of a television show.

Among other things, this episode indicates the way in which religion is often a target of satire in *Futurama*. The citizens of the year 3000 (including the Planet Express crew) generally appear remarkably unreligious, perhaps because the fizzled apocalypse of 2443 has removed much of the terror that earlier drove religious fervor. Christmas, for example, has become merely Xmas, with no religious component. In fact, it has become an object of dread, with a murderous rogue robot Santa Claus patrolling the streets on Xmas Eve looking for sinners to exterminate. In addition, in "The Day the Earth Stood Stupid" (February 18, 2001), we learn from an ultra-advanced race of aliens who have been around since the beginning of time that all Earth religions are wrong.

At least one Planet Express employee does get religion in the course of the series, however. In the episode "Hell Is Other Robots" (May 18, 1999), Bender becomes an electricity junkie, then turns to religion in an effort to get clean. He joins the Church of Robotology (clearly a takeoff on the Church of Scientology) and becomes so self-righteous that Fry, Leela, and the others have to work to try to lure him back into his old ways. They succeed, causing him to be sent to Robot Hell—an actual physical place of torture built by the Church of Robotology beneath an old amusement park. Luckily, the others are able to rescue him once again, but only after Castellaneta's Robot Devil nearly destroys them all.

The title of this episode (a reference to the line "hell is other people" that appears in Jean-Paul Sartre's classic existentialist play *No Exit*) indicates the sometimes highly literate nature of the allusions in *Futurama*. On the other hand, this episode actually has very little to do with the Sartre play. Indeed, the titles of *Futurama* episodes (again following a trend set by *The Simpsons*) often allude to previous works in only the most superficial of ways, usually just for the sake of a bad pun. Thus, the title of "Parasites Lost" (January 21, 2001) clearly refers to John Milton's *Paradise Lost*, but the episode is actually a takeoff on the science fiction film *Fantastic Voyage* (1966)—perhaps filtered through the four-part *Doctor Who* episode "The Invisible Enemy" (October 1977). Here, the rest of the crew create tiny robot duplicates of themselves so that they can go inside Fry's body to try to rid it of the intestinal parasites he picked up from eating a sandwich he bought from a vending machine in a truck-stop restroom. Still, even the jokey title references in *Futurama* can have some significance. Thus, the title "I, Roommate" (April 6, 1999) evokes Isaac Asimov's classic collection of robot stories, *I, Robot* (1950)—which provided the title and much of the inspiration for Alex Proyas's 2004 film of the same title—even though the episode (about Fry and Bender sharing an apartment) has little to do with Asimov's stories. Nonetheless, it is useful to keep Asimov's stories in mind because they help to establish the extent to which the role played by Bender in *Futurama* actually builds on a long tradition of robot tales in science fiction. Indeed, it may be no coincidence that Bender and *Futurama* appeared amidst a flurry of science fiction films about robots—including Chris Columbus's *Bicentennial Man* (1999) and Steven Spielberg's *Artificial Intelligence: A. I.* (2001)—indicating a renewed fascination with the topic at the turn of the century.

In addition to the way in which various motifs within *Futurama* comment directly on popular culture and other aspects of our contemporary world, the program also includes a sort of indirect commentary in the way it represents popular culture as having changed very little in a thousand years. Thus, despite all the other changes, television still seems to be the dominant medium, while television programming seems to have changed relatively little. Leela sums it up in "The Day the Earth Stood Stupid" with her reaction when she learns of a race of evil "brain spawn" that travel the universe attempting to wipe out all consciousness: "My god! They're like flying televisions!" The most important future television program embedded within *Futurama* is the all-robot soap opera *All My Circuits*, a particular favorite of Bender. The convoluted plot of this program is quite similar to the plots of soap operas in our contemporary world—except with robots as the principal characters. Meanwhile, we also get extensive looks at the advertising of the year 3000, which again looks pretty much like advertising in our own world. The products of the future—such as Bachelor Chow, Glagnar's Human Rinds, Mom's Old-Fashioned Motor Oil, and the allusive Soylent Cola and Soylent Chow (referring to the 1973 film *Soylent Green*)—may seem futuristic, but in many ways they are no more far-fetched than the products of our own capitalist system.

As opposed to the utopian future vision of programs like *Star Trek* (in which universal affluence has eliminated capitalist competition, at least on earth), *Futurama* depicts a future world of ruthless capitalists devoted to the making of profits, no matter what. Thus, the ostensibly sweet old Mom (of the Old-Fashioned Oil) is a wealthy and ruthless tycoon who, under the aegis of her umbrella conglomerate Momcorp, also owns a whole range of companies, including the gigantic Mom's Friendly Robot Company. She is not above programming her robots to help her achieve world domination—or using the most unscrupulous of means to drive competitors out of business (which bodes ill for Planet Express, given that she also owns the world's largest delivery service). In this, of course, she is no different from many corporate executives of the twentieth and twenty-first centuries. Thus, in the episode "Futurestock" (March 31, 2002), when a ruthless, unscrupulous corporate shark from the 1980s, identified in the episode simply as "That Guy," is thawed out from cryogenic storage, he fits right in in the thirty-first century. Adopting Fry as his protégé, That Guy (modeled on Gordon Gekko, the villainous stock manipulator of Oliver Stone's 1987 film *Wall Street*) manages to oust Farnsworth as the CEO of Planet Express and to take over the company so that he can try to make it more competitive with Mom's Delivery Company. When his image-is-everything approach actually seems to be working, Mom responds with a takeover bid to buy all Planet Express stock. This takeover seems sure to put the entire Planet Express crew out of work, but that turns out to be just fine with them because they all own Planet Express stock, the price of which has skyrocketed thanks to That

Guy's management style and rumors of the takeover. Unfortunately, That Guy suddenly drops dead of the disease that had caused him to be frozen back in the 1980s. (There is now a cure, but he has been too busy trying to make money to take the time out to get it.) That leaves Fry in charge of the company; he promptly torpedoes the stock sale and promises to return Planet Express to its old inefficient management style. The price of the stock plummets, and everyone is left right back where they started.

Futurama began airing in 1999, the year Fry was originally frozen, and continued through five seasons into the summer of 2003, making it one of the longest-running science fiction series of recent years, as well as an unusually long-running prime-time animated series. It has subsequently been a hit on the Cartoon Network's late-night Adult Swim block, as well as a success in the DVD market. The return of the once-canceled *Family Guy* to the Fox lineup in May 2005 fueled speculation that *Futurama* might some day return as well, but as of yet there seem to be no plans for such a revival. As of this writing, rumors persist that a series of four made-for-DVD *Futurama* movies will go into production in the summer of 2006. In the meantime, *Futurama* has lived on in merchandising (with a variety of products available via the Internet) and in a comic book inspired by the series.

With the cancellation of *Futurama* by Fox in 2003 after *Family Guy* had been canceled in 2002, and with a flurry of short-lived programs such as *Clerks; God, the Devil, and Bob; Dilbert;* and *The Oblongs* canceled before that, it appeared that the surge in prime-time animated programming that marked the turn of the century was at an end. That appearance was deceiving. Not only would *Family Guy* soon return to the air on Fox, but the late-night Adult Swim block on the Cartoon Network continued to produce a variety of innovative new animated programs as well as providing a venue for the rebroadcast of animated programs (including *Futurama* and *Family Guy*) that had previously been canceled on other networks. In addition, cable channels such as Comedy Central, Sci Fi, and the Independent Film Channel (IFC), encouraged by the ongoing critical and commercial success of programs such as *South Park*, would soon get into the act with new prime-time animated programs as well. The next chapter discusses *South Park* itself, while the final chapter surveys the wide variety of new animated programming that began to appear on cable networks in the first years of the twenty-first century.

CHAPTER 6

You Can't Do That on Television: The Animated Satire of *South Park*

The *Simpsons,* like *The Flintstones* before it, was an animated series oriented toward an adult audience but still designed to be relatively kid-friendly family fare. After all, animated television programming had long been considered a form designed primarily to attract younger viewers, an orientation that, with minor exceptions (such as 1972's *Fritz the Cat*) also included feature films dating back to the first Disney classics of the 1930s. However, the proliferation of cable television networks in the 1980s and especially in the early 1990s opened up a number of opportunities for programs that did not fit into conventional generic niches. Animated programs of the early 1990s such as Nickelodeon's *Ren and Stimpy* and MTV's *Beavis and Butt-head* appealed not only to their ostensible target audiences of elementary schoolers and adolescents, respectively, but to college students and older adults as well. Eventually, the success of these programs enabled the rise of Comedy Central's *South Park*, an animated series that uses its inappropriateness as a crucial source of ironic humor, helping to launch a whole new generation of animated programs intended primarily for adult audiences.

Ren and Stimpy, with its dog and cat central characters and its old-fashioned animation style that looks back to the classic Warner Brothers cartoons of the 1940s, would at first glance seem an almost formulaic children's cartoon, perfect for the six- to seven-year-old demographic initially envisioned by Nickelodeon. But the demented and often vicious Ren and the excrementally fixated Stimpy are not your father's cartoon dog and cat, while the animated style derives most of its energy from its deviations from its old-school base, veering into outrageous caricature to produce grotesque sight gags that were hardly the stuff of traditional animated children's programming. The show was a hit, partly due to older audiences introduced to the show through cross-airings on Nickelodeon's sister Viacom network, MTV, soon after the August 1991 debut of the program. But the MTV audience was not quite what Nickelodeon had in mind, and the network quickly became alarmed at the increasingly mature content of the show. Despite the success of *Ren and Stimpy* with viewing audiences, the network quickly came into conflict with series creator John Kricfalusi and his Spumco animation studio when it censored several episodes. Midway through the second season, Nickelodeon gave Kricfalusi and Spumco the boot altogether, seizing control of the program and attempting to divert it into tamer and more acceptable directions.

The program remained in production until 1996, but many loyal fans of the original show were disappointed if not infuriated by the new turn in the program, and it is on the strength of the early Kricfalusi episodes that the cult reputation of the program rests. Indeed, Kricfalusi was brought back with the resurrection of the series as the *Ren and Stimpy Adult Party Cartoon* on Spike TV (another Viacom network) in June 2003, and the new series, with its adult target audience, was designed to allow Kricfalusi's vision to proceed relatively unencumbered. The new show, however, along with Spike's plan to produce a block of animated programs to compete with Cartoon Network's Adult Swim, met with a fairly quick demise and was soon canceled.

In the midst of *Ren and Stimpy*'s run on Nickelodeon, sister network MTV began to broadcast episodes of Mike Judge's *Beavis and Butt-head*, an animated series that became one of the most-talked-about products of American popular culture in the mid-1990s. The object of scorn (and even lawsuits) on the part of parents, *Beavis and Butt-head*, with its teenage metalhead protagonists, raunchy humor, and music-video tie-ins, gained a loyal following among college students and adolescents. The series also drew considerable attention from serious academic critics, who obviously found the program fascinating, despite the fact that they usually proclaimed it a typical example of MTV faux-subversion, designed not to foment rebellion among its young viewers but to sell them products marketed by its corporate sponsors.

The self-consciously simplistic animation of *Beavis and Butt-head* could not come close to the outlandish, cutting-edge animation of *Ren and Stimpy*, but Judge's show went well beyond *Ren and Stimpy* in taking on controversial subject matter. Appearing first as a pair of short features on the MTV late-night program *Liquid Television* in 1992, *Beavis and Butt-head* (with both of the main characters voiced by creator Judge) began broadcasting as a stand-alone weekday afternoon program in March 1993. It was an immediate hit, even though many saw its depiction of Beavis and Butt-head as incredibly stupid slackers who did nothing but watch music videos as an insult to MTV's core audience. It was, of course, anything but. Beavis and Butt-head did not represent MTV viewers: They represented the popular perception of MTV viewers while at the same time congratulating those viewers on being clever enough to get the joke and laugh at those who thought they were stupid enough not to.

Beavis and Butt-head were indeed stereotypical sex-crazed teenage boys, though they also had counterparts in the culture of American stupidity-as-humor going back at least as far as the legendary Three Stooges and including such contemporaries as the central characters of the Farrelly brothers film *Dumb and Dumber* (1994). Their closest equivalents, though slightly more mature than the animated duo, were Wayne and Garth of the *Wayne's World* films (released in 1992 and 1993) and *Saturday Night Live* skits. The format of *Beavis and Butt-head* was simple. Brief narrative segments featuring the brainless antics of the socially maladjusted teenage duo were interspersed with clips from music videos, interrupted by the comments of the two as they sit on Butt-head's tattered couch watching the videos on television. Beavis and Butt-head were hardly brilliant critics: Their judgments typically involved simple conclusions about whether videos were "cool" or "sucked," with "cool" generally meaning that the videos featured extensive displays of violence or naked female flesh. But their comments were sometimes insightful and could be quite humorous, somewhat along the lines of a more immature version of the kibitzing onlookers in the *Mystery Science Theater 3000* television series who heaped sarcasm on science fiction films of the 1950s.

After a two-year-old girl in Ohio was killed in a fire set by her five-year-old brother, the children's mother claimed that the boy had been inspired by the Beavis's pyromaniacal tendencies. The subsequent round of lawsuits, expressions of outrage by media-watchdog groups, and even attention from Senate hearings brought *Beavis and Butt-head* into the very center of the public consciousness. Without admitting any sort of responsibility for the burning death, MTV pulled several fire-oriented episodes of *Beavis and Butt-head* from the broadcast rotation and eliminated references to fire in other episodes. They also moved the cartoon into a late-night time slot, which probably suited its core audience of young adults better, anyway. Perhaps most tellingly, they added the following disclaimer to the beginning of each subsequent broadcast: "Beavis and Butt-head are not role models. They're not even human, they're cartoons. The things they do could cause a person to get hurt, expelled, arrested . . . possibly deported. To put it another way, don't try this at home."

This disclaimer, while perfectly appropriate on the surface, was also clearly designed (in the mode of the show as a whole) to congratulate the show's audience for being smart enough to know perfectly well that Beavis and Butt-head were cartoons, while at the same time taking a sarcastic slap at the show's critics for being stupid enough to believe that audiences of *Beavis and Butt-head* couldn't distinguish slapstick cartoon humor from reality. Indeed, while the controversy over the show might ultimately have contributed to its 1996 demise (when Judge himself decided to stop making new episodes before moving on to the more mainstream, but still edgy, *King of the Hill*), for a time all the fuss took the show to new heights of prominence. Beavis and Butt-head themselves went on to become major media stars, remaining so even after the show was canceled. In December of 1996, for example, they "starred" in the successful feature-length theatrical film *Beavis and Butt-head Do America*, and the next March they even made an appearance as presenters on the prestigious Academy Awards broadcast. They have also occasionally appeared in cameo roles in such shows as the Cartoon Network/Adult Swim series *Robot Chicken* and *Space Ghost Coast to Coast*. *Beavis and Butt-head* also gave birth to an interesting spin-off animated show, *Daria*, which aired on MTV from 1997 to 2001. The title character of that program, bespectacled teenager Daria Morgendorffer, had been an occasional character on *Beavis and Butt-head*.

David Letterman, an avowed *Beavis and Butt-head* fan, often mentioned the show on *Late Night with David Letterman*. He even provided some of the voicing in the film, indicating his support for the *Beavis and Butt-head* phenomenon. And the episode "Late Night with Butt-head" (April 14, 1994) included a hilarious parody of Letterman's late-night program, with Butt-head as Letterman and Beavis as Letterman's band-leader and sidekick Paul Shaffer. Through such motifs, *Beavis and Butt-head* often went well beyond music videos in its commentary on American television culture.

If *Beavis and Butt-head* sought to celebrate tastelessness, partly as a way of satirizing the pretentious bourgeois tastes of its self-righteous critics, *South Park*, which began airing the year after *Beavis and Butt-head* went out of production, brought tastelessness to the level of an art form. *South Park* was created by Trey Parker and Matt Stone, who have continued to write, direct, and edit the series throughout its run, which has now stretched through nine seasons on Comedy Central, with three more already under contract. Set in the small, relatively affluent Colorado town of the title, *South Park* focuses on the misadventures of a group of third-graders (who finally become fourth graders in the fourth season). These are, however, anything but your typical cartoon children. The most important character, and the one who has oddly emerged as an audience favorite, is probably the fat, greedy Eric Cartman (voiced by Parker), a foulmouthed bigot who hates virtually everyone. The central point of view of the series, however, is that of Stan Marsh (Parker) and Kyle Broflovski (Stone), loosely based on childhood versions of Parker and Stone, respectively. The final member of the central foursome is the impoverished Kenny McCormick (Stone), whose frequently obscene lines are muffled by the fact that he constantly has the hood of a parka wrapped tightly around his head. He also has the misfortune, apparently simply because he is poor, of getting killed in nearly every episode through the fifth season, usually in some grotesque fashion. However, in the uncharacteristically poignant "Kenny Dies" (December 5, 2001), near the end of the fifth season, Kenny dies of a terminal illness, partly because the government has effectively eliminated the stem cell research that might have developed a cure for his condition. Kenny then returns at the end of a sixth season, after a sequence of several episodes in which his resurrection is posited as a possibility. This sequence illustrates a growing tendency over the years for *South Park* to include semicontinuous plot arcs, or at least for later episodes to refer to events in earlier episodes (as opposed to much animated television, which is entirely episodic and in which the events of any given episode tend to have no real consequences in later episodes). In the sixth-season finale, "Red Sleigh Down" (December 11, 2002), Kenny simply walks on at the end, perhaps resurrected by Santa Claus's Christmas magic, then resumes his previous role, though he dies less frequently in subsequent episodes.

South Park announced from the very beginning that it was not going to be conventional family-oriented animated fare. The first word of dialogue spoken in the series is "Goddammit," which young Kyle shouts in response to the fact that his baby brother Ike has followed him to the school bus stop, where he waits with Stan, Cartman, and Kenny. (The last bit of dialogue in the episode, incidentally, is Cartman's exclamation, "Son of a bitch!") Soon afterward, Cartman calls Ike a "dildo," though none of the boys, except Kenny, their group expert on sex and profanity, knows what a dildo is. Kyle then proceeds to demonstrate the game of "kick the baby," in which he boots little Ike like a football, first into a group of mailboxes and then through the closed window of the arriving school bus.

The main plot of this episode involves the fact that Cartman (though he himself thinks it was just a dream) has been abducted by aliens, who inserted and left a probe in his anus. As a result, whenever he farts, which he does frequently in this and other episodes, flames shoot out of his ass, much to the amusement of the other children. Meanwhile, the aliens kidnap Ike, and the boys spend much of the episode trying to rescue him, finally succeeding after Cartman recalls the alien ship by signaling it using an 80-foot satellite dish that emerges from his anus. In between, numerous local cows are vivisected by the aliens, Stan vomits every time classmate Wendy Testaburger (Mary Kay Bergman, credited as Shannen Cassidy) speaks to him, the school cook Chef (Isaac Hayes) sings a sexually suggestive song as a way of giving advice to the boys, and Kenny is killed and eaten by rats after being zapped by the aliens, trampled by a herd of cows, and run over by a police car. In one classic *South Park* moment in the episode, Cartman complains to his mother that their pet cat is "being a dildo." "Well, then," sweetly responds Mrs. Cartman (Bergman), "I know a certain kitty kitty who's sleeping with mommy tonight."

In the course of the next several episodes, the boys continue to employ an almost unending stream of profanities, Chef continues his horny (but often wise) ways, and their teacher Mr. Herbert Garrison (Parker), appears more and more unhinged, as when he attempts to assassinate television personality Kathie Lee Gifford in "Weight Gain 4000" (August 27, 1997). Garrison also supplies the boys with misinformation while attempting to deal with his own substantial problems of gender identity, which include his ongoing love affair with Mr. Hat, a hand puppet that he wears on his right hand at all times. To top things off, in "An Elephant Makes Love to a Pig" (September 10, 1997), Kyle's pet elephant has sex with Cartman's pot-bellied pig, apparently resulting in a pregnancy. But when the babies are born, they turn out to look suspiciously like Mr. Garrison. Meanwhile, the boys try to deal with the fact that Stan's dog is patently gay, Stan's ancient grandfather tries desperately but unsuccessfully to commit suicide, and mutant turkeys attack and nearly destroy South Park at Thanksgiving.

South Park then established its irreverent style once and for all with the now almost-legendary episode "Mr. Hankey, the Christmas Poo" (December 17, 1997), surely the most outrageous Christmas special in the history of animated television to that time. Political correctness is a consistent object of satire in *South Park,* and the plot of this episode concerns the attempts of the people of South Park to find a politically correct way to celebrate Christmas without offending any groups who may, perhaps, see the holiday differently than the majority. One of these groups is Jews, and the attempt to find an alternative Christmas celebration is in fact triggered by Sheila Broflovski's vehement complaints that public support for a Christian holiday is offensive to the town's Jewish community, which apparently here consists entirely of the Broflovski family, though later episodes feature a larger Jewish contingent in the town.

His mother's activism only serves to make Kyle feel more left out than he already does at Christmas. He, of course, has Hanukkah, but that seems to him a poor substitute for the Christian holiday that all of his friends celebrate. He does, however, find what seems to him a rewarding nonreligious way to relate to Christmas when he is visited by Mr. Hankey the Christmas Poo, a dancing and singing anthropomorphized turd who "comes out of the toilet every year and gives presents to everybody who has a lot of fiber in their diet."

Unfortunately, Mr. Hankey at first refuses to sing or dance for anyone but Kyle, so his parents and friends think he is merely playing with feces. In the meantime, everyone in town thinks the boy is crazy when he proposes the turd as an alternative Christmas icon. Eventually, Kyle is declared by school counselor Mr. Mackey to be a "sick little monkey" and committed (by the other boys) to an asylum, South Park Mental House. In the meantime, Cartman performs one of the patented musical numbers that have become one of his trademarks, in this case a rousing ditty entitled "Kyle's Mom Is a Bitch."

The town's new nonoffensive Christmas celebration—complete with music by minimalist composer Philip Glass—is so awful that it triggers a riot. Meanwhile, when Chef learns that the other boys have committed Kyle to an asylum because of Mr. Hankey, he assures them that Mr. Hankey is indeed real. Then (after an inserted mock live-action commercial for a Mr. Potatohead–like Mr. Hankey toy), Chef and the boys are visited by Mr. Hankey himself, who stops the riot by exhorting the crowd to respect the true spirit of Christmas, then leads the townspeople to the mental house to rescue Kyle, who now becomes a local hero as the people of South Park sing the Mr. Hankey song, their new Christmas anthem. All seems well, and Stan, as he often does, even reiterates what he sees as the lesson of the episode—that Jewish people are okay. Still, something doesn't quite seem right to Cartman, Stan, and Kyle. Then as the inscription "THE END" appears at the top of the screen, we realize that Kenny (after several close calls during the episode), is for the first time still alive as an episode ends. Kenny himself jumps and shouts with glee as it becomes clear that he has indeed survived the episode.

The exact meaning of this episode is a bit hard to decode. It is certainly irreverent in its treatment of Christmas, and one could even interpret it to suggest that all the hoopla about Christmas in our society is really only so much excrement. And yet the ultimate restoration of the Christmas spirit in South Park, even if spearheaded by a singing turd, is about as close as *South Park* ever comes to being sentimental and nostalgic. *South Park* would go on to complicate and elaborate its dialogue with Christmas in subsequent holiday specials, which may not be surprising in that, to a very real extent, the series itself actually began as a Christmas card. In 1991, Parker and Stone made a crudely animated student film called *Jesus vs. Frosty* that drew the attention of Fox executive Brian Graden, who commissioned the two to create a short animated film, *The Spirit of Christmas*, that he could send out as a video Christmas card. That project led to subsequent negotiations with Fox for an animated series; the failure of these negotiations ultimately led to the airing of *South Park* on Comedy Central.

The four central kids of the *South Park* cast are supplemented by the inclusion of a number of the boys' friends and classmates. Perhaps the most prominent of these is Leopold "Butters" Stotch (Stone), a meek and submissive child who has apparently been cowed by his parents' obsessive concern with discipline. He is also extremely gullible, which tends to make him vulnerable to pranks on the part of the other kids, especially Cartman. The unfortunate Butters was even born on September 11. Other recurring child characters include the hyperactive Tweek (Stone), made jumpy by the fact that his parents keep him hopped up on caffeine; Craig (Parker), who is constantly in trouble for flipping people off, which he does obsessively and apparently unconsciously; and Token Black, also known as Token Williams (Adrien Beard), who is the show's token black and also the richest kid in town. The class also includes Phillip "Pip" Pirrup (Stone), a British child generally abused by the other children largely because he is a foreigner. As his name indicates, Pip is based on the central character in Charles Dickens's novel *Great Expectations*. In fact, his most prominent role in the series occurs when he appears as the central character in the episode "Pip" (November 29, 2000), which departs from the usual *South Park* format (none of the main characters even appear) to present an episode-long fractured version of the Dickens novel.

Girls tend to play a secondary role in the series, though Wendy Testaburger is a fairly prominent character. Perhaps the most controversial of the secondary characters in *South Park* is Timmy (Parker), a young boy who is confined to a wheelchair and virtually unable to speak anything except his own name—which he often shouts with great enthusiasm. Though originally described in the show as "retarded," Timmy at times seems quite intelligent. He figures prominently in numerous episodes, as in

"Timmy! 2000" (April 19, 2000), in which he first joins Mr. Garrison's class and is diagnosed with ADD (attention deficit disorder), then treated with Ritalin, eventually causing the entire town to be dosed with the drug after the other children also feign ADD when they realize that Timmy's condition has caused him to be excused from normal schoolwork. Timmy also enjoys a brief moment of rock stardom when he becomes the frontman for the local band "Lords of the Underworld," rhythmically shouting his name while the other members of the band play backup. One of Timmy's most controversial episodes is "Cripple Fight" (June 27, 2001), in which he becomes the rival of another disabled child, Jimmy (Parker), a would-be stand-up comedian who can only stand up with the help of crutches and who speaks with a stutter. To the backdrop of a narrative that satirizes the homophobia of the Boy Scouts, while at the same time attacking those who would want to force the Scouts to accept gays into their ranks, the two boys become engaged in a violent fistfight that leaves both unconscious. Timmy does, however, get the last laugh when he gets Jimmy kicked out of the Scouts by falsifying evidence that Jimmy is gay.

In addition to the children who form the heart of the show, local citizens of South Park who are prominent in the series include the dim-witted policeman, Officer Barbrady (Parker); the local mad scientist (and Marlon Brando look-alike) Dr. Alphonse Mephesto (Parker); the bumbling but ambitious Mayor McDaniels (originally Bergman, then Eliza Schneider—credited as "Blue Girl"); the narrow-minded local Catholic priest, Father Maxi (Stone); and even Jesus Christ (Stone). In addition to Chef, Mr. Garrison, and Mr. Mackey, prominent adults at South Park Elementary School include Principal Victoria (Bergman, then Schneider, then Gracie Lazar) and Miss Diane Choksondik (Parker), who replaces Mr. Garrison as the boys' teacher when they move to the fourth grade. (Mr. Garrison's various indiscretions have finally led to his being fired by the school system, though he will shortly return.) In addition to her amazingly obscene last name, Miss Choksondik is also distinguished by her preposterously pendulous breasts, which tend to escape her clothing whenever she raises her arms, to the revulsion of everyone within sight.

The families of the four central boys in *South Park* also play important roles in the series. Stan's parents are Randy and Sharon, which were also the names of Parker's parents. Moreover, Randy Marsh, like Randy Parker, is a geologist. Kyle's (Jewish) parents are named Gerald and Sheila, which were also the names of Stone's parents, though Gerald Broflovski is a prominent local attorney, while Stone's father was an economist. Some episodes actually focus more on the parents than on the children, as in "Two Guys

Naked in a Hot Tub" (July 21, 1999), when the adults of South Park gather for a party to celebrate an impending meteor shower. Authorities somehow conclude that the party is actually a gathering of cult members preparing for a mass suicide in conjunction with the shower, so heavily armed and highly incompetent ATF agents move in to surround the house, threatening to kill everyone inside in order to prevent the suicides. The obvious referent here is the 1993 ATF-FBI raid on the headquarters of the David Koresh–led Branch Davidian cult in Waco, Texas. That this raid has become a favorite cause célèbre of right-wing extremist groups antagonistic toward the U.S. government would seem to align the politics of South Park with such groups. However, the point of view of the show is not so easily pinned down, and the funniest part of this episode involves an incident within the party in which Gerald Broflovski and Randy Marsh, perhaps having had a little too much to drink, watch each other masturbate in a hot tub. Marsh then spends the rest of the episode in a frantic state of homophobic anxiety, wondering if this incident makes him gay—until it is revealed that all of the men at the party have at one time or another watched another man masturbate.

Cartman's doting mother Liane is a single mother who dresses and speaks demurely but is apparently a drug-addicted prostitute. She is prominent in numerous episodes, though her most important appearance in the show is in the notorious two-part sequence "Cartman's Mom Is a Dirty Slut" (February 25, 1998) and "Cartman's Mom Is Still a Dirty Slut" (April 22, 1998). These episodes address the fact that Cartman's father is nowhere to be seen, initially suggesting that even Liane has no idea who Cartman's father actually is. In the first of these episodes, Cartman (surrounded by a culture that glorifies the importance of fathers) begins to show signs of serious psychological damage due to his lack of a father. He asks his mother about his father, whom she claims is a Native American man, Chief Running Water, whom she met at a "drunken barn dance" years earlier. Unfortunately, she herself was so drunk at the dance that she remembers very little about the encounter. Cartman goes to the reservation to seek out his putative father, who assures him that his mom is a slut, but that he, Running Water, did not have sex with her at the party, though a young Chef, just arrived in town, did.

Cartman then tries to turn African American to get in touch with his newly discovered roots, until Chef also assures him that he is not his father. Eventually, it turns out that Liane had sex with virtually every young man at the dance, including most of the men who now feature as characters in the show (even Mr. Garrison and possibly even Jesus), as well as the entire 1989 Denver Broncos football team. Dr. Mephesto runs a DNA test to determine the identity of Cartman's father and is about to announce the results when the episode comes to a sudden halt, while a voiceover announcer assures viewers that the identity of Cartman's father will be identified in the next episode of *South Park* in only four weeks time.

This parody of the season-ending cliffhanger then got an additional twist when the next episode aired five weeks later—on April 1. As an April Fool's Day joke, which was not appreciated by viewers, many of whom were enraged at the prank, this episode did not identify Cartman's father at all, but was instead devoted entirely to a special episode of *The Terrance and Phillip Show* (entitled "Terrance and Phillip in Not Without My Anus"), featuring a pair of flatulent Canadian comedians much admired by Stan, Kyle, Cartman, and Kenny. The angry viewer response to this episode caused Comedy Central to move up the scheduled date for the showing of the actual follow-up episode, which finally solved the mystery of Cartman's paternity—though still in a way that was largely a joke on the viewers who were so anxious for this information. With all of the candidates lined up in a single room, Dr. Mephesto prepares to makes his long-awaited announcement, but is then shot down by a mysterious assailant. Chef and the boys manage to drive Mephesto to the hospital on treacherous mountain roads in a heavy snowstorm. As Mephesto lies in a coma, various subplots unfold, including Liane Cartman's efforts to sleep with enough politicians (up to and including President Bill Clinton) to get the abortion laws changed to allow her to have her son Eric aborted, even though he is already eight years old. She succeeds in getting Clinton's support, only to learn that she had misinterpreted the word abortion: She actually wanted to have the boy adopted—so that he could have a father at last. In the end, however, she decides to keep Eric with her. Finally, Mephesto recovers, only to announce that Liane is Eric's father: She is a hermaphrodite who impregnated another woman at the barn dance. Unfortunately, this now leaves open the question of the identity of Cartman's mother, but by this time the boy gives up in frustration and decides to leave this question unanswered.

In addition to the various residents of South Park, numerous celebrities also pass through the town from time to time, usually becoming the targets of outrageous satire, typically aimed at what Parker and Stone obviously see as the pretentiousness and self-importance of such figures. Liberal show-business personalities are often skewered for their political activism, as when Rob Reiner's antismoking activism comes under fire in "Butt Out" (December 3, 2003). Other celebrities, however, get skewered on general principles, perhaps more as a comment on the American cult of celebrity than on the celebrities themselves. Thus, Barbra Streisand, another noted liberal celebrity, is transformed into a giant, Godzilla-like monster in "Mecha-Streisand" (February 18, 1998), though this development would appear to be more a comment on Streisand's own sense of herself as a huge star than on her liberalism. Meanwhile, Robert Redford and his Sundance Film Festival are lampooned in "Chef's Salty Chocolate Balls" (August 19, 1998), in which the festival is moved to South Park, nearly leading to the destruction of the town. This episode comments specifically on the commercialization of the Sundance Festival, but also skewers independent films in general, characterized here, years before *Brokeback Mountain*, as being mostly about "gay cowboys eating pudding." The comic highlight of the episode, however, is Chef's endeavor that gives the episode its title: Trying to cash in on the festival, he invents a new confection, then hawks it by singing a song that invites customers to suck on his salty chocolate balls. All ends well, though, as Mr. Hankey, who nearly dies from festival-related pollution in the town's sewers, but is invigorated by sucking on one of Chef's tasty balls, returns to save the town and restore the ecology of the sewer in which he lives. The musical turd also becomes a celebrity in his own right when an independent film starring Tom Hanks (who couldn't, we are told by Cartman, "act his way out of a nutsack") is made featuring Mr. Hankey, played by a monkey, as a central character.

South Park takes several pot shots at onetime sweethearts Ben Affleck and Jennifer Lopez, culminating in the outrageous episode "Fat Butt and Pancake Head" (April 16, 2003), which depicts Lopez as a skanky tramp and Affleck as a no-talent idiot. Here, Cartman paints his fist to make a hand puppet of Jennifer Lopez, in the mode of the work of the Spanish ventriloquist Señor Wences. Cartman then uses the puppet in a school presentation that goes over well, despite the fact that it is filled with ethnic stereotypes. Then, however, the puppet seems to take on a life of its own and even manages to steal the real J-Lo's recording contract, as well as her boyfriend. Affleck falls madly in love with Cartman's fist and even has sex with it, while Lopez assaults the fist so violently that it has to be hospitalized. She herself, her show-business career ruined, ends up working in a fast-food taco restaurant.

Clearly, the *South Park* celebrity satires can get downright mean-spirited—especially when they are aimed not at major stars such as Streisand, Redford, and Hanks, but at lesser lights whose careers are perhaps not going so well. In "Cartman Gets an Anal Probe," for example, Ike is urged to dive off of the alien ship, plunging downward in "imitation of David Caruso's career." In "Cartman's Mom Is Still a Dirty Slut," actor Eric Roberts has fallen on such hard times that he comes to South Park to play a very minor role in the *America's Most Wanted* reenactment of the shooting of Dr. Mephesto—and then is eaten by the locals who get stranded with him without food due to the snowstorm. The famously overweight Sally Struthers is shown soliciting contributions to buy food for starving Ethiopians, but then eats all the food herself, eventually being transformed, in "Starvin' Marvin in Space!" (November 17, 1999), into a giant, Jabba the Hut–like blob. And Rosie O'Donnell, another somewhat rotund star, is the butt of humor in "Trapper Keeper" (November 15, 2000), a parody of the *Terminator* films with a spoof of *2001: A Space Odyssey* thrown in as well. Here, Cartman's fancy high-tech school notebook turns into a gigantic, monstrous killing machine, growing rapidly larger and more grotesque as it assimilates everything in its path. O'Donnell (a well-known liberal—and lesbian—activist) also comes to town to interfere in the politics of a kindergarten class election. Residents then have trouble distinguishing between O'Donnell and the monstrous Trapper Keeper, but the latter is destroyed when it is unable to cope with the toxic effects of attempting to assimilate the actress and talk-show host. Perhaps the most vicious personal attacks in all of *South Park* occur in the episode "The Biggest Douche in the Universe" (November, 2002), which zeroes in on television psychic John Edward, literally granting him the title that is also that of the episode.

In addition to such celebrity satires, *South Park* often takes glee in assaulting beloved American institutions. Some of the most memorable episodes of *South Park* have been Christmas episodes, beginning with the legendary "Mr. Hankey" special in the first season. The second-season *South Park* Christmas special "Merry Christmas, Charlie Manson!" (December 9, 1998) seems to critique the commercialization of Christmas with its presentation of Mr. Hankey as a new icon of the holiday. Here, Mr. Hankey merchandise is hawked in malls all over America (or at least Nebraska), and Mr. Hankey imitators are prominent in those malls, displacing Santa Claus. The episode also riffs on the beloved Christmas classic *It's a Wonderful Life*, which Charlie Manson, newly escaped from prison, declares to be just another lie, like the spirit of Christmas itself. On the other hand, even Manson begins to get into the spirit when he watches a remake of *The Grinch Who Stole Christmas*, featuring an all-turd cast; he then replaces the notorious swastika tattoo on his forehead with a smiley face. He even sings a sentimental Christmas song as police, having just shot and killed Kenny while apprehending Manson, take him back to prison. The episode then ends as all the principals visit Manson in prison and sing a straightforward rendition of "Hark the Herald Angels Sing," though this potentially sentimental ending is immediately undermined by Stan's trademark, partly bleeped declaration, "Dude, this is pretty f**ked up, right here!"

The ongoing *South Park* dialogue with Christmas takes another turn in the third-season holiday special "Mr. Hankey's Christmas Classics" (December 1, 1999), in which Mr. Hankey hosts a sequence of 10 somewhat fractured Christmas carols performed by various regular *South Park* characters, leading the boys ultimately to conclude that the true meaning of Christmas is getting presents. This conclusion could be taken as a critique of the commercialization of Christmas of the kind now almost as much a part of the Christmas-season routine as Santa Claus himself. However, the fourth-season special, "A Very Crappy Christmas" (December 20, 2000), is an all-out enthusiastic endorsement of Christmas-time commercialization. Here, the boys attempt to counter the town's flagging Christmas spirit by making their own brief animated film (based on the original video Christmas card made by Parker and Stone in 1995). Ultimately, this film helps them to restore Christmas in South Park—which means that everyone in town scurries out to the stores to buy presents. The commercialization of Christmas is a good thing, this episode concludes, because holiday shopping provides a crucial boost to America's consumer-driven capitalist economy.

Almost shockingly, season five of *South Park* did not include a Christmas special, but the next three seasons did include such a show. In the sixth-season episode "Red Sleigh Down," Santa is shot down over Baghdad, then captured while trying to bring Christmas to Iraq. He is ultimately rescued by Jesus and the boys, though Jesus is killed in the effort. Subsequently, Santa restores the magic to Christmas in South Park, noting that Jesus died in order to save him and predicting that, in the future, Jesus might become a significant part of the Christmas celebration. In "It's Christmas in Canada" (December 17, 2003), Ike Broflovski's birth parents come from Canada to reclaim the boy, just as the Broflovskis are celebrating Hanukkah. In an extended pastiche of *The Wizard of Oz*, Kyle and the other boys then travel to Canada to retrieve little Ike, on the way discovering that Canada is a lot like Oz. Ultimately, the episode is a spoof of the efforts of the Bush administration to blame virtually all of the world's evils on Saddam Hussein, when it turns out that all of the trouble has been caused by Saddam, who has covertly taken over Canada as the new prime minister. Finally, "Woodland Critter Christmas" (December 15, 2004) is one of the darkest of all the *South Park* Christmas specials—which is only to be expected given that the episode consists of a Christmas story made up and narrated by Cartman. Here, after various misadventures in which the antichrist is born and nearly destroys the earth as we know it, the episode seems to end happily, but Cartman's story is topped off by a coda in which he informs us that Kyle, a key character in the narrative, died of AIDS two weeks after the events of the story.

The ninth season of *South Park* lacks a Christmas special per se, though "Bloody Mary" (December 7, 2005), aired during the Christmas season, deals centrally with the related issue of Catholic reverence for the mother of Christ. One of the main satirical targets of this episode is Alcoholics Anonymous (AA)—and the general culture of therapy in which behavioral problems such as excessive drinking are treated as diseases for which the sufferers bear no individual responsibility. Here, Randy Marsh is arrested for driving under the influence and forced as part of his punishment to attend AA. Unfortunately, the AA message that he is the helpless victim of a disease is the last thing Marsh, who tends to be a hypochondriac, needs to hear. He surrenders to the disease, drinking constantly and spending his time in a constant drunken stupor, much to the horror of his son Stan.

This episode also lampoons the religious orientation of the 12-step program of AA, which makes the official endorsement of the program by the legal system highly questionable. It is, in fact, the treatment of religion in "Bloody Mary" that has made it perhaps the most controversial *South Park* episode yet. Just as Marsh is being told that he must seek supernatural help to combat his addiction, word comes that a statue of the Virgin Mary in the nearby town of Bailey is bleeding. Such phenomena are conventionally taken by the Catholic Church as manifestations of the holy nature of the Virgin Mother, so pilgrims flock to the statue from miles around. Marsh is among those who come to Bailey in the hope of being cured of various afflictions by the blood of the Virgin, which appears to be coming from the statue's ass. Indeed, when he is blessed with the blood by a priest, Marsh finds that he is suddenly able to stop drinking.

Pope Benedict himself comes to Bailey to investigate the apparent miracle. Examining the rear end of the statue, he is liberally sprayed with blood. Upon closer investigation, however, he finds that the blood is coming not from Mary's ass, but from her vagina. As a result, he declares that the blood is not holy and that the phenomenon is not a miracle because it is nothing out of the ordinary for a "chick" to bleed from her vagina. Disappointed, Marsh begins to descend back into alcoholism, until Stan points out that he obviously can control his drinking because he did so when the thought he had been miraculously cured. Marsh finally sees the logic of Stan's argument and realizes that he needs neither miracles nor AA, but simply a bit of self-discipline.

Given the subject matter of this episode, it was understandably greeted with outrage by many Catholics. Indeed, it was considered so offensive that the Catholic League has petitioned Comedy Central to bury the episode—never to rebroadcast it or even release it on DVD. This reaction, of course, is pretty much the one Parker and Stone seemed to be going for—and one that seems to support the point, made frequently in the series, that religions have a nasty tendency to try to force their views on others rather than accepting the freedom of thought that is supposedly a central part of the ideology of America. If there is a central message in *South Park* it would seem to be support of freedom of thought and expression and condemnation of precisely the kind of censorship embodied in this Catholic reaction, in which given groups would demand that certain ideas never be expressed because they disagree with them. Thus, virtually the entire feature film *South Park: Bigger, Longer, and Uncut* (1999) is devoted to a critique of the hypocrisy and misguided values of a movie ratings system that seems designed to protect the public from offensive language while allowing graphic violence to be shown freely.

Some of the seemingly gratuitous offensiveness of *South Park* as a whole can be attributed to an attempt to make a similar point. After all, the show seems able to present all sorts of vulgar material as long as certain key words are bleeped out (even though it is generally clear to most viewers just what those words are). This phenomenon is addressed directly in the episode "It Hits the Fan" (June 20, 2001), which reacts to the fact that a character in the "serious" cop drama *NYPD Blue* had recently said "shit happens" on the air—to a largely positive response from viewers and critics. In the *South Park* episode, a character in a cop drama similarly says "shit," which makes the word suddenly acceptable (because the show is considered serious art), leading to an epidemic in the use of the word on television—and in the society at large. Indeed, a counter in the lower corner of the screen records the number of times "shit" (or variants such as "shitty") is spoken (unbleeped) during the episode. By the end of this episode, the counter is up to 162. In the meantime, however, repeated public articulation of this curse word literally brings down a curse on American society, which is nearly destroyed, until Chef and the boys manage to intercede and lift the curse. Stan and Kyle, in the "we've learned something today" speech that ends many episodes, explain that we need, in the future, to limit our use of curse words.

Among other things, the plot of this episode mocks those sanctimonious critics who might think it would bring about the end of the world if the language on television weren't heavily censored. In addition, the frequent use in this episode of the word "shit," which gradually loses its shock value with repetition, makes the point that censorship itself increases the power of profanity by making it more unusual. Indeed, a show such as *South Park* works largely because it is unusual, continually violating the expectations that viewers know would normally be associated with an animated program featuring a central cast of small children.

South Park revels in its own sense of being transgressive, which can be seen from the fact that every episode begins with a parody of attempts to "protect" the public from being exposed to offensive material by flashing on the screen a disclaimer (echoing the disclaimer of *Beavis and Butt-head*) that advises *everyone* not to watch the following episode. This disclaimer (which looks as if it had been typed on a computer screen, complete with a flashing cursor at the end), reads as follows:

ALL CHARACTERS AND
EVENT\S IN THIS SHOW—
EVEN THOSE BASED ON REAL
PEOPLE—ARE ENTIRELY FICTIONAL.
ALL CELEBRITY VOICES ARE
IMPERSONATED. . . . POORLY. THE
FOLLOWING PROGRAM CONTAINS
COARSE LANGUAGE AND DUE TO
ITS CONTENT IT SHOULD NOT BE
VIEWED BY ANYONE

This warning, of course, drives away no one who would enjoy *South Park*, which takes a great deal of pleasure in its presentation of offensive material, in the long artistic tradition of "shocking the bourgeoisie." Its intentional flouting of middle-class values exposes the shallowness and hypocrisy of those values, especially when they act to suppress individual liberty even as they are espoused by those who are supposedly proponents of democratic freedoms.

South Park's consciousness of its own vulgarity can also be seen in its inclusion within the show of the *Terrance and Phillip Show*. This show, which plays much the same role in *South Park* that *The Itchy & Scratchy Show* plays in *The Simpsons*, is even more lowbrow than *South Park* itself. In fact, *Terrance and Phillip* essentially consists of nothing more than the two title characters attempting to fart on each other. *South Park*, however, gets an amazing amount of mileage out of this simple premise. In the episode "Death" (September 17, 1997), for example, Kyle's mother, believing the show to be a bad influence on her children, leads a parents' crusade against the program that ultimately takes them to the headquarters of "Cartoon Central" (apparently a combination of Comedy Central and the Cartoon Network), the network that broadcasts the show—though in later seasons *Terrance and Phillip* airs on a network called HBC. Rebuffed by network executives, the parents, by this time themselves plagued by explosive diarrhea, begin to commit suicide by catapulting themselves one after another against the side of the building, until the network gives in, replacing *Terrance and Phillip* with reruns of Suzanne Somers in *She's the Sheriff.*

This episode, very much like the *Simpsons* episode "Itchy & Scratchy & Marge" (December 20, 1990), lampoons parents and other groups who would protest against programs such as *South Park* itself, suggesting that these protests, if successful, can only lead to the most insipid of programming. *Terrance and Phillip,* of course, is ultimately restored to the air and goes on to play a prominent role in several additional episodes, especially the notorious "Terrance and Phillip in Not without My Anus," as well as the later "Terrance and Phillip: Behind the Blow" (July 18, 2001), which, among other things, refers to the controversy over the "Not without My Anus" episode. This episode, incidentally, also takes a shot at cultural snobs when it shows Phillip performing in *Hamlet,* which turns out to look just as ridiculous as *Terrance and Phillip* itself. Terrance and Phillip also play a central role in the theatrical film *South Park: Bigger, Longer, & Uncut* (1999), in which the controversy over a theatrical film based on their program leads to all-out war between the United States and Canada—and nearly to the apocalyptic destruction of the entire earth.

The *South Park* theatrical film, by the way, is very much a musical—and even garnered an Academy Award nomination for best original song. Since that point, music, mostly composed by Parker, has become an increasingly important part of the television series as well. Cartman's performances join Chef's as the centerpieces of this phenomenon, and several episodes show the mean-spirited fat boy attempting to break into show business, thus repeating an established cartoon motif that goes all the way back to *The Flintstones.* In "Something You Can Do with Your Finger" (July 12, 2000), for example, Cartman cons the other boys into joining him to create a boy band, "Fingerbang," which he hopes will finally bring him the wealth he constantly seeks. The boys don't succeed in getting rich, of course, though the episode is quite successful in lampooning the entire boy-band phenomenon.

Cartman achieves his greatest commercial musical success in the episode "Christian Rock Hard" (October 29, 2003), where he attempts to make money by becoming a Christian rock singer. As Cartman himself explains the project, "It's the easiest, crappiest music in the world, right? If we just play songs about how much we love Jesus, all the Christians will buy our crap!" He bets the other boys that his Christian rock band can get a platinum album before their regular rock band, then seemingly succeeds, producing top-selling Christian rock songs by ripping off regular rock songs, replacing words like "baby" and "honey" with "Jesus." In a typical *South Park* example of mock racial stereotyping, Cartman is aided in his quest by the fact that he recruits Token to play bass guitar, which he does brilliantly, thanks to his great natural rhythm, even though he has never played before. It doesn't help, however, that Cartman also recruits the always-honest Butters, who keeps explaining to people that they aren't really Christians, but are just pretending to be. Kyle, Stan, and Kenny, meanwhile, are slowed down when they are arrested by the FBI for downloading music from the Internet (and thus making rich rock stars slightly less rich). Afraid that their own music will also be downloaded free from the Internet, depriving them of income, the boys go on strike and refuse to play. In the meantime, Cartman scores a big hit with his album *Faith+1*, despite the fact that its sometimes-suggestive lyrics indicate that Cartman really, really loves Jesus. Chastened, Stan and Kyle decide to resume playing, just for the music, money or no money—though they are unable to convince *Metallica*, Britney Spears, and other rock stars to join them. In the end, however, Cartman loses his bet because the Christian rock industry doesn't give out gold and platinum albums, but only gold, frankincense, and myrrh albums, echoing the gifts of the three magi to the infant Christ in the New Testament. Enraged, Cartman flies into an obscene tirade against Christian music and even Christ himself, ruining his burgeoning music career.

This episode is highly typical of *South Park* in that the show's attempt to shock middle-class sensibilities can perhaps best be seen in its consistently irreverent, even openly blasphemous attitude toward religion. Much of the satire of religion in *South Park* focuses on the fact that Jesus Christ (apparently the "real" Christ) is a resident of the town, where he spreads his message by hosting his own local cable access show. The soft-spoken Jesus is typically ignored by the general public, though he does occasionally come to the fore, as when, in the episode "Are You There God? It's Me, Jesus" (December 29, 1999), the world's millennial anticipation focuses on the town of South Park with the expectation that Jesus and his father might perhaps perform some sort of spectacular miracle to celebrate the coming of the new millennium. "Hundreds, if not thousands" of spectators gather outside Jesus' modest house, which looks pretty much the same as all of the other houses in South Park (except Kenny's, which is even more modest). As they wait anxiously for Jesus to appear, a television news reporter explains during his live coverage of the event, "If Jesus comes out of his house and is not scared by his shadow, it means the next thousand years will be filled with peace and love."

Jesus does appear, but finds that the crowd expects more from him than he can provide. The *South Park* Jesus seems seriously lacking in superhuman powers, as when he loses a magic contest to illusionist David Blaine in "The Super Best Friends" (July 4, 2001). Jesus does, however, manage to convince an aging Rod Stewart to perform a concert in Las Vegas, then arranges for the entire crowd from South Park to be flown to Vegas for the event. Unfortunately, Stewart is so ancient that he is unable to do much more than drool, moan, and poop his pants, so the concert is a bust, causing the crowd to riot and construct a cross on which to crucify Jesus once again. Luckily, Jesus' reluctant father finally appears to save the day, though the crowd is a bit taken aback to discover that God is a small, fat, weird-looking monkey-like creature with an ugly green reptilian head. Nevertheless, they are cheered when God agrees to answer any question posed to him by the crowd.

Unfortunately, the episode's hilarious subplot kicks in just as the people are about to be granted this gem of godly wisdom. In turns out that Cartman has contracted an intestinal virus that causes anal bleeding, which he interprets as his first menstrual period, then brags to the other boys that he has now reached puberty. Given his hermaphroditic mother, perhaps it is not surprising that Cartman is a bit confused about gender, but even the usually worldly Kenny believes this bit of misinformation, gleefully announcing that he, too, has reached puberty after he also contracts the virus. Kyle doesn't contract the virus, but decides to lie, claiming that he also has had his period, leaving lonely Stan believing he is the only one of the boys not to have reached manhood. Thus, when God offers to answer a question at the end of the episode, Stan emerges from the crowd and demands to know why he hasn't gotten his period. God assures him that boys don't have periods and explains the misunderstanding. He then announces that he will answer another question in 2,000 years, then disappears, returning to heaven. As the episode closes, the enraged crowd sets upon poor Stan for using up their divine question.

Some of the most outrageous religious satire in *South Park* occurs in the two-part sequence "Do the Handicapped Go to Hell?" (July 19, 2000) and "Probably" (July 26, 2000). In the first episode, the boys (except Kyle, of course) misbehave in church, causing the angry Father Maxi to deliver a graphic sermon about the horrors of hell. Absolutely terrified, the boys resolve to change their ways—though we have meanwhile been treated to a glimpse of hell in which Satan hosts a festive luau for the inhabitants there, who include such celebrities as George Burns, Frank Sinatra, Dean Martin, Michael Landon, Walter Matthau (who had died only 18 days before the episode aired), Tiny Tim, and even film reviewer Gene Siskel. Numerous figures from the world of politics are represented as well, including Mao Zedong, Adolf Hitler, Princess Diana, President John F. Kennedy, and even Kennedy's son, John Jr. All of these celebrities are easily recognizable, because, as is often the case in *South Park*, their heads are represented by actual photographs of them, placed atop animated *South Park*–style bodies. However, the most important political figure in the episode is Iraqi President Saddam Hussein, who turns out (as viewers learned in the *South Park* feature film a year earlier) to have formerly been the abusive gay lover of Satan. Satan himself is depicted as a basically kind and sensitive soul, tormented by the fact that he finds the evil Saddam so sexually irresistible.

Meanwhile, back in South Park, the boys attend a Sunday-school class in which a nun attempts to explain to them about eating the body and drinking the blood of Christ in the sacrament of communion, causing them to stare in disbelief, finally leading Cartman to declare "Oh, come on now, this is just getting silly." To make matters worse, they are told that they must confess all their sins—which amount to a considerable list, especially in the case of Cartman, whose vast array of transgressions includes placing a piece of ham between his butt cheeks before feeding it to Father Maxi in a sandwich and urinating in some holy water with which the priest sprinkled his own forehead to bless himself for the next week. Hearing this list, the furious Father Maxi breaks through the screen separating him from Cartman and tries to strangle the boy, who concludes that he has been attacked by the angry hand of God for his crimes.

Cartman's report of this incident makes him, Kenny, and Stan even more concerned about going to hell, to the point that they manage also to terrify Kyle, especially after they convince him that, as a Jew, he is bound to go to hell after he dies—an interpretation that the priest endorses. As Father Maxi puts it, "If you don't go to hell for crucifying the Savior, then what the hell do you go to hell for?" The boys also become concerned that Timmy will go to hell because he can't say anything except his name, and therefore cannot go to confession. To top off the first episode, Cartman, Stan, and Kenny attempt to baptize Timmy, Kyle, and Ike with a garden hose, then rush back down to the church for another confession, only to discover the priest having sex in the confession booth with Mrs. Donovan, one of his parishioners, whom the priest immediately declares a temptress from hell.

Shocked, the boys decide in the second episode that the Catholic church is too corrupt to save them from hell. Instead, Cartman becomes a hellfire-and-brimstone preacher and starts his own revivalist, child-centered church. The town's children, now all terrified of hell, flock to the new church and become so devoted to it that they stop attending school. However, in what can be taken as a comment on evangelists in general, especially the television evangelists on whom Cartman models his histrionic performances, Cartman has not really found religion, but is simply using his church as another in his long line of schemes to make money. The scheme collapses, though, when Jesus himself comes to the church and urges the children to forsake the church; he then sends Cartman to Mexico (apparently considered to be worse than hell) as punishment. In hell, Satan, still unable to choose between Saddam and his new, wimpy nice-guy lover Chris (Dian Bachar), finally decides (on the advice of God) that he needs to go it alone until he can learn to be comfortable with himself. Meanwhile, to get Saddam off his back, he manages to convince God to let Saddam into heaven, which otherwise turns out to be open only to Mormons. This does not, however, mean that God is a Mormon. In fact, we learn in the episode that God is actually a Buddhist.

Mormons, incidentally, frequently figure in *South Park*, which typically makes the point that Mormons are, as a whole, good people, even though their religion is based on false premises. The most extensive treatment of Mormonism in *South Park* occurs in the episode "All About the Mormons?" (November 19, 2003). Here a Mormon family moves to South Park and proves to be so ultra-nice that the Marshes are nearly won over to Mormonism. However, the more Stan learns about the history of Mormonism, the more it is clear to him that the religion is preposterous, based on forgeries and lies. He manages to win his family away from the seductions of Mormon niceness, though the Mormon family continues its nice ways.

South Park's ongoing satire of the Catholic Church continues in "Red Hot Catholic Love" (July 3, 2002), which responds to the ongoing public revelations of the high incidence of sexual abuse (especially of young boys) among Catholic priests—and to the Church's attempts to hide evidence of that phenomenon, protecting the priests, rather than the children. In this episode, it turns out that Father Maxi is apparently the *only* Catholic priest in the world who doesn't sexually abuse young boys. Meanwhile, revelations about this phenomenon cause all of the Catholic parents of South Park to turn away from the Church and to declare themselves atheists. In keeping with the tendency in *South Park* to satirize both sides of any given issue, these atheists are represented as ridiculous figures. Meanwhile, Father Maxi carries his fight against sexual misconduct all the way to the Vatican, where it turns out that secret Church documents actually *require* priests to sexually molest young boys. Indeed, the Vatican itself turns out to be the seat of a collection of bizarre high Catholic officials who worship a giant spider instead of God and who are completely out of touch with the outside world. Maxi manages to get the document changed (destroying the Vatican in the process) and to pave the way for a new era of Catholicism, though the principal message in this episode (much like the show's judgment about Mormons) is that Catholics are mostly good decent people and that Catholicism itself is not necessarily bad, even if it has long been ruled by bad men enforcing bad policies.

Speaking of bad Catholics (at least according to *South Park*), one of the show's most vicious personal satires occurs in the episode "The Passion of the Jew" (March 31, 2004), which lambastes both the 2004 film *The Passion of the Christ* and its maker, Mel Gibson. Here, Kyle's viewing of the film (which has in fact been widely criticized as anti-Semitic) makes him feel guilty to be a Jew. Stan and Kenny, however, are merely revolted. Declaring that the movie is nothing more than a disgusting snuff film, they demand their money back. Refused, they head for Hollywood to demand a refund from Gibson himself. Cartman, of course, is already anti-Semitic, if largely only to irritate Kyle, so the film only inflames his existing tendencies. Cartman had already dressed as Hitler for Halloween in the first-season episode "Pink Eye" (October 29, 1997); here he dons a Nazi uniform and becomes the leader of a local group dedicated to exterminating all Jews. Cartman's efforts, though, are thwarted by Gibson himself. It turns out that the actor-director is an insane, sadomasochistic freak. When Stan and Kenny grab their $18 and head for home, he chases them all the way back to South Park, where he makes such a preposterous spectacle of himself that his credibility and his film's popularity are ruined once and for all, causing Cartman's group to collapse.

Such antics clearly set *South Park* apart from such wholesome predecessors in the cartoon tradition as *The Flintstones*, though the series (which engages in parodies of and dialogues with a variety of works of popular culture, much like *The Simpsons*) frequently nods to its cartoon predecessors. In the very first episode, for example, the aliens use the probe in Cartman's ass to send signals that cause him to start dancing and singing "I Love to Singa," a song by Harold Arlen and E. Y. Harburg that formed the basis of a classic Warner Brothers *Merrie Melodies* cartoon short of that title in 1936. *South Park* is, in fact, consistently conscious of its relationship with the cartoon tradition, even if that relationship is usually subversive. Sometimes, as with the spoof of *Hamlet* in "Terrance and Phillip: Behind the Blow," *South Park* even engages in dialogue with high culture. In "Scott Tenorman Must Die" (July 11, 2001), one of the most outrageous of all *South Park* episodes, Cartman is humiliated by an older boy, Scott

Tenorman, and gets revenge by arranging it so that the boy's parents will be killed. Cartman then steals the bodies and gets his revenge in a way that echoes predecessors such as *The Texas Chainsaw Massacre 2*, but most directly recalls Shakespeare's *Titus Andronicus*, perhaps filtered through Julie Taymor's 1999 film adaptation of that play, *Titus*. Cartman, having failed in his efforts to train a pony to bite off Scott Tenorman's penis, uses the flesh of the deceased Tenorman parents to make chili, which he then tricks Scott into eating. Yet this horrifying episode, which is Cartman's darkest moment in the series, ends as Cartman's head gleefully bursts through a target-like design of concentric circles on the screen, announcing "That's all, folks!" in the manner of Porky Pig in the old *Looney Tunes* cartoons, perhaps reminding us that many such classic cartoons had a dark side in their own right.

One of the most hilarious (if somewhat troubling) riffs on such classic cartoons in *South Park* occurs in the episode "Osama Bin Laden Has Farty Pants" (November 7, 2001). Here, the boys are inadvertently transported to Afghanistan, where they run afoul of bin Laden and his al Qaeda guerrillas. Then, as bin Laden himself murderously pursues Cartman, we are treated to an extended sequence in which the al Qaeda leader does his best imitation of Elmer Fudd, while Cartman imitates Bugs Bunny. That this parody of the classic Bugs Bunny chase sequences also includes an openly racist portrayal of bin Laden as a ludicrous, bumbling, dim-witted camel-lover with a tiny penis (and ends with bin Laden being bloodily and spectacularly killed) is not surprising in a show that consistently mocks the whole notion of political correctness. In this case, however, the racist caricature of bin Laden, which foreshadows similar depictions of Arabs and Muslims in the 2004 Parker and Stone film *Team America: World Police*, enriches the dialogue between *South Park* and *Looney Tunes* by reminding us of the fact that classic characters such as Bugs Bunny were used in numerous highly racist cartoons in the 1930s and 1940s, especially in pro-American, anti-German, and, especially, anti-Japanese cartoons during World War II. In any case, this episode ends on an uncharacteristically conformist note, even if it espouses a particularly unsentimental version of patriotism. Having established that Afghan children probably have good reason to hate the United States, the American kids still decide to root for the American side, simply because it is "our team"—just as they also root for the Denver Broncos. Indeed, young Stan even declares, echoing the conformist rhetoric of "America, love it or leave it," that anyone who doesn't want to root for his own team should "get the hell out of the stadium!"

The episode "Simpsons Already Did It" (June 26, 2002) both acknowledges an important predecessor and mimics the style of that predecessor, addressing the frustration of Parker and Stone that so many of the ideas they have come up with over the years turn out already to have been used on *The Simpsons*. Here, Butters's frustration at being constantly bullied by almost everyone causes him to attempt to transform himself into a dangerous supervillain, Professor Chaos. Unfortunately, he continually finds that all of his ideas for wreaking havoc in South Park have already been used on the *Simpsons*. Butters becomes so obsessed with *The Simpsons* that he begins to perceive those around him as *Simpsons*-style characters, drawn in the distinctive *Simpsons* animation style. In the end, however, on the advice of Chef and others he comes to the very postmodern conclusion (as, presumably do Parker and Stone) that he need not worry about being scooped by *The Simpsons*, because at this point every idea has already been used somewhere and that the best we can hope for is to create inventive pastiches of our predecessors.

This switch in animation style calls attention to the fact that, if much of the humorous impact of *South Park* clearly derives from the fact that its content and language violate so many of the conventions of the cartoon genre, the same might also be said for the show's distinctive animation style, which is so crude as to itself constitute a running joke. The initial episode described above was animated by Parker and Stone using stop-action photography of construction cutouts. Subsequent episodes were animated by computer, mimicking the same style, though the animation has become slightly less crude over the years. Among other things, this computer animation allows episodes of the show to be produced very quickly, allowing it to address extremely current issues. For example, the episode "Best Friends Forever" (March 30, 2005), which won *South Park* its first Emmy Award, showed the oft-killed Kenny being kept alive with a feeding tube, addressing the issue of whether those in his extreme condition should simply be allowed to die in peace. This issue was, at the time, especially in the public eye because of the Terri Schiavo case, and this episode ironically aired 12 hours before Schiavo was finally allowed to die. Clearly, the short response time of *South Park* also has potential drawbacks. "Two Days before the Day after Tomorrow" (October 19, 2005) spoofs the 2004 Roland Emmerich film *The Day after Tomorrow*—precisely the kind of blockbuster that the series often makes light of. But it also makes light of the tragic flooding of New Orleans due to Hurricane Katrina at the end of August 2005, still then a bit too recent to be funny. After all, as *South Park* itself concluded in the episode "Jared has Aides" (March 6, 2002), tragedies can't be effectively joked about until approximately 22.3 years after they occur.

In addition, especially in later seasons, *South Park* occasionally switches momentarily into other styles of animation, as if to make the point that the show could employ a more sophisticated style if Parker and Stone so chose. Probably the best example of animation style-switching in *South Park* occurs in the episode "Good Times with Weapons" (March 17, 2004). The boys acquire some ninja-style weapons at a local fair, then pretend to be superpowered warriors. The animation style switches to Japanese animé, and sometimes even to widescreen, to reflect what the boys are imagining— though their imaginations ultimately get away from them, causing Kenny to hurl a throwing star that lodges in the eye of poor Butters, who is pretending to battle them as Professor Chaos. Cartman, meanwhile, starts to believe he has the power of invisibility, which causes him to display himself nude in front of the entire town. The wounded Butters suffers a series of other abuses as well, but the punch line of the episode (another *South Park* critique of misguided censorship) occurs when it turns out that the townspeople are far more shocked and concerned about Cartman's nudity than Butters's injury. As Stan sums it up, "I guess parents don't give a crap about violence if there are sex things to worry about."

Of course, *South Park* addresses a wide variety of political issues in addition to its ongoing concern with the prudery of American censorship. Many episodes, in fact, are devoted to specific political issues—or at least to satires of the groups who espouse specific points of view on those issues. "Rainforest Schmainforest" (April 7, 1999) satirizes environmental activists dedicated to the salvation of the rainforest. Here, the boys get into trouble at school and are forced, as punishment, to join a traveling choir group called "Getting Gay with Kids," which is about to embark on a tour of Central America to raise awareness about the plight of the rainforest there. The group travels to Costa Rica to help save its rainforest, but they discover once they arrive that the rainforest is a horrid place whose products are mostly harmful to mankind. After encounters in the forest with dangerous plants and animals, violent weather, leftist guerrillas, and a tribe of savage pygmies, even Miss Stevens, the enthusiastic choir teacher (voiced by Jennifer Aniston), becomes an advocate for the destruction of the rainforest by the end of the episode, especially after she and the kids (their guide having been killed by a snake) are all saved by a kindly construction crew working to clear the rainforest with bulldozers.

"Rainforest Schmainforest" is unusual for *South Park* in that it does not take place in Colorado. It is also unusual among early episodes in that Kenny survives the episode. He is killed by a lightning strike, but then revived by a girl in the choir who has developed a crush on him. It is, however, typical of the depiction in *South Park* of political activists as self-righteous, self-serving hypocrites who generally have no real understanding of the issues they are promoting. That the majority of these activists tend to be associated with political views to the left of center has led many to associate *South Park* with conservative political views. This view is summed up in Brian Anderson's book *South Park Conservatives: The Revolt Against Liberal Media Bias* (Washington, D.C.: Regnery Publishing, 2005), which argues that *South Park* is part of a growing revolt against what Anderson sees as the traditionally liberal bias of the media. For him, *South Park* is an attempt to convey the conservative agenda (or at least to debunk the liberal agenda) for a new generation of young, hip, Republicans-to-be.

Yet the political viewpoint of *South Park* is not easy to pin down. Other episodes seem to lampoon the conservative agenda, as in the apparent rejection of gun culture in the episode "Volcano" (August 20, 1997), where gun-loving rednecks are shown to be bloodthirsty killers who revel in the deaths of innocent and defenseless animals. Similarly, "A Ladder to Heaven" (November 6, 2002) ridicules the Bush administration's rationale for invading Iraq, several months before that invasion would undermine its own rationale by finding that there were no weapons of mass destruction in Iraq. This episode also lampoons country music star Alan Jackson for attempting to cash in on sentiments surrounding the 9/11 bombings to increase the sales of his music. In the episode, reports that there are weapons of mass destruction in heaven, built by Saddam Hussein after he was sent there in the episode "Probably," cause the United States to consider bombing heaven. When President George W. Bush reports on the situation to the U.N., he is asked whether he is high or just incredibly stupid. He assures them that he isn't high. Indeed, Bush is consistently depicted in *South Park* as a bumbling idiot, much as he had been in the short-lived Parker and Stone live-action series from 2001, *That's My Bush*. On the other hand, a final scene in the episode shows that Saddam is, in fact, building weapons of mass destruction in heaven, right under the nose of a God who is apparently too dim-witted to realize what is going on.

Even an episode such as "Rainforest Schmainforest," however clear it might be in its rejection of radical environmentalism, does not clearly support the conservative alternative. For one thing, the critique of environmentalism in the episode is not well thought out and ignores the crucial role played by the rainforest in the global ecology. *South Park* is satire, not political manifesto. Moreover, Miss Stevens's sudden antipathy to the rainforest (complete with a stream of bleeped-out expletives) is clearly an irrational response to her recent traumas in the forest, making her new antienvironmentalist stance appear at least as ridiculous as her former proforest stance. Meanwhile, in some ways, the most seemingly reasonable political statements of the episode are actually made by the leader of the leftist guerrillas whom the choir meets in the rainforest. Unlike the choir, which is playing at politics, these guerrillas are engaged in a real-world, life-and-death political struggle, and their leader has no patience with the political posing of the choir. He thus excoriates Miss Stevens as a typical example of the rich, white Americans who "waste food, oil, and everything else because you're so rich, and then you tell the rest of the world to save the rainforest because you like its pretty flowers."

In other words, there is considerable reason from the content of the episode itself to interpret the rejection of environmental activism in "Rainforest Schmainforest" as coming from a radical leftist perspective rather than a conservative perspective. This is not to say that the real political agenda of *South Park* comes from the far left. For example, a similar critique of environmentalist activism in "Terrance and Phillip: Behind the Blow" (July 18, 2001) allows much more room for interpretation as supporting a conservative agenda. Here, environmentalists are depicted as sinister and dangerous—and as wrongly blaming all the world's woes on Republicans. But then Republicans are not really depicted positively in this or any other episode, even if they may come in for a bit less heat than do their critics.

Clearly, the politics of *South Park* cannot easily be pigeonholed in terms of a simple liberal vs. conservative opposition. In fact, the show quite frequently lampoons both sides of any given issue. For example, it features prominent gay characters in a number of episodes, often in positive ways, though (refusing to acknowledge sacred cows of any kind) it also has fun at the expense of these characters and openly mocks the notion that gays or any other minority are above criticism simply because of their minority status. Thus, in "The Death Camp of Tolerance" (November 20, 2002), the quest for "tolerance" of minorities gets out of hand (suggesting that the same thing has happened in the real world), and anyone criticizing any member of any minority is sent to a Nazi-like concentration camp for retraining.

In "Die, Hippie, Die" (March 16, 2005), a huge hippie music festival threatens to make South Park the hippie capital of the world. At first, the local authorities welcome the newcomers, even jailing Cartman (who has hated hippies all his life) when he attempts to drive them away. But, when things get out of hand, they have to release Cartman and ask his help in ridding the town of hippies. In a sequence that pastiches the film

Armageddon (1998), Cartman succeeds in averting disaster, and South Park returns to normal. In this episode, the criticisms of capitalism spouted by the hippies are so clichéd that they appear silly, even if accurate. At the same time, Cartman's paranoid horror of the hippies is ridiculous as well, so both sides end up being skewered.

Perhaps the classic case of such two-sided lampooning in *South Park* occurs in the episode "I'm a Little Bit Country" (April 9, 2003), which satirizes both the supporters and the opponents of the then-recent U.S. invasion of Iraq. Here, the town of South Park is virtually torn apart as the townspeople line up on opposite sides of this issue. Then, when the boys are assigned by Mr. Garrison to do a report on how the founding fathers might have felt about the invasion of Iraq, Cartman manages to travel back in time to 1776 to consult the founding fathers themselves. There, he learns that the notion of free speech is really just a ruse. In the midst of a debate over whether to go to war with England to fight for independence, Benjamin Franklin points out that allowing citizens to protest against war would mean that, "as a nation we could go to war with whomever we wished, but at the same time act like we didn't want to." Another debater agrees, noting that we could have "an entire nation founded on saying one thing and doing another!" Cartman then brings this message back to the present, healing the rift that had separated South Park's adults. Elaborating, he points out that the people who are for the war "need the protestors, because they make the country sound like it's made of sane, caring individuals." On the other hand, he concludes, the protestors need the warmongers, because "if our whole country was made up of nothing but soft, pussy protestors, we'd get taken down in a second." The adults buy his argument, then join together in song to celebrate their new solidarity. Revising the old Donnie and Marie theme song that gives the episode its title, they declare that there's no reason why the country-music-loving hawks can't get along with the rock-loving peaceniks, culminating in the final line that summarizes the convenience of the do-one-thing-say-another ethos of America, "Let a flag for hypocrisy fly high from every pole, cause we're a little bit country, and a little bit rock and roll!" Then, as if to back away from the potentially subversive implications of this conclusion, the townspeople suddenly forget about this issue and declare that what's really important is that this is the hundredth episode of *South Park*—which, in fact, it is.

What can be discerned about the politics of *South Park* is that the show is radically individualist and antiauthoritarian, consistently opposed to those of any political persuasion who would declare their view of the world as the only possible one. If any particular political philosophy comes close to that of *South Park*, it would be libertarianism, a philosophy that is itself difficult to place in terms of conventional left vs. right oppositions. Parker, in particular, has been quite vocal in his own espousal of libertarianism, which supports the maximization of individual freedoms and minimization of government interference in the lives of individuals. Libertarians typically oppose most government-sponsored social programs, though many have seen this aspect of libertarianism as problematic and harmful to the less fortunate. Libertarians also support unrestrained free-market capitalism, which many have seen as highly irresponsible given the historical evidence that such laissez faire capitalism doesn't work and inevitably leads to economic collapse.

In any case, *South Park*'s support of capitalist free enterprise is clear in episodes such as "Gnomes" (December 16, 1998), in which Harbucks Coffee Company, a large corporate chain of coffee bars and transparent stand-in for Starbucks, decides to open a franchise in South Park, which threatens to put the small mom-and-pop coffee store run by Tweek's parents out of business. This episode thus seems poised to critique the heartlessness of mighty corporations as they steamroller smaller businesses, homogenizing the American landscape and depriving towns like South Park of their once-distinctive local character. Mr. Tweek attempts to conscript the boys in his effort to mount a protest against Harbucks, leading to a public referendum on banning the corporation from operating in town. In the end, however, it turns out that Harbucks actually makes far better coffee than Mr. Tweek. Meanwhile, the boys conclude that big corporations are good because their superior resources are necessary for the development of useful products such as cars and computers. This lesson may be ironized a bit by the fact that the boys learn it from a group of gnomes engaged in a project to make money by stealing underpants and then converting them into profit through a means they have yet to figure out, but the procorporate (and antiactivist) message of the episode is nevertheless clear.

In "Something Wall-Mart This Way Comes" (November 3, 2004), the opening of a new Wall-Mart [sic] in South Park essentially destroys the local economy, driving virtually all the local stores out of business. The locals mobilize to protest against the Wall-Mart, but are unable to drive it out of town, especially as they themselves are unable to resist the store's low prices. Even burning it down doesn't stop the new megastore, which by this time has clearly evolved into a malevolent entity with a mind of its own, beyond the control of its corporate owners. Ultimately, Stan, Kyle, and Kenny are able to destroy the heart of the monster (Cartman, of course, sides with the Wall-Mart). That heart, however, turns out to be a mirror, making the point that the power of Wall-Mart comes from the consumers who shop there. Wall-Mart itself is thus freed of any culpability for the damage it does. Indeed, the episode stipulates that K-Mart, Wall-Mart, Target, and all other such stores are part of a single consumerist phenomenon. The real culprit, according to the episode, is all of us, who flock to these stores just to save a few dollars. As Randy Marsh puts it, "If we like our small-town charm more than the big corporate bullies, we all have to be willing to pay a little bit more." Consumer greed, though, is a powerful force. After the death of the Wall-Mart, all of the people of South Park begin shopping at Jim's Drugs, one of the few small local stores still in operation. As a result, Jim's itself grows into a new superstore, starting the entire cycle over again.

For a show that relies largely on surprising, if not shocking, audiences with its willingness to go into uncharted territory, *South Park* has remained amazingly fresh over the years, even if it has had to push the envelope farther and farther to continue to achieve the same effects. In the meantime, its success has spurred other programs to push the envelope as well, and it seems clear that a program such as *Family Guy*, whose more direct forebear is *The Simpsons*, would not be possible without the groundbreaking precedent provided by *South Park*. In addition, the early years of the twenty-first century have seen a number of new programs that seem overtly designed to attract audiences by flouting the conventions of television animation, much in the mode of *South Park*. The existence of these programs is testament to the importance of *South Park* as a cultural phenomenon; the fact that none of them has had the ongoing success of *South Park* shows just how inventive that program has managed to be for what is now nearly a decade on the air.

CHAPTER 7

Pushing the Animated Envelope

In the *South Park* episode "Clubhouses" (September 23, 1998), young Kyle is discouraged when his mother forces him to cease watching *Terrance and Phillip* and to switch instead to the seemingly more wholesome *Fat Abbot Show* (transparently based on Bill Cosby's *Fat Albert*). To his surprise, however, Kyle finds that the new show is, if anything, even raunchier than *Terrance and Phillip*. After viewing a nonstop stream of profanities on the part of the beefy Fat Abbot, Kyle exclaims with obvious glee, "Wow! Cartoons are getting really dirty!" To an extent, of course, Kyle is really talking about *South Park* itself, but it is also the case that numerous programs have followed the lead of *South Park* in this direction. Programs such as *Family Guy* and *American Dad* clearly draw much of their energy from venturing into unexplored territory, attracting audiences with the promise of transgressive content never before seen on network television, animated or otherwise. Meanwhile, the growth of cable networks has offered opportunities for programs such as Comedy Central's *Drawn Together*, Sci Fi's *Tripping the Rift*, Spike-TV's *Stripperella*, and IFC's *Hopeless Pictures*, following in the footsteps of *South Park*, to push the animated envelope even farther. In addition, the Cartoon Network's late-night Adult Swim block, while not strictly prime time, has offered a number of opportunities for experimentation with new kinds of animated programming that will probably influence the prime-time animated programs of the future. It has also given new life to several animated programs that previously failed to find an audience on other networks.

Drawn Together began broadcasting with an abbreviated eight-episode season in the fall of 2004. Typically scheduled to run immediately after *South Park*, the program is clearly designed to build upon the success of its illustrious predecessor by attracting much of the same audience. Though it builds heavily upon precedents in animated television, *Drawn Together* is specifically structured as a parody of "reality" television, primarily of MTV's pioneering *Real World*, plus a touch of the somewhat similar *Big Brother*. In the show, eight animated characters from very different cartoon universes are drawn together into a single house, where they must all learn to coexist, despite their very different backgrounds, personalities, and animation styles. These characters include Princess Clara (voiced by Tara Strong), a generic fairytale princess from the Disney universe in the mold of Sleeping Beauty. Princess Clara is beautiful and musically talented, but bigoted and hopelessly naïve about sex. Her counterpart from the other side of the cartoon tracks is Foxxy Love (Cree Summer), described in the show's intro as "a mystery-solving musician with a sweet ass." The African American Foxxy is a streetwise ghetto girl who wears a long tale and ears for a hat that identify her point of reference as Hanna-Barbera's *Josie and the Pussycats*, whose Valerie Brown became, in 1970, the first regularly appearing African American cartoon character on American television. The third female character of the group is Toot Braunstein (Strong), an overweight black-and-white 1920s sex symbol in the vein of Betty Boop. Toot's monstrous appetite leads her to devour virtually everything in her path—and occasionally to expand to mammoth proportions as a result of her overeating.

The male characters are led by Captain Hero (Jess Hartnell), seemingly a macho superhero in the mold of superman, but one whose sexuality becomes increasingly ambiguous as the show proceeds, partly thanks to his growing friendship with the effeminate Xandir (Jack Plotnick), an openly gay adventurer reminiscent of any number of video game characters, especially Link from "The Legend of Zelda." The third male member of the cast is the crass Spanky Ham (Adam Carolla), an incredibly uncouth "Internet download" given to openly masturbating, urinating, and defecating whenever and wherever the mood strikes him. He is also a practical joker and con artist, perfectly happy to exploit the other members of the cast for his own personal gain. The final two members of the cast are of indeterminate gender. One is Ling Ling (Abbey McBride), a "sociopathic Asian trading card battle monster," modeled on the Pikachu character from the Pokemon universe. The other is Wooldoor Sockbat (James Arnold Taylor), a "fucking annoying wacky whatchamacallit," apparently derived from the children's cartoon character SpongeBob SquarePants, but with a touch of extreme animation reminiscent of series such as *Ren and Stimpy*.

Each episode of *Drawn Together* features segments of main narrative interspersed with confessional interviews in which individual characters give their personal points of view on the action, a structure derived directly from *Real World*. In addition to the comic incongruity derived from the interaction among such completely different cartoon characters, *Drawn Together* relies heavily on sexual and scatological humor for its effects. In "Dirty Pranking Number 2" (December 8, 2004), for example, the entire episode revolves around Spanky's favorite practical joke: ordering pizza, then defecating on it and complaining to the delivery person that he didn't order the pizza "with sausage." Extreme irreverence is also a key element of the program. Thus, in "Clara's Dirty Little Secret" (November 3, 2004), the title refers to the fact that Clara's vagina has been turned into a horrible tentacled monster due to a curse from her wicked stepmother. In addition, a spiteful Toot convinces Clara that she is pregnant from kissing Foxxy. In her confessional interview, Foxxy comments on this development: "Poor pitiful Clara. So incredibly gullible she'll believe anything you tell her." To illustrate the extremes of nonsense that Clara is willing to swallow, the camera then cuts to Clara talking to Wooldoor, who is dressed as a priest. Clara then responds to what Wooldoor has been telling her: "He died on the cross for our sins you say. Yeah, I can see that."

Drawn Together also derives considerable humor from its send-up of the reality-show genre, moving beyond *Real World* and *Big Brother* to include other programs as well. For example, "The One Wherein There Is a Big Twist, Part 1" (December 15, 2004), the cliffhanger conclusion to the first season, is primarily a parody of Donald Trump's *The Apprentice*. Here, Bucky Bucks (Chris Edgerly), a preposterous juvenile caricature of Trump (inflected through the cartoon character Richie Rich), puts the *Drawn Together* cast through their paces, with disastrous results. The *Drawn Together* house is destroyed and the characters find themselves on a helicopter about to crash in the jungle as the episode ends. Then, in part two of the episode (October 19, 2005), the opening episode of the second season, the copter crashes on a tropical island, where the characters are suddenly approached by an animated Jeff Probst, propelling them into the universe of the *Survivor* program.

Stripperella, which ran for a single 13-episode season that stretched from June 2003 to April 2004 on Spike-TV, resembles *Drawn Together* in that much of its comic effect derives from its parodic relation to specific cartoon predecessors, this time to the whole cartoon tradition of superheroes. It also parodies James Bond spy thrillers, somewhat in the mode of the *Austin Powers* films. *Stripperella* was created by Marvel comic-book legend Stan Lee (who also created such stalwart superheroes as Spiderman and the Fantastic Four), so it is very much an insider's parody of the superhero genre that serves more as a tribute than a mockery, despite the fact that the campy program is perfectly aware of the basic silliness of the whole superhero tradition.

The premise is simple: Shapely exotic dancer Exotica Jones (voiced by Pamela Anderson, whose 1996 film *Barb Wire*—itself based on a comic book—is a clear predecessor to the series) secretly doubles, for reasons never really explained, as Stripperella, a scantily clad crime-fighting super-hero. Though she is barely even disguised, no one seems to be able to recognize that Exotica is Stripperella, despite the fact that she is constantly being summoned via her vibrating belly ring away from her strip club to respond to various emergencies. Stripperella lacks genuine superpowers, but is a hero more in the Batman mold, battling an array of supervil-lains with the aid of her superb athletic ability and a variety of high-tech paraphernalia, though her gadgets are more reminiscent of Bond than of Batman. Also more like Bond than Batman, Stripperella is not a free agent, but works for a secret crime-fighting organization, under the leadership of one Chief Stroganoff (Maurice LaMarche), aided by two comically leer-ing geeky scientists, Hal and Bernard (Tom Kenny and Greg Proops), who develop Stripperella's various crime-fighting devices.

Stripperella includes extensive scenes of cartoon stripping in the Tender Loins Gentlemen's Club (their motto: "The Best Cervix in Town"), where Exotica and her fellow dancers work for the mild-mannered owner, Kevin Calhoun (Kenny). The most important of the other strippers in the club is Exotica's friend Persephone (Serena Irwin), who generally speaks with an accent, but whose accent inexplicably changes from one episode to the next. Professional wrestling impresario Vince McMahon also does a turn as Dirk McMahon, the somewhat shady owner of a rival club. The bulk of the show, however, is devoted to Stripperella's battles with a string of supervillains, ranging from the penny-pinching Cheapo (LaMarche), whose idea of a big heist is to steal a gem of cubic zirconium worth $300, to the evil (but ugly) cybervillain Queen Clitoris (Irwin), who uses her computer skills to wreak havoc in society—and to help her abduct the handsome Armando (voiced by romance novel cover model Fabio Lanzoni), the world's greatest lover.

Stripperella has its amusing moments, as when both Anderson and boy-friend Kid Rock appear as themselves in an episode with the Bondian title

"You Only Lick Twice" (July 24, 2003). Responding to Exotica's suggestion that some people think she looks like Pam, Kid Rock responds that he thinks Pam looks like Stripperella instead—and that Pam should play Stripperella if they ever make a TV show about the latter's exploits. Episodes are also occasionally spiced with allusive gags in the mode of *The Simpsons* or *Family Guy*. Thus, in "You Only Lick Twice," Chief Stroganoff calls in an air strike on the island of the evil Queen Clitoris, ending as a nuclear bomb is dropped with a cowboy riding it like a bronco in reference to the famous scene from Stanley Kubrick's classic 1964 film, *Dr. Strangelove or: How I Learned to Stop Worrying and Love the Bomb*, in which Major T. J. "King" Kong (Slim Pickens) drops from a plane riding a bomb like a wild bronco. Similarly, "Pushy Galore," the name of the villain in "Everybody Loves Pushy" (July 10, 2003) echoes that of Bond girl Pussy Galore in the 1964 film *Goldfinger*. Meanwhile, when Stripperella invades the fashion knockoff factory of Galore (Jill Talley) in this episode, we find that the facility echoes the candy factory of *Willy Wonka and the Chocolate Factory*, complete with singing sweatshop workers who resemble the Oompa Loompas of the film. All in all, however, *Stripperella*'s sometimes amusing but virtually nonstop barrage of double entendre ultimately wears thin; it was pretty much a one-joke show that was probably fated for a short run from the very beginning, something an update in the look of the show and of Stripperella herself midway through the one and only season couldn't change.

Tripping the Rift is just as risqué as *Stripperella*, but has other resources that make it a more flexible show. It also relies significantly on parodies of predecessors, this time with a focus on its forebears in the science fiction genre. It focuses on the crew of the starship *Jupiter 42*, which is controlled by an artificial intelligence named Spaceship Bob (voiced by John Melendez) as they move about on the fringes of the law in an interstellar "Confederation" that lampoons the United Federation of Planets of *Star Trek*, complete with ships that look like the *Enterprise* and self-righteous Confederation functionaries who wear *Star Trek*–style uniforms. The Confederation is opposed by the evil Dark Clowns—led by the comically sinister Darph Bobo (Terrence Scammell). This opposition creates a sort of galactic Cold War rift between the two sides, though the "good" Confederation generally turns out not to be much better than the evil Clowns. The crew of the *Jupiter 42* essentially travel about in this rift (thus the title of the series) siding with neither the Confederation nor the Clowns.

The *Jupiter 42* is one of the fastest and most advanced ships in the galaxy. Unfortunately, Spaceship Bob suffers from agoraphobia (fear of wide open spaces), which is a serious handicap in outer space. The ship is captained by a self-serving, three-eyed, tentacled purple blob called Chode (voiced by Stephen Root), an unscrupulous schemer with a bad attitude. The pilot is T'Nuk (Gayle Garfinkle), a fat, ugly, four-legged, three-breasted female with an overactive libido, while Chode's libido is taken care of by Six of One (Carmen Electra), a supervoluptuous android designed specifically for sex. Modeled on the sexy Seven of Nine from *Star Trek: Voyager,* Six is also the most sensible and altruistic member of the crew; somewhat in the mode of the beautiful Jadzia Dax from *Star Trek: Deep Space Nine,* she is also highly intelligent and doubles as the ship's science officer. The ship's chief engineer is the depressive and outrageously gay robot Gus (Maurice LaMarche), vaguely reminiscent of C-3PO from the *Star Wars* films, with a dash of the robots from the film *I, Robot* (2004). The final crew member, though he seems to have no particular function on the ship, is the green space lizard Whip (Rick Jones), a teenage slacker who likes to use the ship's computer systems to play video games.

Employing a style of computer-generated animation that makes the series look rather like a video game itself, *Tripping the Rift* specializes in sophomoric sexual humor, much of it focused on the depiction of Six as a jiggling, bobbling collection of erotic body parts. However, the program sometimes aspires to more sophisticated forms of humor, especially in its parodic engagement with the science fiction tradition whose rules it so overtly violates (somewhat in the mode of its live-action predecessor, the *Lexx* series). One of the show's finest episodes, for example, is *2001 Space Idiocies* (April 15, 2004), an obvious reference to Stanley Kubrick's classic science fiction film *2001: A Space Odyssey* (1968), which the episode extensively lampoons. Most of the action of this episode occurs on the planet Kubrickia, where Darph Bobo has employed Chode to install a black monolith that helps Bobo, along with his white-armored gang of *Star Wars*–style storm troopers, to establish himself as the reigning god of the simple, primitive people who inhabit the planet. Chode completes the installation—to the music of Richard Strauss's *Also Sprach Zarathustra,* of course—then Bobo enslaves the Kubrickians, forcing them to work to mine their planet's substantial supplies of gold for Bobo's gain, at the same time disrupting their own smoothly functioning agrarian culture. In return Bobo offers the Kubrickians the benefits of modernization: "junk food, cigarettes, drugs, alcohol, violent entertainment, pollution-spewing factories, and gangsta rap."

Seeing the damage that has been done on Kubrickia, Six insists that the crew of the *Jupiter 42* try to set things right on the planet and finally manages to convince Chode to make the effort (though he hopes, at the same time, to score some gold for himself). Leaving Whip in charge of the ship (which he then uses, in classic teenager-left-home-alone fashion, to take a joyride and host a wild party), the others go down to the planet, where Six keeps the storm troopers busy sampling her sexual services while Chode works to appropriate the mined gold for himself. Chode, Gus, and T'Nuk are eventually captured by Bobo and locked in a dungeon, but Six manages to free them. They all make their way back to the ship, where Bobo, disguised as a Rasta disc jockey, has infiltrated the party and managed to upload a new control program into the *Jupiter 42*. This uncooperative program, which is called Hal, then takes over the ship and refuses to execute anyone's commands (including Bobo's), in the meantime insisting on calling everyone "Dave." Asked what it does, Hal simply explains, "I'm a computer program that refuses to do things." A horrified T'Nuk then responds, "Be careful. It sounds like it's from Microsoft!" But where it's from, of course, is *2001: A Space Odyssey,* in which the HAL 9000 computer attempted to take over spaceship *Discovery,* battling against Dave Bowman, the last surviving human crew member.

With Hal in control and refusing to act, the ship's orbit is decaying and they seem doomed to crash on planet Kubrickia. Then, at the last moment, a Confederation battleship, answering a distress call sent out by Six using the antennae built into her oversized breasts, swoops in, destroys the black monolith, and rescues the *Jupiter 42*. But the planet has hardly been liberated. The black monolith of the Dark Clowns is merely replaced by a Confederation white monolith, which displays a nonending series of advertisements, signaling that the "freed" people of the planet are now subject to a more subtle enslavement by consumer capitalism. Indeed, they are now forced to continue their slave labor in order to be able to afford to buy the various commodities that are now offered to them by a troop of Confederation salesmen that emerges from the monolith, though they are assured that their situation has been vastly improved because they are now "wage slaves" instead of "slave slaves."

Silliness aside, *2001 Space Idiocies* makes a number of potentially important points. First, its irreverent treatment of Kubrick's *2001: A Space Odyssey* (a truly great film that nevertheless may take itself a bit too seriously) is a quintessential example of its lampooning of the sometimes overly self-serious genre of science fiction. Second, its treatment of the exploitation of the Kubrickians by first the Dark Clowns and then the Confederation satirizes the history of our own planet. Bobo's reign on Kubrickia can be taken as a commentary on the colonial era in Earth history, when Western powers such as Great Britain and France directly imposed political control on most of the "underdeveloped" parts of the globe. The Confederation takeover then signals the coming of the postcolonial era of capitalist globalization, in which the U.S.-led West has practiced a more subtle form of economic exploitation in the formerly colonized world.

Of course, these two aspects of the episode tend to work against one another, with the parodic suggestion that science fiction should not be taken too seriously tending to undermine the satirical commentary on colonialism and neocolonial capitalism. On the other hand, by calling attention to its intertextual relationship with *2001: A Space Odyssey,* the episode points out that the film's narrative of alien intervention in the evolutionary development of the human race also serves as a displaced reenactment of the history of colonialism and its aftermath on our planet. The episode thus probably inadvertently calls attention to the film's blindness to its own underlying colonialist assumptions, a situation that is symptomatic of the unconscious depth to which these assumptions have been absorbed into the mindset of the West.

If *Tripping the Rift* may sometimes make points that are more serious than its surface appearance would imply, IFC's *Hopeless Pictures* is probably the most genuinely adult-oriented animated program to have appeared as a regular series on American television—even though it is animated in a crude style that makes it look as if it had been drawn by a child. Because of the HBO-like liberal standards of IFC, *Hopeless Pictures* can employ frank language, explicit sex scenes, and even full-frontal nudity, which takes it well beyond *Drawn Together* and *Tripping the Rift* in its presentation of such adult material. However, unlike those programs, *Hopeless Pictures* employs this risqué material as a realistic and natural (if often comical) part of its subject matter—rather than simply as a source of sophomoric humor. In the tradition of films such as Robert Altman's *The Player* (1992), *Hopeless Pictures* is a biting but hilarious satire of the Hollywood film industry and of the vain, venal, back-stabbing characters who inhabit it. It is, however, an oddly affectionate form of satire, produced by a group of Hollywood insiders who clearly enjoy the opportunity to take humorous jabs at their own industry (and the frustrations they have experienced within it), but still love the industry—and the movies it makes.

Hopeless Pictures was created by Bob Balaban, a character actor who has regularly appeared in Hollywood films since 1969—and whose uncle, Barney Balaban, was the president of Paramount Pictures from 1936 to 1964. Balaban (who has also directed and produced) thus approaches the subject matter of *Hopeless Pictures* as a knowledgeable insider. The show is also vaguely scripted by Balaban, but largely relies on the improvisational skills of its superb cast of voice actors. Central in this regard is veteran comic actor Michael McKean, who provides the voice for the central character of the series, Mel Wax, the head of struggling Indie studio Hopeless Pictures (named for Wax's parents, Hope and Les Wax). As Balaban puts it in his voiceover introduction to each episode, "his life is a mess, and you should be glad you're not him." Indeed, virtually the entire plot of *Hopeless Pictures* is given over to the unending stream of disasters that plague Wax, both personally and professionally.

Wax's parents are deceased, though their ghosts still haunt him, constantly complaining of his failure to live up to their expectations. His personal problems, at least in the brief nine-episode first season (first broadcast in the late summer and fall of 2005), center on his impending divorce from his fourth wife, Sandy (Lisa Kudrow), who, infuriated by his constant philandering, is determined to take him for everything he's worth in the divorce settlement. That, of course, doesn't stop him from continuing his philandering with various neighbors, actresses, and even with his own studio's head of development, Traci Mink (Jennifer Coolidge), a former Miss Bikini Car Wash and the ex-wife of the king of Bahrain.

None of Wax's relationships are meaningful, of course, and Mink herself sleeps around with various writers and directors, thus expressing her admiration for their creative talents. She also has phone sex with Dr. Harold Stein, the staff psychiatrist of Hopeless Pictures. In an inspired bit of intertextual casting, Stein is voiced by comedian Jonathan Katz, who had voiced the psychiatrist-protagonist of *Dr. Katz: Professional Therapist*. Dr. Stein is, in fact, reminiscent of the earlier Dr. Katz, though with an added Hollywood edge that often pushes his behavior beyond the bounds of professional ethics. In addition to having sex with patients, he is the author (under the transparent pseudonym of "Dr. Teins") of the book *Shrink Rapped: Confessions of a Hollywood Shrink,* which reveals the deepest secrets of many of his patients, including Wax, who frequently consults the therapist, but generally only on the phone while driving in his car, which is, in fact, his standard situation.

In episode seven, Wax, furious about the revelations of the secrets of "Mel Paraffin" in *Shrink Wrapped,* buys the movie rights to the book just so he can make sure it never it never makes it onto film. Then, however, Nora Ephron (voiced by herself) announces to Wax that she would like to write and direct the film version of the book. Wax, who has been trying throughout the first several episodes to convince Ephron to direct a film for his studio, in unable to resist the opportunity, despite the personal embarrassment it might bring him. Meanwhile, Wax continues to pursue other projects as well, always looking for that one big "tent-pole" film that will at least put his studio into the black and onto the map.

Programs such as *Drawn Together, Tripping the Rift,* and *Hopeless Pictures* take advantage of the more liberal standards of cable television to push the animation envelope, just as *South Park* had done before them. In many ways, however, the Adult Swim block is the true mover and shaker of adult-oriented television animation in the early twenty-first century. Animated television programming in general entered a new era with the addition of the Cartoon Network (CN) to the Turner Broadcasting cable empire in October 1992. Turner had purchased the Hanna-Barbera animation studio the year before, so CN was equipped with a large ready-made library of programming that provided its initial fare. Nevertheless, the prospects of broadcasting animated programs on a 24-hour-a-day schedule also offered opportunities to reach new kinds of audiences with new kinds of animated programming. In particular, it was obvious that the late-night audience for CN would differ substantially from the typical Saturday-morning cartoon audience, and CN quickly moved to begin to develop new programming that would appeal to young-adult and especially college-age viewers, rather than children. Programs such as *Space Ghost: Coast to Coast,* which brought back the hero of a classic Hanna-Barbera cartoon from the 1960s and 1980s, this time as a bumbling talk-show host, proved a big hit with late-night audiences. Meanwhile, programs such as *South Park* had demonstrated the rich possibilities offered by adult-oriented, cartoon bawdiness. So, in September 2001, CN established the Adult Swim late-night programming block, which quickly grew to a nightly event, providing what would become a crucial venue for the airing of risqué, adult-oriented comedy programs and animé-inflected and often ultra-violent action programs.

Adult Swim runs from 11 P.M. to 6 A.M. and so is not, strictly speaking, prime-time programming. However, much of its programming (*Family Guy* and *Futurama* have been particularly important core programs for the block) originated in prime time. But even these recycled programs have an element of the new, reaching audiences that they had not reached in their initial runs. In addition, Adult Swim's original programs have been among the most innovative animated programs on television, so the block has become a major source of potential new directions for prime-time animated programming. Animated Swim specializes in brief, 15-minute programs that in some ways exemplify the fragmentation of postmodernist culture. On the other hand, the brevity of these programs also allows an entire episode to be played out between commercial interruptions, so in some ways the brief programs of Adult Swim are less fragmented than more conventional network programming. The brevity of Adult Swim programs also contributes to the block's experimental feel: With such brief programs it possible to try more different things—and less disastrous if a given experiment falls flat.

Many Adult Swim programs employ innovative and unusual techniques of animation. In *Tom Goes to the Mayor*, for example, the main characters are represented by computer-processed black-and-white photographs of live actors. These photographs (sometimes enhanced with very limited movement) are then superimposed on a more conventional animated background, producing what are essentially a series of stills conveying the usually ridiculous story lines. The result can sometimes be rather interesting, though it seems unlikely that the style will catch on in many other programs.

Robot Chicken, another highly unusual Adult Swim series, employs stop-motion animation of a variety of models and action figures on miniature sets to string together sequences of essentially unrelated brief skits, most of which are outrageous spoofs of well-known moments from popular culture. As such, *Robot Chicken* is one of the most fragmented of all Adult Swim programs—though narrative coherence is seldom a major consideration for programming on the block. Meanwhile, the irreverent engagement with popular culture in *Robot Chicken* is just a slightly exaggerated version of the tendency of most Adult Swim programs, in good postmodernist fashion, to be constructed of bits and pieces borrowed from earlier works, especially earlier animated programs.

Ultimately, this engagement with other works from popular culture in *Robot Chicken* is significantly more interesting than its stop-motion animation style. Indeed, Adult Swim programs in general are probably more interesting for their innovative content than for their experimental advances in animation technology. *Space Ghost* draws its central characters from the earlier Hanna-Barbera children's cartoon series *The Space Ghost and Dino Boy* and even recycles a great deal of animated footage from that show, making for an extremely inexpensive production. However, *Space Ghost Coast to Coast* draws in significant ways on nonanimated programming as well. In particular, its format is a fairly accurate pastiche of the late-night talk show genre and includes most of the elements that audiences have come to expect from that genre—with the added defamiliarizing effect of casting the show with animated characters. *Space Ghost* (voiced by George Lowe) hosts the show, while most of the rest of the cast consists of villains he had battled in the earlier Hanna-Barbera series. These include the evil mantis—though Space Ghost thinks he is a locust—Zorak (voiced by C. Martin Croker), who leads the band and provides the host with a sidekick, playing an evil version of Paul Shaffer to Space Ghost's clueless version of David Letterman. The space pirate turned dim-witted adolescent space cat Brak (Andy Merrill) often hangs about the studio as well, sometimes doing Beavis and Butt-head imitations with a friend. The other key regular character is the director Moltar (also Croker), another old enemy of Space Ghost who despises his current boss. (Zorac and Moltar are both apparently being forced to work for Space Ghost as punishment for their former crimes.)

The antics of Space Ghost and his fellow cast members occasionally make for high hilarity. *Space Ghost* himself still has his muscular physique, which he delights in showing off to his guests, who usually aren't impressed, and he can still fly, become invisible, and shoot a variety of power rays from his armbands (usually to zap Zorak), but he is presented mostly as a comically self-absorbed buffoon. Zorak, Moltar, and Brak have their moments as well, and at its best the show can be quite interesting even apart from the interviews with actual human guests. For example, in "$20.01" (February 9, 1996), Space Ghost tries to replace Zorak and Moltar with an advanced "MOE 2000" computer, but his inept interviewing of guests Penn and Teller and Joel Hodgson (of *Mystery Science Theater 3000*) causes the computer to attempt to do away with him and take over the show, just as the HAL 9000 computer had attempted to replace what it saw as the unreliable human crew of spaceship *Discovery* in *2001: A Space Odyssey*. From that point, the show becomes an overt and highly amusing pastiche of *2001*, ending with its own version of the film's Starchild: a baby Zorak.

Space Ghost, in fact, references a variety of films and television programs, as when the show mimics a variety of Quinn Martin television productions from the 1970s (especially *Charlie's Angels*) in the episode "Jacksonville" (October 16, 1996). All in all, though, the send-up of the talk show genre is probably the most interesting aspect of *Space Ghost*. This is especially true of the show's engagement with *Late Night with David Letterman*. In the episode "Late Night" (October 23, 1996), for example, Space Ghost mimics the mannerisms of Letterman throughout the episode; he even claims to be from Indiana and calls upon his mother for a remote report from an ice planet, just as Letterman's mother reported from the 1994 Norway Winter Olympics on *Late Night*. This episode also features take-offs on of a number of classic Letterman bits, including a "Big 10 List," the reading of viewer mail, and "Stupid Zorak Tricks." While interviewing guest Janeane Garofalo, Space Ghost even reprises Letterman's notorious "Uma-Oprah" routine from the 1995 Academy Awards show. Meanwhile, the opening sequence of the show is changed to mimic that of *The Late Show*. In fact, scripted by former Letterman writers Steve O'Donnell and Spike Feresten, this episode features a number of inside, behind-the-scenes references to the Letterman show that most audience members would not even recognize.

As with any talk show, the guest interviews are the heart of *Space Ghost Coast to Coast*. In fact, while many guests were unknown or obscure, the show was able to get a fairly impressive (and varied) list of guests, even if it generally lacked huge A-list stars. Offbeat and hip guests like Garofalo, Judy Tenuta, Bobcat Goldthwaite, Timothy Leary, William Shatner, Weird Al Jankovic, Jim Carrey, Sandra Bernhard, Jon Stewart, the Ramones, David Byrne, Rob Zombie, Alice Cooper, Ben Stiller, Michael Moore, Carrot Top, Bob Odenkirk, and David Cross might be expected to appear on such a show, as might one-time luminaries such as Mark Hamill, Dr. Joyce Brothers, Jimmie Walker, Bill Mumy, Catherine Bach, and the casts of the *Batman* TV show and *Gilligan's Island*. There are also predictably a number of guests from the cartoon world, including Mike Judge, Matt Groening, and H. Jon Benjamin (from *Dr. Katz* and *Home Movies*). The talk-show world is represented as well, with such guests as Bill Carter (author of *The Late Shift*, a book on the battle between Letterman and Jay Leno to succeed Johnny Carson as host of the *Tonight Show*) and former Letterman writers Merrill Markoe, Feresten, and O'Donnell. In the episode "Fire Ant" (December 10, 1999), even rival talk-show host Conan O'Brien makes an appearance, as do some of the great figures from talk-show history, including Joe Franklin and Steve Allen, though alas a planned interview with Carson, the greatest figure from that history, falls through when Moltar fails to pick up the satellite feed because he is too busy watching reruns of *CHiPs* on his monitor.

Space Ghost also featured relatively incongruous appearances by such straitlaced figures as Donny Osmond, Pat Boone, Charlton Heston, and astronaut Buzz Aldrin. But then the whole idea of a one-time animated superhero playing host to live talk-show guests is in itself a bit strange. The guests (for obvious reasons) are not actually interviewed by Space Ghost but respond to questions posed by a human interviewer—apparently sometimes dressed in a Space Ghost costume. Their responses are then taped for display on the television screen on which they appear when seemingly interviewed by Space Ghost. The awkwardness of this process can sometimes be quite funny, not to mention the fact that the questions posed by Space Ghost on the actual show are not necessarily the ones the guest answered in the pre-interview, so that the answers sometimes seem entirely inappropriate to the question.

Despite its ostentatious silliness, *Space Ghost Coast to Coast* actually requires a certain amount of sophistication, and especially familiarity with television, on the part of its viewers. It even occasionally includes literary allusions. In "Sleeper" (July 28, 1995), for example, Zorak refuses to obey Space Ghost's commands, declaring, in the mode of the title character of Herman Melville's classic story "Bartelby the Scrivener," that "I would prefer not to." Surprisingly, Space Ghost catches the reference and in fact responds to Zorak, "You're not a scrivener. You're a locust." Indeed, while this literary allusion may seem a bit esoteric, "Bartleby" is widely taught in college literature classes, indicating the show's understanding that many of its viewers are college students. Space Ghost seems very much aware of its audience, and the show has a special relationship with its viewers, relying in a particularly extensive way on a hip audience that is in on its particular form of humor. Some episodes of the show are about nothing but the show itself (so that Space Ghost joins the list of programs lampooned by Space Ghost), as in "Woody Allen's Fall Project" (December 25, 1996), which consists entirely of a series of re-enactments of moments from earlier programs, this time with live actors (including Andy Merrill as Space Ghost) playing the roles of both the cartoon characters and the former guests.

The first episode of Space Ghost aired on the Cartoon Network on April 15, 1994. New episodes continued to be produced through the establishment of Adult Swim and then on into the fall of 2004, when the last episode aired on November 7, 2004 (for a total of 99 episodes). In addition to running for more than 10 years in its own right, Space Ghost spawned two spin-offs. From 1995 to 1998, Cartoon Planet aired original episodes on CN, featuring Space Ghost, Zorak, Moltar, and a then little-known Brak as they struggle to produce a cartoon show on the Cartoon Planet. More interesting was The Brak Show, which mimics the family sitcom format and thus enters into dialogue with a rich tradition of animated programs from The Flintstones to Family Guy.

After a pilot broadcast in December 2000, the program began regular broadcasting when Adult Swim went on the air in September 2001. In its early episodes, The Brak Show was clearly designed as a pastiche of 1950s sitcoms and was assembled out of bits and pieces that made reference to those programs, for example, featuring opening titles such as Leave It to Brak and Brak Knows Best, invoking specific predecessors. The dim-witted early-adolescent humanoid space cat Brak (still voiced by Andy Merrill) is a fairly original character who recalls a number of 1950s teenage characters, though Wally Cleaver may be his closest predecessor, even if his younger brother Sisto, whose appearances, until he is eaten by cannibals, are limited to walking across the screen while farting, has little in common with the Beaver. However, Brak's parents, simply known in the series as Mom and Dad (voiced by Marsha Crenshaw and George Lowe), seem to have more specific precedents. Dad, for example, looks human, except that he is tiny in size and speaks with a comically exaggerated Spanish accent that recalls

Desi Arnaz in the legendary *I Love Lucy* show. The apron-wearing Mom, meanwhile, recalls the stock housewife figure of the 1950s sitcom, such as June Cleaver or Donna Reed. Zorak (still voiced by C. Martin Croker) is also a regular, appearing as Brak's neighbor and bullying "friend," somewhat in the mode of Eddie Haskell from the *Leave It to Beaver* show, though Zorak, still a psychopathic sadist, is more evil than any of the characters from 1950s TV. Various science fiction elements—such as the presence of the neighbor Thundercleese, an anime-style killer robot—go well beyond the bounds of 1950s sitcoms as well, and as the show proceeded, it tended to stray from its roots, becoming more and more bizarre.

Vaguely similar in conception to *Space Ghost* (but funnier and more daring) is the series *Harvey Birdman: Attorney at Law*, created by Michael Ouweleen and Erik Richter. Like *Space Ghost*, *Harvey Birdman* spoofs a well-established television genre (in this case the courtroom drama), while recycling a second-string Hanna-Barbera cartoon superhero from the past. In the 1967–1968 series *Birdman and the Galaxy Trio* (canceled after only a short run because of pressure to reduce violence on TV), ordinary human Ray Randall is given superpowers by Ra, the god of the sun; he then fights evil using his ability to fly and to shoot solar ray beams from his fists, periodically recharging his powers with solar energy. In *Harvey Birdman: Attorney at Law*, the Birdman returns as a somewhat incompetent attorney who uses his questionable legal skills to defend various other Hanna-Barbera characters from the past when they run into legal difficulties of various kinds.

In the pilot episode of *Harvey Birdman*, entitled "Bannon Custody Case," Harvey represents Dr. Benton Quest against his "partner" Race Bannon for custody of young Jonny Quest and his pal Hadji, with lots of innuendo suggesting that Dr. Quest and Bannon may have been involved in a longtime homosexual liaison. It first aired in December 2000 and was rerun as part of Adult Swim's first night of programming. The series then ran intermittently over the next two years; its first "season" (comprising nine episodes) lasted until June 2003. The 11-episode second season then ran from January to November 2004. A third season began in July 2005, running through October, with each episode airing several times per week.

The premise of *Harvey Birdman* allows any number of former cartoon "stars" to make appearances on the program, usually in situations that are very different from the ones in which we are accustomed to seeing them. In the episode "Trio's Company" (April 18, 2004), for example, former Hanna-Barbera crime sleuth Inch High, Private Eye, keeps popping out of Harvey's fly, with reminders that private detectives are also called "dicks." These often extremely risqué situations create a tremendous ironic sense, while the program's constant insistence on pushing the envelope of allow-able animated action drives the program with a "What's next?" energy. Still, the character of Harvey remains dominant in most episodes and provides a strong center for the program. Thus, in the two-parter "Deadomutt" (May 25 and June 1, 2003), Harvey himself is accused of the gruesome murder of cartoon robot dog Dynomutt, sidekick of former superhero and Harvey's current legal rival, the Blue Falcon. "SPF" (May 9, 2004) focuses on the tribulations of the title character as he comes to grips with the knowledge that sunlight can cause skin cancer, then discovers that shielding himself from the sun makes it impossible for him to recharge his powers. He finds that a strong dose of tanning cream, provided by his psychotic legal aid, Peanut, will restore his strength, but then he has to cope with addiction to the cream, which he needs in larger and larger doses in order to remain functional.

Gruesome murder, skin cancer, and drug addiction are not exactly the conventional stuff of children's cartoons, but they are they typical fare for *Harvey Birdman*, which gets a great deal of mileage precisely out of the seeming mismatch between its subject matter and animated program-ming. Thus, much of the humor of an episode like "The Dabba Don" (July 28, 2002) derives from the amusing incongruity of seeing Hanna-Barbera superstar Fred Flintstone on trial as a racketeering mob boss. The episode ties into more contemporary popular culture as well, including an open-ing sequence that revamps the famous opening of *The Flintstones* to mimic the opening of *The Sopranos*. The episode contains other references to *The Sopranos* as well, as when we find that Fred owns a strip club called Dabba Doo!—as opposed to Tony Soprano's Badda Bing! The episode spoofs other classics of "gangster" culture as well; in one hilarious scene that reprises a classic moment from *The Godfather*, Harvey, reluctant to accept an invi-tation to become the "godfather" to Freddy Flintstone's daughter Pebbles, awakes to find a horrifying (sort of) warning left beneath the covers of his bed: the head of famous cartoon horse Quick Draw McGraw. One of the major ironies of this episode is that, looking back on the original *Flintstones* program, one finds that much of the subject matter there dealt with crime and corruption, so that recasting Fred as a mob boss is not as unlikely as it would first appear. On the other hand, as the episode ends, we find that Fred is not the boss of the local mob after all. The real boss is the seeming innocuous Barney Rubble!

While programs such as *Space Ghost* and *Harvey Birdman* featured fac-similes of Hanna-Barbera characters from the past, other Adult Swim series, such as *The Venture Brothers* and *Sealab 2021* have been constructed as pastiches of entire Hanna-Barbera programs. *The Venture Brothers* is an extended irreverent parody of *Jonny Quest*, with dashes of the Hardy boys and a variety of other predecessors thrown in as well. Created by Jackson Publick (a pseudonym of Christopher McCulloch), formerly a writer for the off-beat Saturday-morning cartoon series *The Tick*, the show features teenagers Hank and Dean Venture (voiced by McCulloch and Michael Sinterniklaas, respectively), essentially splitting the role formerly played by Jonny. Like Jonny, their father is a scientist, though Dr. Thaddeus S. "Rusty" Venture (James Urbaniak) is only a would-be superscientist, struggling to live up to the legacy left by his own father, Dr. Jonas Venture (Paul Boocock), a true superscientist, as well as a he-man adventurer in the mold of Doc Savage. The Ventures' bodyguard, filling the role played in *Jonny Quest* by Race Bannon, is the ultramasculine secret agent Brock Samson (Patrick Warburton), who spends most of his time getting Dr. Venture and the boys out of a variety of jams, usually largely of their own making.

This main cast is supplemented by a variety of other wacky characters, including an array of often incompetent "super" villains who provide opposition to Samson and the Ventures. Most important among these is the Monarch (voiced by McCulloch), Dr. Venture's self-declared nemesis, who is totally dedicated to the destruction of Dr. Venture and Venture Industries, the conglomerate that was founded by Jonas Venture and that Thaddeus Venture now heads. The Monarch is, however, even more ineffectual than Rusty Venture, as is suggested by his rather unthreatening choice of the butterfly as his emblem of evil—he was raised by Monarch butterflies and wears a butterfly costume. Another important character is Dr. Girlfriend (voiced by Doc Hammer, along with Publick one of the show's principal writers), Monarch's beautiful girlfriend, characterized by her preposterously deep voice (perhaps because Samson once cut her throat in an earlier encounter) and her tendency to sympathize with Rusty.

The Ventures also have a number of allies on the show, including their neighbor and tenant Dr. Byron Orpheus (Stephen Rattazzi), a necromancer whose powers actually occasionally work. His daughter Triana (Lisa Hammer), a world-weary Goth-punk teenage girl, is one of the more sensible characters on the show. She is also reasonably tolerant of the fawning crush that Dean Venture has on her. Also important is boy-genius Master Billy Quizboy (Doc Hammer), an expert on prosthetics who works for Conjectural Technologies, along with the albino scientist Mr. White (McCulloch), who looks a bit like Andy Warhol and also has a crush on Triana.

The Venture Brothers very effectively parodies *Jonny Quest* and the entire Cold War action-adventure genre of which it was a key example. However, the humor of the show is effective even without reference to this original, partly because the show also draws upon a number of other more contemporary works of popular culture. For example, the episode "Ice Station—Impossible!" (September 18, 2004) begins with an especially direct link to *Jonny Quest* as Race Bannon crashes to earth after a battle with a planeload of terrorists over possession of a vial of "Goliath Serum," a deadly formula developed during the Vietnam War by Dr. Richard Impossible (Stephen Colbert), former college teacher of Rusty Venture. Samson (a colleague of Bannon) and the brothers discover the dying agent, in the course of which Dean becomes infected by the serum, which is designed to turn an infected animal into a superpowerful walking bomb.

In the meantime, Rusty, Master Billy, and Mr. White have traveled to a top-secret arctic base to join Impossible's high-level government-sponsored think tank. There, however, Venture discovers Impossible's family secret: A laboratory accident has strangely transformed him and his family. Impossible, for example, is now an elastic man whose body can extend itself and take on various shapes. Mrs. Sally Impossible (Mia Barron) has skin that becomes invisible. Her brother Cody tends to burst into flames whenever exposed to oxygen, and her "retard" cousin Ned has become a huge, hulk-like "walking callous." In short, the four parodically mirror the powers of the Fantastic Four of comic book and eventually feature film fame, though the parody is also filtered (as their uniforms featuring a large dotted "i" emblem indicate) through the feature film *The Incredibles* (2004), itself highly derivative of the *Fantastic Four* comics.

To protect his secret, Impossible decides to kill Rusty by exposing him nude in the arctic. However, Samson and the boys, seeking an antidote to the Goliath Serum, arrive in the nick of time, saving Venture and then demanding that Impossible produce the antidote. When he says there is none, Venture, aided by White and Master Billy, works to develop one of his own and is apparently successful, though Impossible claims that Dean simply recovered it on his own and that Venture has merely discovered the formula for ranch dressing. In any case, all ends relatively well, with the silliness of the entire episode nicely pointing up the basic silliness of the cultural artifacts being parodied.

The Venture Brothers ran in 14 half-hour episodes in the fall of 2004, after a pilot that aired in February 2003. It is slated to begin a second season in the spring of 2006. It is similar in spirit to *Sealab 2021*, an overt riff on *Sealab 2020*, an ecologically minded animated science fiction action-adventure that ran on NBC in 1972. Indeed, *Sealab 2021* even opens with the main title of the original series, then shows the second zero clicking over to a one.

Sealab 2021 aired three episodes in December 2000 and then aired a fourth episode on Adult Swim's opening night in 2001. It then became a staple of Adult Swim's lineup, finishing its fifth season in 2005.

Like its 1970s predecessor, *Sealab 2021* features a group of scientists and adventurers stationed in a high-tech undersea research lab. Unlike its straightforwardly serious, even somber predecessor, *Sealab 2021* plays as high farce, with little attention to scientific accuracy or verisimilitude. For example, the entire undersea installation quite often blows up at the ends of episodes, only to be magically restored, with crew intact, by the beginning of the next. The animation style of *Sealab 2021* is self-consciously similar to that of its predecessor; in fact, actual footage from the original show is frequently shown, often with hilarious results due to the changed context. In this sense, familiarity with the original series adds humor to the second, though it is by no means necessary to be familiar with *Sealab 2020* to enjoy *Sealab 2021*.

In the early seasons of *Sealab 2021*, the undersea station is commanded by Captain Hazel "Hank" Murphy (voiced by Harry Goz), a well-meaning buffoon whose stupidity, childishness, and adolescent sexual preoccupations make him something of a joke to the other crew members. He is also a joke to audiences, providing much of the show's humor until Goz's death during the production of the third season forced the lab to find, via a help-wanted ad, a new commander in the person of former football coach Bellerophon "Tornado" Shanks (voiced by Goz's son Michael). Other key crew members include brilliant African American cyborg scientist Dr. Quentin Q. Quinn (Brett Butler), sexy blonde marine biologist and sometime religious fanatic Debbie DuPree (Kate Miller), steroid-popping Latino muscle man Marco Rodrigo Diaz de Vivar Gabriel Garcia Marquez (Erik Estrada), the profoundly stupid pretty-boy Derek "Stormy" Waters (Ellison Henican), and the scheming, wisecracking communications technician Jodene Sparks (Bill Lobley).

Sealab 2020 had been an attempt at intelligent programming for children; *Sealab 2021* is intentionally stupid programming for adults, often featuring bogus scientific premises and plot structures that make no sense. In addition to its obvious reliance on the original *Sealab*, the series is chock full of allusions to other science fiction television series and films. For example, the episode "Lost in Time" (September 30, 2001) includes several allusions to *Star Wars*. Further it derives its plot from a 1992 episode of *Star Trek: The Next Generation* ("Cause and Effect")—except, of course, that it warps the plot toward silliness. Here, Murphy's attempts to steal free cable cause the cable company to blast Sealab out of existence, producing a shock wave that causes a time warp resulting in a loop in which Quinn and Stormy repeatedly try to prevent the catastrophe but repeatedly fail, so that the station is blown up over and over again. In the process, the episode introduces a number of the kinds of paradoxes that are central to science fiction stories of time travel (such as the *Star Trek* episode on which it is based), except that here the paradoxes are ludicrous and nonsensical rather than thought provoking.

One of the most representative *Sealab 2021* episodes is "Red Dawn" (December 7, 2003), which spoofs the Cold War orientation of *Sealab 2020*, while at the same time presenting a kind of alternative history of the twentieth century that makes a mishmash of real history, treating some of the most important people and events of the past century as buffoons and jokes. As the episode begins, Murphy has been unaccountably transformed into a Lenin-like figure who addresses a large gathering of uniformed followers, spouting Marxist slogans, but clearly, as one would expect from Murphy, having no real understanding of what he is saying. When not making speeches, Murphy continues to spout Marxist-Leninist-Stalinist clichés, but is more concerned with promoting his own image than in building socialism aboard Sealab. Other works of Cold War satire are introduced as well, as when Murphy introduces a large hog who wanders by as "Napoleon, Minister of Agitprop." Quinn catches the reference to George Orwell's novel *Animal Farm* and tries to explain to an inattentive Murphy that *Animal Farm* was an *anti*-communist allegory. Orwell's *Nineteen Eighty-Four* (often also taken as anticommunist allegory, but aimed by Orwell equally at Soviet communism and Western industrial capitalism) comes into play as well, as when Murphy proudly displays his ability to spout "Newspeak," the official language used by Orwell's totalitarian government to manipulate perceptions of reality and thus help control the general population.

Quinn circulates among the other crew members to try to convince them that Murphy's devotion to communism is misguided, but finds them too stupid to understand what he is saying. Quinn himself is arrested and forced to build an atomic bomb for Murphy, while Debbie DuPree (who by this point in the series is growing increasingly ditzy in classic dumb blonde style) is ordered to use her sexual charms to gain support for the party. She then travels to the mainland and begins to sleep with both President John F. Kennedy and his brother Bobby, though she is unable to convince them to drop their plans to make a preemptive strike against Sealab. In any case, the Sealab bomber, piloted by a reluctant Quinn, is launched first, leading to an American launch in response. Quinn contacts Washington and assures them that he wants to defect rather than bomb them; the clownish Kennedy (he is at this point wearing the pope's hat) believes him, but learns that his own bombers cannot be called back.

By this time, the episode is growing more and more reminiscent of *Dr. Strangelove*, with side references to the more serious companion piece, *Fail-Safe* (1964), and the later Cold War thriller *War Games* (1983) thrown in as well. Sealab is seemingly destroyed in the American assault, as the phone on which Murphy is speaking to Kennedy goes dead just as the American bombs were scheduled to hit. Kennedy announces to Quinn that the lab has been destroyed—unless, of course, Murphy's phone just melted spontaneously—but Quinn takes this news with a shrug, since the facility is routinely destroyed in the series, after all. However, when he learns that the Kennedys have been cavorting with his beloved Debbie he becomes furious and decides to bomb Washington after all. Following *Stripperella* in mimicking the famous *Dr. Strangelove* scene, Quinn drops from his plane riding the bomb like a bronco as it falls onto the city below, blasting it out of existence. Meanwhile, a cut back to Sealab shows that, for once, the facility has not, in fact, been destroyed—Murphy's phone really did simply melted spontaneously.

Sealab 2021 runs in 15-minute episodes, as does *Aqua Teen Hunger Force* (*ATHF*). *ATHF* originated as an episode of *Space Ghost: Coast to Coast*, though that episode was not aired until New Year's Eve, 2002–2003, two years after "Rabbot," the pilot episode of *ATHF* itself, had aired on December 30, 2000. *ATHF* began to appear regularly on Adult Swim in September 2001. It is now in its fourth season, though Adult Swim "seasons" are irregular and of varying length.

ATHF is, in many ways, the quintessential Adult Swim show. The show is highly absurdist in its orientation, depending for its effect on an intertextual dialogue with previous animated programming—and indeed with contemporary popular culture as a whole, and especially science fiction. It is thus intended for a relatively hip, well-informed audience who can understand these dialogues; but it is also aimed at an audience of relatively young (perhaps college-aged) viewers who are not bothered by the show's complete lack of seriousness, however sophisticated its intertextual construction might be. Like much Adult Swim programming, *ATHF* is a hit-or-miss affair. Devotees of the show love it; others find the show almost unwatchable.

Even the title—*Aqua Teen Hunger Force*—makes no sense, but is merely designed to sound like the typical titles of animated programs, especially those involving crime-fighting superheroes. The main characters are themselves icons of American popular culture. They are, in fact, anthropomorphized fast-food items, including Frylock (a box of french fries that inexplicably floats about in mid-air), Master Shake (a milkshake), and Meatwad (a ball of hamburger meat with shape-shifting abilities, though it can generally transform itself only into a hotdog or an igloo). Master Shake seems to regard himself as the leader of the group, though he is in fact a bit slow-witted and spends most of his time loafing in front of the television, the programming of which he seems unable to distinguish from reality. Frylock is the most intelligent of the three: He possesses superpowers and is able to use his french fries as sensing devices or as weapons; he can also shoot energy rays from his eyes. He is vaguely African American (his fries look a bit like dreadlocks) and acts very paternally toward the childlike, single-toothed Meatwad.

These three characters live together in a dilapidated rental house in New Jersey next door to the hairy-armed, beer-bellied Carl Brutananadilewski, a walking cliché of Jersey working-class "manliness," with his stereotypical souped-up car, white muscle shirt, and gold pendant necklace. Mostly, the three "heroes" just hang out, tormenting their human neighbor, though they occasionally have to mobilize to act as detectives or superheroes, solving crimes or battling alien invaders and miscellaneous various monsters, many of which are inadvertently created in the laboratory of Dr. Weird, a mad scientist whose various whacked-out experiments are featured in the opening of each episode of the first two seasons. These battles are often inconclusive and largely beside the point, merely providing a framework for the show's never-ending pastiche of earlier animated television and its barrage of one-liners and allusions to popular culture as a whole.

For example, in the first-season episode "Revenge of the Mooninites," the alien Mooninites, Ignignokt and Err (a couple of two-dimensional roughly pixellated recurring characters reminiscent of the primitive graphics of 1980s computer games), arrive on earth to work as much mischief as possible. Always willing to be a bad influence on the young, the Mooninites recruit the impressionable Meatwad to join them by promising to help him win enough tickets at a local arcade to get a 10-speed bicycle. They win the tickets by cheating, but then, to Meatwad's disappointment, use them to buy a magical belt that is supposed to give them the powers of 1970s/80s supergroup Foreigner. They then use those powers to aid them in their attempts to score as much pornography as possible, beginning with a raid on Carl's extensive collection, which they steal after immobilizing Carl in a block of ice as music from the Foreigner song "Cold as Ice" emanates from the guitar-shaped buckle of the belt. Similarly, they foil the efforts of Frylock to stop them by ruining his eyesight with the song "Double Vision." Eventually, Carl manages to escape from the block of ice and to snag the belt while the Mooninites bask in his backyard above-ground pool. He then uses the Foreigner song "Hot Blooded" to heat the water in the pool until the Mooninites are forced to flee back to the moon. Carl then tries to use the belt to reverse the effect on Frylock's eyes, but inadvertently activates the song "Head Games" and turns his own head into a Connect Four rack.

The absurdity of this episode is typical of the series as a whole, as is the engagement with science fiction (in the spoof of the alien invasion genre) and popular culture (in the use of the music of Foreigner). Among other things, one could see the motif of the Foreigner belt as a comment on the cultural power of popular music, but surely the real point of the episode is its own senselessness, which has a certain entertainment value in its own right, while also suggesting the pointlessness of most other television programming.

Not all Adult Swim programs are so silly. One of the most interesting programs to appear recently on Adult Swim is *The Boondocks*, which began airing in November 2005 and continues to air (in half-hour episodes) as of this writing. Created by Aaron McGruder based on his comic strip of the same title, *The Boondocks* is one of the most genuinely political programs to have appeared on American television. Though its political vision is filtered through the eyes of a child protagonist, *The Boondocks* addresses a number of serious social and political issues, most of them centering on race and racism, topics that are widely acknowledged to be central to the texture of American society but that are seldom addressed in any serious way in American television programming. As with the *Boondocks* comic strips, the show employs a sometimes biting mode of satire that is considerable more mature than that typically found in cartoon television, though its barbs are aimed as much at the failings of African Americans to stand together for their own good as at the racism (conscious or otherwise) of white Americans. The show is also quite topical, though not as much as the daily comic strip, which can by its nature react more quickly and directly to current events.

The protagonist of *The Boondocks* is young Huey Freeman (Regina King), a 10-year-old, Afro-wearing black radical. Huey, as befits his age, sometimes gets a bit carried away in his zealous pursuit of black causes, but he generally serves as the show's moral center and can be taken essentially as a spokesman for McGruder himself. Huey's young brother, eight-year-old Riley (also King), is also politically aware but considerably more immature in his attitudes. He is heavily influenced by gangsta rap and other aspects of contemporary African American culture that Huey looks on with suspicion as harmful to the efforts of black Americans to work together to build better collective lives for themselves.

The two brothers grew up in inner city Chicago, but now live with their grandfather, Robert Freeman (John Witherspoon), in the "boondocks," the distant, relatively affluent, mostly white Chicago suburb of Woodcrest. Freeman is a former civil rights activist and a former associate of Dr. Martin Luther King, though the strength of his commitment to the cause was perhaps a bit questionable even then. In his elderly years, he prefers peace and comfort to political activism, spending most of his energy dreaming of finding the woman of his dreams after years of being alone. He has moved the boys to the suburbs in the hope of providing them with a wholesome environment in which to grow up, though the move also threatens to alienate them from their own culture.

The episode "Return of the King" (aired on January 15, 2006, the 77th anniversary of the birth of Dr. King) is typical of the political vision of *The Boondocks*. The show is based on a sort of "what-if" alternative history premise, stipulating that King was not killed when shot in 1968, but instead lay in a coma until regaining consciousness in the year 2000. In 2001, shortly after the 9/11 bombings, King then appears on the television show *Politically Incorrect* (which was itself canceled because of host Bill Maher's comments on the bombings) and is asked about the proper U.S. response to the terrorist attacks. True to the nonviolent attitude that had made him a national hero in the 1960s, King responds that, as Christians, we should simply turn the other cheek and forgive our attackers. The country erupts in outrage, and King is branded a traitor and al Qaeda sympathizer. King finds other aspects of twenty-first century America difficult as well. Concluding that he is out of place in the gangsta-rap inflected black culture of our own time, he opts to move to Canada, where he hopes his philosophy of nonviolence will be more acceptable.

The Boondocks features a variety of other characters as well, perhaps most notably Robert's friend Uncle Ruckus (Gary Anthony Williams). Apparently named for Uncle Remus from *Song of the South*, Ruckus might as well have been named Uncle Tom. He is a self-loathing black man who regards African Americans as naturally inferior and who attributes all things good to the wondrous powers of white people. Through such depictions, *The Boondocks* has stirred considerably controversy through the airing of its first few shows, though probably more for its frequent use of the word "nigga" than for the specifics of its political content. Still, the show was nominated for an NAACP Image Award for best television comedy series in January 2006. Nevertheless, it remains to be seen whether the show, despite its intelligent writing, excellent animé-style animation, and sharp satirical humor, will have a long run on television—though the comic strip, also quite controversial, has shown considerable staying power.

The Boondocks was originally pitched to Fox, but that deal eventually fell through (probably because of the political content), leading to the move to Adult Swim. Other programs have actually aired on other networks before moving to Adult Swim in syndication. Such recycled programs include relatively successful shows such as *Family Guy* and *Futurama*, which play on Adult Swim as syndicated reruns. In addition, some Adult Swim programs began on other networks and then were picked up by Adult Swim, where they continued in production. One of the most interesting of these was *Home Movies*, which began in 1999 on UPN. The fledgling network had had some mild success with *Dilbert* in its attempt to recreate the success with which earlier struggling networks (such as ABC with *The Flintstones* and Fox with *The Simpsons*) had used animated programming as a means of competing with more established rivals. Created by Loren Bouchard and Brendon Small, *Home Movies* ran for only five episodes on UPN, after which it was picked up by Adult Swim, where it ran for four seasons as some of the most interesting programming on the block. In its first season, *Home Movies* was animated using executive producer Tom Snyder's "Squigglevision" technique that had distinguished the earlier *Dr. Katz: Professional Therapist*, though *Home Movies* later switched to a more conventional look. There were other links to *Dr. Katz* as well. For example, Bouchard had been a producer on that show, while Bill Braudis was a member of the writing staff for both programs.

Perhaps because of its network background, *Home Movies* runs in half-hour episodes. As its title suggests, the series is a variant on the animated family sitcom, though its focus on child characters sometimes reads like a postmodern pastiche of the classic *Peanuts* cartoons. The series focuses on the home life of its eight-year-old protagonist, Brendon Small, voiced by series co-creator Small, on whom the character is based, in a relationship that indicates the general collapse of distinctions between truth and fiction that mark this series. However, Brendon's family is decidedly dysfunctional. His parents are divorced, and his lawyer-father Andrew is initially nowhere to be seen, though he does eventually establish a relationship of sorts with Brendon, complicated by tensions between Brendon and Linda, Andrew's hot young girlfriend and later new wife. Brendon's well-meaning, but neurotic mother (voiced in the first six episodes by Paula Poundstone, then later by Janine Ditullio), often needs more support from Brendon than she provides to him. Brendon, who has his own difficulties in dealing with the challenges of childhood life, does have reliable support from chums Melissa (Melissa Bardin Galsky) and Jason (H. Jon Benjamin), who serve as cast and crew for the various amateur films that Brendon directs as he fumbles his way toward his dream of being a filmmaker. Benjamin, incidentally, had provided the voice of Ben Katz in *Dr. Katz*, while Galsky had served as a staffer. The main cast of *Home Movies* is completed by John McGuirk (also voiced by Benjamin), Brendon's bullying, alcoholic soccer coach, an all-around loser who constantly exploits his relationship with Brendon, but who somehow manages to be oddly sympathetic. The show features numerous minor characters as well, including the children's fourth-grade teacher, Mr. Ronald Lynch (voiced by Ronald Lynch) and Dwayne (Small), a slightly older neighbor with his own rock band called "Scab." Jonathan Katz (as Melissa's father, Erik, a real estate agent) makes frequent guest appearances as well.

Many of the episodes of *Home Movies* show Brendon simply dealing with ordinary childhood problems, often badly. In "The Art of the Sucker Punch" (May 10, 1999), Brendon defends Jason from Shannon, a local bully, only to get bullied himself. In "Brendon Gets Rabies" (May 17, 1999), Brendon and Paula take care of a neighbor's cat, only to have it escape and contract rabies, which it gives to Brendon. Occasionally, even Brendon's filmmaking skills even get him into trouble. In "It Was Supposed to be Funny" (September 9, 2001), Brendon makes a video tribute to Melissa's ancient grandfather, but can't resist making fun of the old man. Pretty much the same thing happens in "The Party" (February 3, 2002), in which Brendon makes a video celebrating the birthday of classmate Fenton Mulley, only to portray Fenton as a whiney idiot. In "Curses" (February 22, 2004), Brendon makes a movie about a foulmouthed robot (reminiscent of *Futurama*'s Bender) that becomes a big hit with the neighborhood kids but outrages their parents because of its language.

Though not directly based on any specific precedent, *Home Movies* is often highly allusive, as in "Definite Possible Murder" (March 21, 2004), which spoofs the Alfred Hitchcock classic *Rear Window* (1954). Here, Brendon is laid up with a leg injury, then can't resist spying on the seemingly suspicious and possibly murderous activities of neighbor Raymond Burley, just as Hitchcock's L. B. Jefferies (Jimmy Stewart) spies on a neighbor played by Raymond Burr. Brendon, meanwhile, is a versatile filmmaker whose work tends to be derivative all sorts of film genres. In "History" (March 10, 2002), for example, he and his crew are engaged in making a science fiction space opera entitled "Starboy and the Captain of Outer Space," one of their more elaborate productions.

"History" is a particularly illustrative episode of *Home Movies* in more ways than one. Brendon and Jason play Starboy and the Captain of Outer Space, respectively, as they battle to save the human race from a transhistorical group of villains (vaguely reminiscent of the heroes from the

League of Extraordinary Gentlemen graphic novels and film) made up of George Washington (played by Brendon), Picasso (Jason), and Annie Oakley (Melissa). And, if the collapse of historical boundaries that brings these eighteenth-, nineteenth-, and twentieth-century figures together suggests a postmodern disregard for temporal sequence, it also arises from the sheer ignorance of Brendon and his crew. For example, per Brendon's script, George Washington is correctly identified as the first president of the United States, but he was born in 1492, freed the slaves, and was impeached for shooting Abraham Lincoln. Picasso, meanwhile, cut off his ear ("in a major shaving accident") and mailed it to an ex-girlfriend. Annie Oakley, finally, is identified as the ward of Daddy Warbucks and as the star of a musical based on her life, thus both confusing Annie Oakley with Little Orphan Annie and collapsing distinctions between the Orphan Annie comic strip, the musical based on it, and the actors who perform in that musical. Continuing the dialogue with stage musicals, one of the first victims of these villains is William Shakespeare, author of the great classic *Cats*. In fact, one sequence of "Starboy and the Captain of Outer Space" is an extended reference to *Cats*, featuring Dwayne as Mr. Pants, an evil singing space cat who helps the villains in their nefarious schemes but is defeated by the heroes. Thus, Brendon's film is itself a musical, collapsing the generic boundary between science fiction and the musical, as did *The Rocky Horror Picture Show*, of which the music in the film is sometimes reminiscent.

Such misinformation might be taken as intentional postmodern play. However, the background narrative in this episode involves Brendon's travails at school, where he is failing abysmally, especially in history, largely because he spends all of his time making films instead of studying. Thus, it becomes clear that much of the misinformation in Brendon's film comes about because he doesn't know any better—and it doesn't help that he is being tutored in history by McGuirk, whose scrambled fund of misinformation deals largely with government conspiracies surrounding alien visitations and research into them at the notorious secret facility, Area 51.

At this writing, Adult Swim continues to provide a home for reruns of series such as *Home Movies. Futurama,* and *Family Guy* remain staples of the block, while the newer *American Dad* has begun to appear there as well, with episodes often appearing on Adult Swim only a week or so after their first broadcast on Fox. More obscure series, such as *The Oblongs* and *Mission Hill,* have also been rebroadcast on Adult Swim. In the meantime, new series continually appear on the block. Recent examples include the detective farce *Stroker and Hoop* (essentially a parody of the old *Starsky and Hutch* TV series, though it moves well beyond that beginning premise), *Squidbillies,* and *12 Oz. Mouse.* The continual flow of such new series, together with the unprecedented number of animated series now appearing either on network TV (especially Fox) or on cable channels such as Comedy Central and Sci Fi, suggests a bright future for adult-oriented animated television in the twenty-first century.

Postscript: Prime-Time Animation in American Culture

Though many still think of cartoons as a children's genre—or at least regard animated programming as less than serious—it is nevertheless the case that animated programming has played an extremely important role in American television history. For example, few television programs have made a bigger impact on American popular culture than *The Flintstones* and *The Simpsons*, whose characters and other images have become some of the most widely recognizable in all of American culture. Part of the ongoing appeal of these programs can no doubt be attributed to their popularity with young audiences, which creates generations of viewers who fondly remember the programs even in adulthood. Still, animated series have, especially in recent years, provided some of the most daring and innovative programming on American television. Perhaps for the very reason that animated programming is not always taken entirely seriously, programs such as *The Simpsons, South Park,* and *Family Guy* have dealt with issues that might otherwise have been deemed too controversial for American commercial television, the sponsors of which are always extremely concerned about offending and possibly alienating audiences and thus losing potential customers.

The proliferation of cable networks in the past two decades has made it possible for animated programming to be even more daring. Such networks need not attract the large audiences that are necessary for commercial success on the major broadcast networks. They can target their programming and advertising for much more limited "niche" audiences, which means that programs such as *South Park*, intended for a hip audience of relatively well-educated young adults, can include material that a broader audience might consider gross, vulgar, and offensive. While this phenomenon sometimes allows animated programs to descend into sophomoric silliness, it also allows such programs to explore genuinely new territory. As a result, animated programs have often been at the forefront of American television, especially in the past decade, when the long-running *Simpsons* has been joined by so many other edgy, satirical, and inventive animated programs.

Index

About the Author

M. KEITH BOOKER is Professor and Director of Graduate Studies in the Department of English at the University of Arkansas. He is the author of numerous articles and books on modern literature, film, and science-fiction, including *Film and the American Left* (1999), *Monsters, Mushroom Clouds, and the Cold War* (2001), *Strange TV: Innovative Television Series from "The Twilight Zone" to "The X-Files"* (2003), *Science Fiction Television* (2004), and *Alternate Americas: Science Fiction Film and American Culture* (2006).